Genesis Days

Eyal Cohen

Producer & International Distributor
eBookPro Publishing
www.ebook-pro.com

Genesis Days
Eyal Cohen

Cover art by Gadi Dadon
Translation: Yossie Bloch

Contact: eyalcohen51@gmail.com
ISBN 9798476829140

THE LOST TREASURES

Genesis Days

EYAL COHEN

Contents

PROLOGUE

It all began on a summer night, one of the more pleasant Safed nights. Several of us friends sat in the yard of the house and the conversation shifted from topic to topic. One of the friends suddenly laughed and said: "Wow, King David was quite a mess." I observed him, in an attempt to understand what he was talking about. I, who became religious later in life, and a Breslover Chasid of twenty years, was surprised by my friend's disrespectful assessment, even though he is not observant of Torah and the commandments; the way in which he spoke of the holy ones of Israel with such contemptuousness was surprising to my eyes. Another friend who sat with us, joined the opinion of our mutual friend in his portrayal of the image of the anointed of God as a tainted individual whose every action was grounded in corrupt interests and characteristics.

Without elaborating, I was shaken to the depths of my soul – as one who researches, studies, and loves the revered image of King David, the pain sliced deep. When I inquired as to from where they drew this distorted historical "knowledge," they said that they read these facts in a specific book (which I don't find appropriate to mention by name), that was written by a woman who in the past was ultra-Orthodox. I attempted to explain, to reason, to clarify, but the reaction was: "That's what she wrote." I asked them: "Did you try to read the Hebrew Bible? The works of the Sages? The commentaries? And the reaction was: "Who has the time and stamina for that! Her book is so easy and pleasant to read!"

It is now many years that I have been learning and teaching the Bible and facing students' questions about their impressions of the great ones of Israel, questions that flow from sources external to Judaism and that cause a distortion of the characters, in an attempt to distort and design anew the collective memory regarding the morality of our people and its revered customs. I took the book which had been spoken of and I tried to read it but because of the nature of the distortion I was not able to continue …

I wanted to chase away the darkness by screaming, but at night when my heart screamed, I remembered that one can only chase away darkness with light.

I had the desire to write in a manner attainable for all, to allow my friends and readers, who do not spend their time in the house of study, to recognize the image of King David through hundreds of sources of tales and books which have accompanied us for thousands of years and to present an innovative commentary.

In my profession I am a scribe of biblical texts (really…). On my agenda was the writing of a Torah scroll. After the preparations and logistical arrangements which were involved in this, I sat myself down to write the Torah scroll, but then something happened… my hands held paper and pen in place of the parchment and quill, and for approximately four consecutive hours I began to write, letters combining into words, transforming into sentences, in turn combining into paragraphs and complete pages. Page after page, folio after folio, the chapters flying off and away. Like a hot, fluid geyser that bursts forth from below the surface of the Earth into the air of the world, screaming to teach and tell of the awesome image and character of King David.

In the evening I sat with my wife. She asked: "Nu…Did you start the writing of the Torah scroll?"

I smiled and answered her: "Yes…and no." My wife laughed; she is not accustomed to evasive answers from me and requested that I explain myself.

I said: "Could you perhaps read what I wrote today and tell me what you think ?"

After a short while my wife returned to me a bit shocked and teary eyed, and told me emphatically: "The Torah scroll will have to wait. You must finish this book; the world needs it."

The writing took approximately two years, in particular the clarification of Jewish sources; the Bible, Talmud, Midrash, Zohar, the earlier and later biblical commentators; tens and even hundreds of books which we included all helped to clarify the image of David, the King of Israel. The book about the life of King David was published under the name "The Love of King David," and it elicited incredible responses from hundreds of thousands of readers, but always with the following questions: "What about the rest of the biblical warriors? What about other books?" So, I started writing about Moses, our Leader and his generation, a project that lasted approximately another two years, which morphed into the title "The Generation of the Wilderness," but before it was published the question arose: "Why don't you begin from the beginning?!" I jumped into the stormy waters and wrote "The Genesis Days," which also took approximately two years. I knew immediately that another question would arise: "But what about the books of Joshua and Judges? You need to connect the Torah with King David!" Another a long, two-year journey, the book "The Days of the Judges" was ready. Now the books are presented to you as the series "The Hidden Treasures," which unwrap the history of the world from the creation story through the life of King David. The question of "What about the book of Kings?" has now reached me, and I am currently on the fascinating journey into the nadirs of the days of the kings...

It stands to reason that it will take at least another two years...

INTRODUCTION

Throughout the world, the Bible is known as the Book of Books. It tells about the Creation of the World and the development of all the creatures in it — up to the formation of nations in general and the people of Israel in particular.

Throughout human history, the Bible has been translated in its entirety into hundreds of languages, and parts of it into thousands of languages. Hundreds and thousands of collections of legends and lore have been compiled over the years about this book, and they have become the legacy of all mankind. Some are based on official, trustworthy sources; others are the product of their authors' imaginations.

The intense thirst to know the biblical story according to reliable sources is growing. However, this remains a challenging endeavor, as the archaic texts and largely inaccessible commentaries bring the vast majority of people to despair, as if drawing from an empty well.

The *Lost Treasures* series seeks to address this dilemma. Anyone who wants to study the biblical story may now do so without having to try and deduce the content of the narrative from hundreds of secondary sources. In response to the modern reader's great desire to gain access to and experience the reality of the ancient world, the series presents the text in readable prose. The reader is brought from the beginning of Creation into the magical world of the Bible and its protagonists, who become flesh-and-blood human beings. Theirs is a suspenseful, moving and sweeping saga, presented by interweaving the lexicon of the Bible with clear and pleasant contemporary language.

The first book in the series, *Genesis Days*, tells of the Creation of the World and the first millennia of humanity.

The second book in this series will take the reader from the arrival of Jacob and to his descendants in Egypt.

I hope that reading this book provides you, dear reader, with a pleasant and exciting experience, both instructive and enlightening.

CHAPTER ONE

Creation

Before there were creatures or emanations , God existed on His own in the world; there was no sense of time or space — just He, and nothing else, existed.

"There can be no king without subjects, nor can a benefactor bestow benefit without beneficiaries," God thought to Himself.

"I will make a people for Myself, to receive My good and to reveal My kingship. A people, who will walk straight upon My path, whose attributes will be exemplary and who will have a positive influence through the good they do: the People of Israel are straight *(yashar)* with God (El). They will be My flock, and they will teach My Will, showing all the creatures I create the correct path to follow, a people who will sense My Being among them, children faithful to their Heavenly Father."

This was simply the force of Divine Will, uncompelled, as there was no one else to compel the Creator.

"I will create tools by which My people may receive the good I wish to bestow upon them. I will create the Torah, to give them laws and statutes to guide My people as to what is desirable and what is objectionable. I will create Heaven and Hell, to reward those who follow My path and to refine those who stray from the path of good. I will even create a Throne of Glory, a spiritual world devoid of any physicality, through which My children will be able to connect to Me. Finally, I will create the Upper Temple, a site at which my Presence will be contracted, so that My children may serve Me."

"Naturally, My children will stumble; they will violate My laws and commandments, so I will create the option of repentance, so that the world will not despair of returning to fulfill My will. There must also be a leader among them, a person of impeccable character, understanding, and wise in fulfilling My will. A person who will guide them to the culmination of perfection; a person who eschews evil, and whose whole aim is to reveal to other people that there is a sovereign and ruler, who created them out of His love for them: a messiah who will direct them along My path."

A great deal of time passed; it was undefined time before the past, present, and future existed. God created and destroyed many worlds, playing with the letters of the Torah, assembling combinations to express what He sought from His handiwork, preparing the tools of Creation itself. Spiritual worlds were created — one above another — one touching and adjoining the next, for the sake of the souls of Israel.

The twenty-two letters of the alphabet are twenty-two spiritual forces, which were combined in various, sundry ways to write the Torah. Each letter vied to be the first in the Torah, as the original point of Creation; but it was the second letter, "*bet,*" which was chosen for this position, as it is the initial letter of blessed ("*baruch*"). This was meant to teach all creations that the "*aleph,*" the first letter, the essence of divinity, could never be fully grasped by any other mind. All the spiritual worlds awaited the Creation of the physical world, so that they might serve their Creator. Silence — far more profound than the mere absence of sound — reigned, waiting without the reality of time.

"*Bereishit*," God pronounced, "In the beginning." This was the first word of the Torah, as an infinite light, which penetrated all the physical elements that filled up all of reality: space, time, and matter were created in one instant. Water (*mayim*) spread throughout the space, expanding further, while the boundless land split even further. Darkness and light served in confusion, chaos, and nothingness; there was a lack of limits or order that prevailed throughout the created Universe. A wind filled the open space with air: oxygen, carbon, and other materials from which creatures would draw out their own sustenance.

"This pure light," God thought to Himself, "is not appropriate for regular people, it is a light by which one can see from one end of the world to another. Such light must be stored away for the righteous who follow My path to enjoy in future times." So, the light was hidden away, and a new light shone, a light without luminaires.

"Light and dark must be separated; they cannot function simultaneously; each one should rule half the time. This will teach My creatures that after the darkness, the light will always break through again; after every bad thing, good arrives." Light and darkness were separated, and each one functioned on its own.

"I will call the light 'Day,' and I will call the dark, 'Night.' ...*And it was evening and it was morning, one day.*" Thus, the unique first day of Creation concluded.

"Let there be a firmament in the midst of the waters." Matter was torn, split, and divided, one part from the other: an upper part and a lower part. A firmament separated from the physical matter came into being above the lower waters, while the upper water existed above it. *"Eish (fire),"* and *"mayim, sham —* (there) is *mayim," "sa* (bear) *mayim —* lifted and suspended by royal decree." Division was created between the upper water and the lower water. The upper waters ascended, cleaving to the rock which hewed them, to distance themselves from the place which would be subject to the lower infirmities. The lower waters also wanted to be included, but for the sake of the upper waters, they remained below. *"And God called the firmament, 'Heaven.' And there was evening and there was morning, a second day."*

"Let the waters under the heaven be gathered together unto one place, and let the dry land appear." The lower waters got mixed up with each other as they retreated from the dry land, and flowed into different gatherings of water to reveal solid land; a dry and arid land, with nothing upon it but earth and clods of dirt. "Let the land put forth herbs and grasses according to their kind, trees with fruit containing seeds for new trees, which will sustain the animals and people I will create." The land sprouted herbs and trees, reaching towards but not yet breaking the surface. *"And it was evening and it was morning, a third day."*

Light without luminaires are likely to confuse people, as if there is some independent existence to light apart from Me. *"Let there be lights in the firmament of the heaven to divide the day from the night."* So, the two great luminaires were suspended above the earth, with the sun and the moon, holding equal in size and intensity.

"Master of the Universe," the moon said. "Can two kings share a crown? How can we be the same size?"

"Because you criticized the sun, I am minimizing you. You will only get your light from the sun," God said, and the moon shrank.

The moon protested: "am I to be punished for telling the truth?"

"Certainly, even were you correct, it is not your place to criticize the sun! However, to put your mind at ease, I will give you a legion of stars, by which My people Israel will count the festivals, the months and the years. *'And it was evening and it was morning, a fourth day.'*"

"Let the waters swarm with swarms of living creatures, and let fowl fly above the earth in the open firmament of heaven." In one instant, without any progenitors, the waters swarmed with life, uncountable fish and sea creatures, massive whales, fish in stunning hues filling the water. Dolphins jumped out of the water with youthful exuberance, chirping back and forth. There were sea snakes and starfish, corals and anemones. There were fish in rivers and fresh water, fish in every hue filling the empty waters. From the mire and mud, every shade and shape of bird emerged: eagles and hawks, parrots and songbirds, birds of prey and nightingales taking wing and flying over the earth. The rooster and the hen together produced fertilized eggs, as well as creatures with the power to bear offspring in their own images. Great sea-monsters were then created but immediately destroyed, to prevent them from reproducing and destroying the world. *"And it was evening and it was morning, a fifth day."*

"Let the earth bring forth the living creature after its kind, cattle, and creeping thing, and beast of the earth after its kind." Dust was kneaded and shaped to create creatures great and small: horses and cattle, rhinoceroses and giraffes, zebras and deer, mice and cats,

dogs and rats, lions and tigers, who burst forth from the kneaded earth and ran the length and breadth of the dry land.

"Everything is ready for the crowning glory of Creation: man, who would repair the world. Man is to have intelligence, understanding, and wisdom, to be able with his mind to explore the goal of his life and try to acquire it; a creature which can overcome his lusts and control his actions, My handiwork who is to rule over the fish of the sea, the birds of the sky, and the animals of the land."

So on the sixth day of Creation, during the first hour of the great first day of the month of *Tishrei*, dust was gathered from the four corners of the earth, as if by the very own hands of the Creator. All of the fundamental elements of Creation were combined in that clump of earth and were brought to the top of the mountain, which was one day destined to be the site of the Lower Temple, built by the people of Israel.

In the second hour, that clump of earth was kneaded into a mass upon the mountaintop. In the third hour, the mass was delineated, separated into limbs, and arranged in correspondence to the creation of the upper worlds. The brain was on top with the ability to think and control. The emotions were found in the heart which was positioned below it. Below the heart, the liver was placed in charge of human passions. The human form was thus completed, a tall and splendid being, utterly perfect — like a twenty-year-old at the apex of strength and beauty — one side male and one side female.

In the fourth hour, God decreed: "now the soul must be placed within it, with the power to think and to speak, and to have a mind which is similar to that of the upper worlds." As it were, the Creator bent over the human being, to breathe the breath of life into his nostrils.

In the fifth hour, man stood on his feet, and considered the Creation in which he had been created. His body was magnificent and resplendent, he was awed by what his eyes beheld: the Garden of Eden, with the beauty of the Creation at the apex of its glory. Trees of all types and species raised their branches, laden with plump, colorful splendid fruit.

God then said to the human being: "whatever I created, I created solely for you. I am the King of the upper worlds, while you are the king of the lower worlds. Be mindful so that you do not ruin and destroy My world! If you ruin it, there is no one to repair it afterwards."

"Lord, why did you create man? You know full well that they are destined to sin before You," the angels asked their Creator. The angels were spiritual creations, appointed by their King, God, to manage things in the physical world.

"True, man is destined to sin, but also to return in repentance. What delight is there in creatures such as you, who cannot defy My word and must follow My path? Only in man do I find delight. Not only that, man has a greater mind than you. Can you give the animals different names? Do you have the ability to assess the nature of each and every creature I have created?" God asked them.

The angels wondered aloud, "does man have this understanding?"

"You shall see very soon!"

In the sixth hour of the sixth day, man stood in the midst of the garden, looking eagerly at the wonder before his eyes. Many sundry animals passed before them, and they instinctively began to name the creatures. "This should be called a dog (*kelev*), because it is faithful, like the heart (*ke-leiv*) of man. This should be called a donkey (*hamor*) because it is so materialistic (*homri*) and physical. This should be called a goat (*eiz*), because it so brazen (*az*) and brash, stealing whatever it finds in front of it…"

Man spent a long time naming all the creatures which passed before them, to reflect the latent abilities each one had. "As for me, I shall be called 'Adam,' because I have been taken from the ground (*adamah*); and my Creator shall be called the Lord because of His dominion over all the creations of the Universe."

Adam thought despondently, "all of these animals are in pairs, male and female; they see each other, they can reproduce — but I am alone! Must I forever live in solitude?! Is there no one among all the creations who could be my mate?! What is the benefit of my being one entity with two sides? How can I reproduce? With whom can I speak? Every creation has its companion, except for me."

"Now," thought God, "after Adam has made the request for a mate, I shall grant it. Adam shall sleep, so the experience will not be painful as I separate them. I do not want this mate to be rejected because the process of Creation is too bloody."

It was in the seventh hour that Adam lay on the ground, distressed by the bitterness of fate, and as his eyes closed, he fell into the deepest of slumbers. Adam was then split in two, front and back, each one becoming its own being, as the sinew and skin covered the rear of each. Though these two were actually destined to reunite in love and become like one body again. From out of his deep slumber, a perfectly formed female arose to gaze at the freshly awakened man, from whom she had been taken.

Adam opened his eyes, and looked at the female hovering over him, who was gazing at him tenderly. A broad smile appeared on his face, and heartfelt joy filled him as he looked at his heart's desire standing before him. The man whispered with much gratitude to his Creator: *"this is now bone of my bones, and flesh of my flesh; she shall be called Woman, because she was taken out of Man."*

The man rose up, and grinned with elation. "Your name will henceforth be Haia," he said to the woman, "because you will be the source of all human life (*hai*) to come." In the eighth hour, Adam and Haia became parents to two sons and three daughters.

However, a malicious eye watched Adam and his wife as they stood among the trees of the Garden, unashamedly. The malevolent observer was jealous of Adam.

In the ninth hour, Adam walked through the Garden of Eden, enjoying the colorful fruit hanging from every branch of the trees; while his heart overflowed with happiness at the good bestowed upon him.

"Adam!" the Creator's voice echoed in his ears. "You may eat of the fruit of any of these trees, except for the tree in the midst of the Garden; from that tree you must not eat, lest you die."

"Now I give you seven more commandments, which you will transmit to all your descendants. These seven commandments will sustain the world and all the creatures in it." Adam listened eagerly to his Commander.

"First of all, you must not worship anything else but Me as divine.

"Second, whenever a woman marries a man, she becomes his wife and his alone.

"Third, you must not take the life of another human being.

"Fourth, you must eschew theft.

"Fifth, you must not blaspheme.

"Sixth, you must establish courts to judge and punish those who violate My commandments.

"As the seventh and last commandment, you must not eat the limb of a living animal. As long as an animal is alive, you may not consume its flesh. When it dies of its own accord, you may eat it; but you may not kill it in order to eat it."

Adam ran to his wife to tell her about the commandments he had just been given. "Listen, my wife, please," he said to her. "The Lord has told me that we may eat from any tree in the Garden, except the tree in the midst of the Garden, which we may neither eat from nor touch. If we violate the Lord's commandment, we will die! Therefore, you must take heed neither to touch nor to eat from this tree."

Adam continued to instruct his wife on the rest of the commandments. He then resumed walking in the Garden — thrilled and rapturous — he was grateful to God for the opportunity to fulfill his Creator's will and to give pleasure to his Maker in some way. Feeling incredibly content, he lay down to doze off.

In the tenth hour, Haia was sitting with their children, playing with her offspring. "We will call you Cain because I acquired (*kaniti*) a man-child from God; we are now partners in the creation of human beings. And we will call you Abel, because, to our dismay, we came to the world in vanity (*hevel*), and in vanity we will be taken from it..."

CHAPTER TWO

The Tree of Knowledge of Good and Evil

"Greetings…" The woman was surprised and startled by the sibilant voice hissing behind her back. "Who are you?" she asked the creature, whirling around.

"My name is Samael, and some call me the serpent (*nachash*)," he chuckled. With its cunning eyes, he considered the woman carefully. "As someone as wise as you must know, I am called the serpent, because I know how to soothsay (*nachosh*). Who are these adorable ones?" he whispered, as he looked at the five children lying on a multicolored bed of leaves.

The serpent approached the woman and gazed at her children — stoking its secret lust for the woman — trying to seduce her. Haia watched, quite astounded, as the serpent approached. It stood on two legs, while it reached for her with outstretched arms. She tried to resist, but she felt an unnatural power when he grabbed her. The seconds ticked by, as the woman understood that something very wrong was happening here. She defied the serpent, "what do you want? Why have you come here?"

"All that concerns me is your welfare," the serpent whispered, enjoying the powerlessness of the woman standing before him. "I want you to experience the truest good which you can experience. I do not want you to be blinded, because you are so goodhearted and innocent. I want you to get what you deserve..."

"What do we deserve? Who would want to blind me?" Her voice started to sound confused.

"Tell me, if you please, weren't you told not to eat or touch the tree in the heart of the Garden? Didn't your foolish husband order you to stay away from the tree, telling you that this what the Lord has commanded?" he asked her mockingly.

The woman defiantly responded to the sniggering serpent: "Yes, the Lord told us not to eat or touch the fruit of the tree; since this is a poisonous tree, and thus it is forbidden for us to come in contact with it."

"Tell me, can you show me this poisonous tree? Can you identify it for me?"

"Of course! Come with me," Haia said to the serpent, who then followed after her. She approached the tree, pointing at it from a short distance. "This is the tree!"

"This is the tree which you are forbidden to touch?! The tree which kills all who come in contact with it?!" the serpent hissed in dismay. "The fruits are so beautiful, a real delight to the eye," he said, as he began to stroke the bark of the tree, to Haia's astonishment. The woman gazed at the tree longingly, her feet bringing her closer and closer to the forbidden tree. "Its fruits are indeed beautiful, far more beautiful than the fruits of all the other trees," she whispered, staring at its luscious fruits.

"From what I understood, God said it was forbidden to touch or eat from the tree, not referring to its fruit. However, it appears to me that Adam may have misled you, that he never received any such command. Now, let's see if I'm right or not!" the serpent said, deliberately pushing the woman with all his strength against the tree.

Haia felt the shove propelling her towards the deadly tree, fright and terror seized her as she grabbed on to the tree to keep herself from toppling over.

The serpent's laughter boomed. "You see? The tree neither kills nor harms; the opposite is true. Whoever fabricates such lies does not have your best interests in mind. This tree is better than all the other trees in the garden, so your husband forbade you to touch it and eat from its fruit. Just as touching the tree is not fatal, eating its fruits is also not fatal. Apparently, your husband does not want you to get what you deserve…"

"Why would he lie to me?" she asked in confusion.

"Oh, you poor naïf," the serpent's voice sounded sad. "If only you knew what awaits when you eat the fruit of the tree, you would not hesitate for even a moment…"

"What will happen?" Haia whispered as she stroked the coveted fruit hanging from the tree.

"If you eat from it, you will become like God! You will be able to create entire worlds! He too ate of these fruits, and by the power of eating the fruits, He created the world!"

"Are you sure?"

"Trust me, you know I'm not lying."

Her hand was already wrapped around the fruit, so the woman simply plucked it. Her eyes opened wide at the sweetness of the fruit of the tree of sin and knowledge.

"You hate me!" Haia shouted at her husband. Adam looked at his wife in amazement. It had only been a little while since he had left her with their young children, and suddenly, he was being greeted with anger and resentment.

"What? Why are you — "

The woman's screams interrupted him: "What have you heard? You hate me and lie to me! You probably want to leave me and marry another woman! Whom do you have your eye on? Do you not have a drop of pity for me and the children? We have been together just a short time, and you're already sowing wild oats! How could you do that to me?" Haia burst into heartrending wails, with tears streaming down her face.

Adam looked at his wife in amazement, trying to figure out what she was going through. "I do not know what you are talking about! Why do you think I hate you? When have I lied to you? What other woman could I possibly marry?"

"Don't you dare say that! You think I don't see her following you, looking at you all the time?!" Haia cried, weeping bitterly.

Adam, his gaze downcast, murmured, "will you just tell me what you mean?" with unconvincing innocence.

"You know very well who I mean! The same one who walks around with the serpent all the time; the female who walks in front of the serpent, while it trails behind. That one, with the sly, come-hither eyes!" Haia screamed, totally out of control.

Adam tried to put a conciliatory smile on his face, "Ah... that one... What is that female to me? That's the serpent's mate! Why would I think of it when I have you, my dear? Do you really think I'd leave you for that? You are my wife, the mother of my children, and my soulmate. Why would I stray anywhere else?"

Adam looked at Haia seriously, "you are everything I have in the world, the bone of my bones, the flesh of my flesh, the joy of my heart and my life."

A choking cry emerged from the woman's throat: "so you love me?" she asked with teary eyes, "you're not looking for another woman?"

"Certainly, my wife! How could there be a more perfect woman than you, the crown of Creation, the culmination and apex of the Maker's actions in forming the Universe?" He said to his wife, in a soft and comforting voice.

"Really...?"

"Nothing but the truth, my soulmate," Adam smiled at his wife calmly.

"Very well... I believe you," said the woman and sat down. "Come, sit with me, and eat something."

Adam sat down in front of his somewhat-relieved wife, and looked at the eye-catching fruit that she had served him. "It looks like the fruit of that tree which is forbidden to us," Adam thought to himself. "But my righteous wife, surely, would not let me eat anything forbidden." Adam looked at his chastened wife soothingly and took a juicy bite of the fruit.

"You know, we are being immodest to walk around like this." Adam told Haia, "we are naked before all, like the beasts of the field."

"You are right, we must sew some garments, at least a belt to cover the modest parts of our body," the woman agreed.

The man and the woman plucked leaves from the fig tree and covered their bodies.

"I still feel naked," Adam told his wife sadly, "not in my body, but in my soul. I feel that something is happening inside me, and I do not know what it is."

In the eleventh hour, a sound was heard in the Garden that sent chills through the body of Adam and his wife. Through a strong

27

wind, the voice of God was heard walking in the Garden that evening. Adam and Haia hid themselves among the trees, in an attempt to conceal their shame and disgrace.

"Where are you?" the call was heard. They both understood that the one question encompassed many others. "Where are you hiding? Where have you ended up? Why are you hiding from me? Do you not know I am omniscient?"

"I heard Your sound in the Garden, and I was afraid because I was naked, so I hid. It is not proper to stand naked before a King, and therefore I was ashamed," Adam murmured, his heart full of wonder at the strange feeling of shame that inundated him.

"Who told you that you were naked? Did you eat of the tree from which I had forbidden you to eat?"

It was with a punch in the gut that Adam realized with shock the nature of the unfamiliar emotions surging through him. He understood where they emanated from and how they had wormed their way into him. Suddenly, the bizarre conversation between him and his wife a short time earlier made sense, along with their reconciliation, as they ate the spectacular fruit his wife had served him.

"The woman whom You gave to be with me, gave me of the tree, and I did eat," he whispered, gazing contemptuously at the shame-faced Haia; even as he recognized that in doing so, he was showing ingratitude for the very thing he had asked God for.

"What is this you have done?" Haia was asked by God.

A torrent of tears poured from the woman's eyes, as she realized what the serpent had done to her and the way it had managed to seduce her into violating her Maker's will.

"The serpent beguiled me, and I did eat," she whispered as she sobbed. "It infected me with the poison of its wickedness and caused me to eat of the fruit of the tree. The evil it injected into me caused

me to make my husband sin, since he knew that my husband would leave me if he found out I had transgressed."

"Because you have done this, cursed are you from among all cattle, and from among all beasts of the field; upon your belly shall you go!" God said in anger to the serpent, as he enjoyed watching his victims, caught in their ruination.

The upright serpent felt invisible hands gripping it and ripping off its arms and legs from its body. A horrible scream was heard from one end of the world to another, as its gleaming multicolored skin was stripped off of its body. The serpent, as it lay on its belly, opened its mouth to defend itself.

"There is no defense for a seducer and an enticer," God replied. The tongue of the serpent was caught, and torn to pieces so that all the creatures of the world would know that no creature should be suborned to sin.

"...And dust shall you eat all the days of your life," the curse continued. "Whatever you eat will not bring you joy. Your food will always be at hand, so that you never need to appeal to Me with any request." The mortified serpent tried to coil within itself to avoid the rage being poured upon it.

"...And I will put enmity between you and the woman, and between your seed and her seed; they shall bruise your head, and you shall bruise their heel." There will be a constant hatred on the part of her seed toward your seed; wherever they see you they will try to crush your head, while you will be able to hurt them only at their heels." Adam and his wife watched the serpent writhing in pain on the ground.

"And you, for causing your husband to sin," God turned to Haia, who was trying to hide from the rage directed at her. *"I will greatly multiply your pain and your travail; in pain you shall bring forth children.'* The pain of childrearing, the difficulties of pregnancy and the agony of childbirth will be your lot. *'...And your desire shall be to your husband, and he shall rule over you. "*

God's fury then turned on Adam. "'And you, because you did not investigate and inspect what your wife gave you to eat; *because you have hearkened unto the voice of your wife, and have eaten of the tree, of which I commanded you, saying: 'You shall not eat of it...' Cursed is the ground for your sake; in toil shall you eat of it all the days of your life. Thorns also and thistles shall it bring forth to you; and you shall eat the herbs of the field.'"*

The tears began to flow from Adam's eyes, causing him to wonder in dismay, "Will I and the animals eat from the same trough?!"

God said to Adam: " *'In the sweat of your face shall you eat bread, 'til you return unto the ground; for out of it you were taken; for dust you are, and unto dust you shall return.'* You shall eat human food, but only after you toil to produce it. And when you die, you will be buried in the earth. You will no longer belong to the upper spheres."

"Until when?" Adam winced.

"Until a man is born circumcised."

Adam looked at his wife Haia; as the light that once shined from her became dimmer and dimmer, and their bodies which had once been enrobed in light were now sheathed in skin only.

"Haia is no longer your name, but Eve, because you have acted like a snake (*hevia*). From now on, you will be associated with the snake, so that you will not sin again."

The skin stripped from the snake was cut and sewn into garments for Adam and Eve.

"If Adam eats from the tree of life, he will live forever and be able to deceive the people who will be born after him, to think that he too is a god," thought the Lord, "so I will banish him from the Garden of Eden, so that he cannot partake in the fruit of the tree of life."

Adam, Eve, and their children were banished from heaven to the material world, to cultivate the land, " *Adamah*," from which they had been taken. The Cherubim — fierce angels of destruction — were placed at the gates of the Garden, who would prevent the unworthy human beings from entering inside there. They wielded *"the flaming sword which turned every way,"* as the opening to Hell which would turn from burning to freezing for the evildoers, if they tried to break through into a place where they did not belong.

Now the day was ending, as the sun about to set on the sixth day of Creation.

The sky took on a reddish hue as the sun set, the distant horizon ablaze. The roar of the animals crying aloud replaced the rustle of the fruit trees, which had been the lot of the inhabitants of the Garden of Eden; this sent tremors through the bodies of Adam and Eve. They shuddered and sweated as the light of the sixth day vanished, and were left looking at the arid earth, totally bare of trees and grass that had filled the place from which they had just been expelled.

Sadness for all the creatures of the earth filled the heart of Adam. "We have sinned against You, Master of the Universe, and for this we deserve death; but how have all the animals and beasts You created sinned? If You do not bring down the rains, the animals of the earth will have no food, and they will all perish. Please, act for the sake of Your Glory, bring down the rains to revive the soul of every living thing," Adam prayed, his hands outstretched, as he searched for mercy from above, towards the ruddy horizon.

Rain then began to fall, watering the arid land, covering the land in pastures and meadows. Trees hidden beneath the surface of the earth, as if waiting for human prayer, burst forth from the bosom of the earth, bearing leaves and fruits. Adam watched the wonder unfold around him, watched the wild animals eagerly eat the fresh grass that had sprouted at the height of its glory on earth. However, his gaze turned to horror as before his eyes, the light dimmed, darkness and gloom beginning to descend upon the earth. He heard the sounds of Eve's frightened crying, the howls of their young children seeking some comfort in their mother's hands.

"The world is being destroyed because of me! Darkness is falling over the whole world!" Adam whimpered in pain. "You devastated Your world because of me. My sins are causing all creation to return to chaos; I ruined Your world instead of guarding it..."

Adam fell asleep. A deep slumber descending on him in the evening. In his dream, he saw the serpent's mate come to him and rub against him. Adam awoke in a panic, his eyes tearing. "I created demons and devils in my sleep," he reflected, dismayed at his inability to guard his mind.

For a long time, Adam and Eve sat in darkness, hours of prayer and supplication lest the land be destroyed. The falling rain washed over their faces, merging with the tears rolling from their eyes. They trembled, paralyzed by the terror of impending death, leaving them broken and desolate. They curled up, crying, trying to shield their children with their bodies, whimpering in voices that rent the heavens.

"It is the Sabbath, the day on which I competed My creation of the universe. It is a day on which all Creation will be blessed. A day on which nothing is made or manufactured, no labor is performed, a day of rest which testifies to the act of Creation. Rest is the final element of Creation; without stopping, there can be no starting. It is the holy Sabbath…"

A light gleamed in the east, cracking the obscurity that enveloped the world, illuminating eyes blinded by darkness. A line of light spreading over the earth shone hope into the hearts of Adam and his wife.

"He does not want to destroy the world; we have sought forgiveness and atonement and found it!"

In awe, the couple watched, inspired by a sense of renewal. *"A psalm, a song for the Sabbath day,"* the melody rose from Adam's mouth. *"It is a good thing to give thanks unto the Lord, and to sing praises unto your name, O Most High."*

Adam and his wife went out to dance in the presence of the Creator of the World. They went on singing and dancing for many hours in honor of their Creator, realizing that their lives had been granted to them with complete mercy. The hours passed, and the sun tilted to the west. "This is probably the way of the world," Adam told Eve as he saw her face darken as she watched the sun set. "After every night there is a day, and after every day, a night."

"But I'm scared," Eve said in a trembling voice as she remembered their last period of darkness. "They wouldn't stop crying the whole night through." A shudder gripped her when she heard a growl from nearby.

Adam got to his feet, took a piece of pottery he had found next to him and threw it at the ominous sound emerging from the dusk, hoping that would drive away the menacing creature. But that potsherd hit another, and a glimmering spark lit up the scene. Adam, gazing in amazement, ran towards the potsherds without thinking about the animal he was trying to drive away. He took two potsherds in his hand and began to beat them together. A spark ignited, lighting the leaves scattered on the ground. The flame drove away the darkness of the gloomy night, instilling confidence in the woman and her children. "Blessed is the Creator of the lights of the fire," the man murmured, watching in astonishment the flickering wonder.

CHAPTER THREE

Cain and Abel

A quiet breeze blew through the stalks of wheat, which kissed each other as they elegantly danced. The rays of the late afternoon sun caressed the extensive pastures. The sound of the sheep's bleating was accompanied by the chirping of the birds, singing as the sun got ready to set.

Cain was busy building an altar to offer a sacrifice to God as his father had commanded. He piled up stones, and on top of them he placed half-rotten stalks of flax along with the roasted barley remaining from his midday meal.

"I have brought You an offering, as my father instructed," Cain said, sneering at his father's command. "If You are hungry, bring down fire from heaven and consume my offering!" Cain, laughing to himself, looked at the offering of leftovers he had placed on the altar he had built.

"Such nonsense!" He thought to himself as he turned his back, returning to his labor. "I do not know what came over my father to tell me to waste my valuable time in order to bring this offering." Cain turned his head to look at the altar; perhaps something was happening. "Apparently my father dreamed that he made a sacrifice, and fire came down from heaven and consumed it. There is no limit to what a person can imagine," he chuckled to himself.

"How did father put it? 'When I first saw the dawn and realized that God would not destroy the world, that he had accepted my repentance, I sacrificed a bull whose horns preceded its hooves — it burst straight out of the ground, head first!'" Cain gestured toward the altar with contempt. "There are more important pursuits than such... vanity! A man has to support himself!" he thought as he turned back to his plow.

Abel, a handsome young man, took a different approach to his brother, carefully placing one stone atop another, arranging them adroitly. His hands caressed the stones with reverence, his heart rejoicing at his father's command. He had a pair of lambs, carefully inspected to be unblemished, thick with snow-white wool. He slaughtered them and placed them on the altar. "It is true that we are not allowed to kill animals, but the prohibition does not apply to animals that we kill in order to eat. Therefore, my father sacrificed, before God, that horns-first bull." Abel looked at the altar in hope, whispering a prayer from the bottom of his heart. "Please, Father in Heaven, accept my offering that lies before You and accept my gift to You."

A loud thunderclap shook the area, making the forest animals flee and the birds take flight. Abel looked at the fire that descended upon his offering, consuming every last trace. "Thank you, Lord," he whispered as he fell to his face, tears of happiness filling his eyes.

Cain who had been on his knees, busy rooting out the thorns and thistles rising from the ground, sprung up, panicked. A pillar of fire descending from the sky was visible to him from afar. Cain began to run towards the fire, to see what was happening.

As he sped towards the column of smoke, towering over everything, he thought in disgust, "it seems to be rising from where Abel is grazing his flock. I hope a bolt of lightning has finished off the bastard. Has he no shame? He takes two wives, and leaves me, the eldest, just one!"

Cain stopped suddenly, looking at his brother Abel, who was bent over the ground in tears; in front of him was the altar above which the pillar of smoke rose. The smell of burnt flesh was in the air. "What are you doing?!" he shouted contemptuously at his brother.

Abel raised his head in amazement, looking at his brother approaching him. "I offered a sacrifice to God, and God accepted my offering," he said innocently.

"I offered a sacrifice to God, and God accepted my offering," Cain imitated his brother mockingly. "Who told you to sacrifice anything? And where did you get your offering?"

"Father told us to make a sacrifice," Abel replied, puzzled at the question. "See, fire came down from heaven and devoured the offering."

"It's just lightning! Stop imagining things. You sound just like father, full of fantasies and tales about the Creator and offerings," he sneered.

Abel, who was bigger than his older brother, got to his feet and looked with disgust at Cain, who was much thinner than him. "You better keep your mouth shut!" he said to his brother, "The Creator and father's sacrifice are not stories and imaginings!"

"Really? Who told you that? Father, perhaps?" Cain burst out laughing. "You burned two sheep, and you think God accepted your sacrifice?! If there is a Creator at all, He is not interested in sacrifices!

If the Creator exists, and He created all creatures, as father told us, then why would He need sacrifices? Is He hungry? And if He is really hungry, will two sheep satisfy Him?"

Abel looked at his brother, trying to figure out what motivated him to speak in such a way, searching for some positive angle from which to approach his brother's heretical declaration. "My dear brother, you may not have understood what father explained. God does not need sacrifices and He is not hungry. Rather, He wants us to approach Him and be willing to sacrifice our bodies and our lives to Him. To prove that we are worthy recipients of the abundance of good He desires to bestow upon us. If we sacrifice all the flocks and herds, it would still not be enough, but we must make at least a token effort. Try it, brother, it is worthwhile for you! Bring an offering to the Lord and see, He will respond to your offering."

"Try?! I tried it, and I tell you there is nothing! I brought a sacrifice and nothing happened!" Cain shouted angrily.

Abel looked at his brother compassionately, realizing the despair he'd felt when his offering had not been accepted. "What sacrifice did you bring, my dear brother?" he asked gently.

"What does it matter? In your opinion, no matter what we sacrifice, it is irrelevant anyway. I sacrificed flax stalks and leftover barley from my lunch. I put everything on the altar and nothing happened. Just a waste of time and energy!" Cain declared.

"No, brother, you had to sacrifice from the best you had, the finest flour and oil, the best fruits and vegetables. God wants to see that your heart is with Him, and that you are willing to give Him the best of the best," Abel explained.

"Stop preaching morality to me, scoundrel!" Cain's face burned with rage. "Are you not ashamed to lecture me? You are a thief! You took two women for yourself, while I, your firstborn brother, was left with one! And even that was not enough. At the height of your audacity, you took Belibera to be one of your wives. I know the evil of your actions, taking Belibera — who is the most beautiful of all women, perfect in every way — to be your plaything. You will have sons and daughters from our sister Ima, but you will make sure Belibera never gets pregnant, to keep her as your plaything, so that her beauty will never fade and she can remain your plaything forever!"

"Why do you call me a thief, brother?" Said Abel sadly. "It is quite obvious that Kalmana should be your wife and Belibera and Ima should be my wives!" Abel tried to reason with his brother: "You and your wife have straight, black hair, while my wives and I have curly light hair. You and your wife have blue eyes, while my wives and I have brown eyes. You and your wife..."

"Shut up already! Stop your nonsense! Do you think it interests me? You're a damned thief, trying to justify yourself now that you've been caught red-handed, claiming that you deserve what you stole. According to you, if father's teachings are indeed correct, then you are a thief, and as a thief, you deserve the death penalty! It's a shame that Father is not applying that law to you. I'd happily do it!" Cain shouted at his stunned brother. Cain turned away and left his brother alone next to his flock.

"I must be cautious around him," Abel thought sadly. "I hope he does not try to do something foolish."

Cain sat in his tent, his wife Kalmana noticing that her husband seemed angry and upset. "What troubles you, my dear husband?" She asked gently, trying to appease her grumbling husband.

"That is none of your business!" He said angrily. "Go out, make me something to eat, and bring me water to drink!" Cain looked at his wife in disappointment, thinking of the differences between her and Belibera, his brother's wife. "And make sure it takes you long enough for me to have a bit of quiet, without you driving me crazy!"

Kalmana went out of the tent quickly, her gaze downcast as she teared up, hurrying to do what her husband had asked, until she remembered his demand and slowed down, so she would not return before the rage had passed. She wanted to escape this place but has nowhere to go.

Cain sat on his mattress, heartsick and angry. He was shame-faced, trying to escape the thoughts troubling his mind. A feeling of disappointment and alienation from his Source flooded his heart. Like a child, he had been rebuffed by his Father, with disgust and rejection; Cain knew he had done something wrong but he found a way to blame it all on the One who had turned him away.

Suddenly, he heard a voice within him: "*why are you wroth? And why has your countenance fallen?*"

Cain sprung to his feet, trying to see who was speaking to him, realizing there was no one he could see.

"Why am I angry? Why am I upset?" he challenged the being surrounding him, defending himself against the One who had humiliated him. "You know full well why! You did not want my offering, but you accepted my brother's offering! Why should I not be furious? Do you play favorites, valuing one soul over another?!"

"You are fully aware that I do not show favoritism," God replied in a conciliatory voice. "*If you do well, shall it not be lifted up? And if you do not do well, sin crouches at the door*. If you improve your behavior, I will happily accept you. If you do not improve your behavior, then it is you who will be responsible for your sin and your eventual punishment."

"But what can I do?" Whispered Cain, shamefaced, knowing that his thoughts were an open book for the being speaking to him. "I cannot stop thinking about her... I cannot stop hating my brother."

"You can do anything! Even though this instinct overpowers you, you can control it! You must not be ruled by your instinct, you must be the ruler and control it. You are the one who decides what you crave and lust for. You can direct yourself wherever you want, you can control your thoughts and desires. This is your ability and your responsibility as a human being, and this is the great task of your life! If you rule over your evil inclination, you will benefit from all the good; and if not, it will rule you — until your final days!"

Cain looked up, staring at his wife Kalmana as she entered the tent, loss and rejection filling his heart, which was still preoccupied with Belibera, his brother's wife. "Let me eat and get out of here!" he hissed angrily at his wife. Kalmana, gaze downcast, put the food in front of her husband, and fled from the tent, humiliated and tearful.

"Thief, why do you herd your cattle on the land that belongs to me!" Cain shouted at his brother Abel. "Do you remember that we divided the world between the two of us? The land and everything connected to it is my domain, and you have everything which moves on its surface. So how dare you herd your animals on the pasture-land that belongs to me?"

Abel sighed from the bottom of his heart, knowing that this was a mere pretext to give his brother an excuse to quarrel with him. "If so, why are you wearing clothes made of wool? Why do you live in a sheepskin tent?" He enquired of the red-faced Cain.

"The area on which the altar stands belongs to me!" Cain challenged him, changing the subject. "Forty years ago, my father built this altar when he brought his sacrifice, and therefore it is mine, because mine is the firstborn rite. Because I am the firstborn, I deserve twice as much of everything on earth, so I take this place to graze my flock." Cain approached the altar with a sharpened rock in his hand, as if he were about to smash the altar's stones.

"I cannot let you do that, my brother," Abel said as he stood between Cain and the altar. "This land is not yours to use!"

Anger flared in Cain's eyes, "You are not just a thief, but a brazen one! You take Belibera for a wife, and now you want to take the land?! Everything connected to the land belongs to me! You only have the things which move upon it."

"According to you," Abel grinned at his brother, "Kalmana should be mine as well. She is not attached to the ground, she moves upon it. Although you do your best to push her down into the dirt with the way you treat her!"

"Adulterer! You have set your eye upon my wife!" Cain screamed as he dropped the sharpened rock and attacked his brother angrily. The sturdy Abel saw his brother running towards him with his eyes blinded by fury and wrestled Cain to the ground. Abel sat on Cain's slender body, one hand gripping both of his brother's hands, as the other clenched into a fist, raised to punch him in the face.

Cain's face was filled with anxiety at the realization that his brother was far stronger and that he was at Abel's mercy. "Please, brother," Cain wept. "Please, brother, forgive me, I do not know what happened to me. We are brothers, do not hurt me; if you injure me, you will be hurting mother and father deeply. And what of the Master of the Universe — what will you tell Him if you harm me? Forgive me, my dear brother, for what I did," Cain pleaded, tears streaming down his face.

Abel looked at his crying brother, feeling pity for him. He let his raised fist fall, rather than pounding the face of his skinny brother. A few moments passed, with Abel still sitting astride his crying brother. "I hope you never repeat this folly," Abel whispered as he got up off his prostrate brother and walked towards his flock waiting for their shepherd.

Cain rose from the ground and shook the dust out of his clothing. He felt the hatred for his little brother, who had just humiliated him, increase exponentially. He watched his brother walk away from him; eyes filled with contempt. Quietly, he approached the sharpened rock lying on the ground. His hands lifted the rock, concealing it behind his back. Silently, he snuck up on his brother, who was tending to his flock.

Abel sensed his brother approaching, but he was confident that his brother would not be able to hurt him. Slowly, he turned to his brother to see what he was up to. Suddenly, Cain pulled out his hand from behind his back, raising it angrily to viciously attack his brother, slashing the palm of Abel's outstretched hand. The next swipe connected with Abel's thigh, splitting open his leg, forcing Abel to the ground in pain. Cain's face appeared demonic as he looked at the sprawled Abel. "Now you will get what you deserve, adulterer!" Cain taunted him, mercilessly smashing the rock into Abel's body as the latter screamed in pain. Blood splattered everywhere, staining Abel and Cain in crimson. Abel screamed in pain, trying to dissuade his brother from the awful act, "brother... what... what will you say to God... if you kill me?"

Horrible laughter burst out of Cain, "I'll take care of that!" Cain struck his prone brother again and again, trying to end his life, but Abel kept writhing. "This beast does not want to die. Father slaughtered that animal by slitting its throat." Cain smiled grimly, "so we will see if it works for this beast as well." Cain hacked at his brother's throat with the sharpened rock. A few seconds passed, and Abel stopped wallowing.

"Now it's all mine," Cain smiled, dropping the rock and heading back to his tent.

Kalmana looked at her husband returning from the field, his clothing dyed red with blood. "Why are you looking at me like that? Get moving! Get me water to bathe, and bring me clean clothes!" he said contemptuously to his wife. "On the way, tell Belibera and Ima, Abel's wives, to come to me! And pack up all of our belongings, I'm tired of living here. We're moving the encampment somewhere else!"

"Did you hear those screams?" Eve asked Adam, terror darkening her features. Eve, who had her own tent far from her husband's, came running pell-mell to see the husband she had avoided for forty years. "It sounds like Abel's voice to me," she whispered in fear, tears streaming down her cheeks.

Adam, fasting and wearing sackcloth as he sat on the ground, looked up at Eve. His eyes were suffused with sorrow, regret, and mourning for the sin which he had committed by eating from the tree of knowledge forty years before. "What...? I heard nothing..." He muttered, his heart numb.

"There were screams from the altar you built," Eve said hysterically. "It sounds to me like something terrible has happened to our baby, Abel!"

Adam got up and followed his wife reluctantly. Birds were circling above the altar, and they greeted Adam and Eve, and clean animals were clustered around the site. Eve dashed madly towards the spot where the animals had gathered, and Adam followed her. The animals scattered in every direction when they saw Eve and

Adam running towards them, revealing the gruesome tableau to the now-bereaved parents. Adam and Eve fell to the ground in grief, as they wept over the loss of their younger son, mourning their bitter fate. The sound of crying could be heard far-off, as the parents embraced the bloody, broken body of their beloved child.

"Cain!" Eve whispered in anguish, knowing of her firstborn's jealousy towards his younger brother.

"Surely, Cain is the one who murdered Abel, our blameless, virtuous son. Abel was capable of repair the universe, our hope to atone for our grievous transgression," Adam cried, knowing that his last chance to fix the damage he had done had now vanished. He knew himself, and he could not overcome his desire; four decades of fasting and repenting could not keep him from running to Lilith, the serpent's mate, whenever he fell asleep.

"What do we do now with the body of our dear son?" asked Adam in a tremulous voice, as he saw the sun about to slip below the horizon.

The raven's call answered his question. Adam and Eve looked up at the sound; it was a raven digging in the ground and placing another raven's corpse in the pit, amid the dwindling twilight. "Apparently, we must do the same," Adam murmured to his wife. The couple began digging a grave with their hands. Finally, they placed their young son in it, their eyes blinded by tears.

"Where is Abel your brother?" The question rang in Cain's ears.

"He does not know!" Cain thought jubilantly. "*I know not; am I my brother's keeper?*" His feigned innocence was repulsive as he argued: "Is that my job? I am not his guardian. Had You but asked me to watch over him, I would have done so gladly."

"The voice of your brother's bloods cries unto Me from the ground," the accusation rang out. "It was not only the blood of your brother you shed, but the blood of the millions of descendants who were to come from him as well!"

Cain's mind worked tortuously, trying to exonerate himself over his brother's murder. "It was not I who killed him, but the evil instinct you gave me that made me do it. You are the Master of everything, and without You no man can do anything, so You let me kill him. In addition, had you but accepted my sacrifice, I would not have been jealous of him, nor would I have killed him. Also, had I ever seen a dead man? How could I know that he would die from my blows?"

The curse was pronounced: *"and now cursed are you from the ground, which has opened her mouth to receive your brother's blood from your hand. When you till the ground, it shall not henceforth yield unto you her strength; a fugitive and a wanderer shall you be in the earth."*

Cain began to cry, overwhelmed by the punishment given to him, trying to turn back God's fury from upon him. "Master of the Universe! You bear all of existence — is my sin too great to bear? I regret what I did. I want to repent," he said, but his heart was not in it.

"Because you have, at least, displayed confession and repentance, I will let you live. However, you must leave immediately and begin your wanderings," God commanded.

"Whosoever finds me will slay me," Cain said, knowing that his protective shadow was gone, and not even the forest animals would fear him.

"You shall not die now, but at the end of seven generations. Now, you shall bear on your forehead a mark of the animalistic crime you have committed," said the voice to Cain.

Cain felt a sharp pain, as if his very skull were splitting open — as a truly beastly horn sprouted from his forehead. "And I give you this dog to guard you! An animal to protect an animal!"

Kalmana, outside the tent, screamed as a terrifying dog curled up at Cain's feet.

A few minutes passed and the vision faded. Cain touched his forehead and looked at his new ally. The sound of crying outside his tent made him jump out of his skin. "Father and mother must be coming to make me pay for Abel's death," he thought apprehensively. Cain rubbed his eyes tightly to make them look reddish; with a tearful voice he moaned bitterly, striking himself in the head as he left the tent. "What have I done? I have killed my brother! I am evil, I too deserve to die! Death is better than life for me!"

Adam and Eve watched their only remaining son weep over the brother he had murdered. The anger that filled their hearts subsided upon seeing his bitter grief over the death of his younger brother. Cain fell at his parents' feet, shrieking, heartbroken. "Please kill me! I deserve to die! There is no place for the wicked like me in the world!" He begged his parents. "Father, you must kill me; avenge your son's blood immediately. Though the Creator forgave me for my sins, you must pour my blood upon the ground for what I did to my dear brother!"

Adam and Eve were left shocked by their son's performance.

"Did... Did the Creator forgive you...?" Adam asked in bewilderment.

"Yes..." Cain wept. "When I confessed the deed and repented, he forgave me for my iniquity," Cain whispered between his sobs.

"What did the Creator tell you?" asked Adam.

"He told me that he had accepted my repentance, but in order to atone for my crime, I must go wandering," Cain replied to his father.

Adam, excited, clapped his head with his hands. "This demonstrates how great repentance is!" He thought to himself. *"It is a good thing to give thanks unto the Lord,"* he said aloud. "You must do now what the Creator has told you. You must gather your belongings, and you and your wife will go together on the journey which has been decreed for you," Adam commanded his son.

"What will happen to Belibera and Ima, the wives of Abel? I must take these poor unfortunate souls with me. It is my fault that they have become widows..." He said to his father, hoping to convince him.

"No!" Adam resolutely ordered. "It is not fitting that after murdering your brother, you will inherit his wives! These unfortunates will have to wait until more sons are born to me and your mother. You will not take them! My offspring will never associate with your offspring!"

With sorrow and heartbreak, Cain collected his belongings and set out with his wife Kalmana on the long journey. His dog walked in front of them, navigating, chasing away the beasts of prey trying to drive him away from any spot where he tried to pitch his tent. He felt the ground vibrate beneath him whenever he tried to settle down in a specific location.

For the first years of his wandering, Cain refused to father children, thinking of the burden that would be placed on him to carry offspring along with him on his endless trek. Then an idea flashed through his mind, convincing him to reproduce. "The decree of wandering is upon me, but not upon my son; I shall have a son, and I shall build a city for him to dwell in. I will even name the city after my son." A year later, Cain and his wife had a son. *"and he builded a city, and called the name of the city after the name of his son Enoch.*

As the years went by, Cain and his wife had more sons and daughters. Their firstborn Enoch, gave birth to Irad, whose son was Mehujael. Mehujael's son was Methushael, who fathered Lamech.

"We dissent! We think it more fitting that You destroy the world You have created and all that is in it, especially man," the supernatural beings Uzza and Azael told their Creator. "Adam was unable to overcome his lusts and because of his sin with mother Lilith, we were created; surely all other men will not be able to restrain themselves and keep from sinning with women," they sneered. "Humans cannot control themselves, they are weak and have no faith and loyalty to You, their only desires are to pursue the pleasures of the world. They are not like us! They are mindless, unable to understand that the pleasures of the world are nothing but a trick, imaginary and illusory. Better that you lay waste to them and put us in charge of Your world. That is the only way the world will reach the improved state You so desire!"

"Then, it seems, we must see how you withstand the test," God decreed. Uzza and Azael were sent down into the world, in human form.

CHAPTER FOUR

Lamech

"Adah!" Lamech the blind shouted at the top of his lungs, to his wife sitting outside the door of the room. Adah entered the room, chastened. "Why do I even have to tell you to bring me and my dear Zillah something to eat! You are so dense that you do not understand that people need to eat! Get moving or you'll have to explain yourself to my fist!" Lamech screamed in the direction of the door.

"Yes, my lord," Adah said, shamefaced, and left the room, seeing the tear in the corner of her sister Zillah's eye, lying at the feet of their blind husband.

"I do not know what to do with this ugly woman," Lamech sighed to her sister. "So what if she takes care of the two boys, Jabal and Jubal? She thinks that because she is a mother to the children, she has to rest all the time."

"I'll get you something to eat, my beloved husband," Zillah said in an attempt to ease some of the burden on her sister.

"God forbid, my dear," said Lamech in shock. "Why should you trouble yourself? It was not in vain that I took you to sit in my shade, but to savor your beauty. If you start working, you will look like Adah! You have to take it easy, or you will ruin your beauty. I gave you that wonderful potion, which spares you from the suffering and sorrow of pregnancy and birth and enduring the burden and onus of bearing babies and raising children. Thanks to me, you, my love, will remain gorgeous forever — no pregnancy, no birth, no responsibilities. For that, your sister Adah exists."

"Well, I have a surprise in store for you," Zillah thought as her lips formed a smile Lamech could not see. "Despite your magic potion," she reflected silently, "I am now with child. So much for your grand plan!"

"Well, my husband, you are the one who decides," she said aloud, grinning mischievously.

The door opened and Adah brought her husband and his wife food to eat. Zillah looked lovingly at her tormented sister; a smile appeared on Adah's face as Zillah gestured to her belly, hinting to her sister that she was now pregnant.

Months passed, and Zillah gave birth to a son and a daughter, Tubal-Cain and Naamah.

Tubal-Cain grew up to be a blacksmith, forging weapons of war. His sister Naamah, who was perfect in her beauty, became re-nowned throughout the land; all the nobles in the area bowed down to Lamech in an effort to win the hand of his stunning daughter. Lamech gloried in the respect and prestige with which he was re-garded for being the father of such a beauty — while her mother's looks had faded with the passage of time.

"Zillah, summon our boy Tubal-Cain. I want to go hunting, and I need him to guide me," Lamech demanded one day. He still resented what pregnancy and childbirth had done to Zillah's beauty. Zillah considered her husband and his misery over the children she had borne him.

"What a fool!" She thought to herself. "He cannot not see me, but he is distressed by my looks. My face is invisible to him, but he is concerned about every wrinkle, mark, and blemish on my body? It is sheer arrogance and conceit on his part. He just wants to display me to his friends because a wife is merely a piece of art. A better a piece of art is sterile and untouched, rather than one that brings more beauty into the world." Her face radiated happiness, as she recalled how awful it had been in the past. Those days when friends and acquaintances would gather in their home for the presentation of Lamech's beautiful wife. Now she was spared the indignity, but her daughter, Naamah, was being put on display for the rich and powerful. "I'll call our son right away," she told her husband, accentuating the term "our son."

Lamech and his son Tubal-Cain set out for the forest. Tubal-Cain led his elderly father, who wanted to preserve his youthful practice of hunting despite his failing eyesight. At the approach of human voices, the thickets in the forest rustled, as the wild animals fled from their invaders. Meanwhile, above their heads, the birds of the forest took flight, making their own escape.

Tubal-Cain presented his father with a new metal bow and arrow. "Father, feel the bow!" He happily said to his father. "I finished making it just yesterday; it's incredibly precise."

Lamech happily felt the bow. "Give me an arrow. When you see an animal, tell me, and aim my hands. I haven't been able to hunt anything interesting in a long time."

The father and son stood quietly in the heart of the forest, merging with the many trees and plants, disappearing into the undergrowth, their rhythmic breathing barely audible. The sound of forest animals and birds could be heard once again. Tubal-Cain touched his father's shoulder, whispering in his ear, "father, prepare yourself, we have a very special animal in front of us." Lamech stretched the bowstring, readying the arrow to fire. His muscles were tense but maneuverable enough to allow his son to aim at the mobile target. "Now!" Tubal-Cain whispered. The metal arrow flew fast, cutting off the leaves of the trees in its flight, approaching its target, slicing open the throat of the strange beast. "Yes!!!" Tubal-Cain shouted, scaring the forest animals from their spots once again, happy that his aged father would return from his hunt triumphant.

"Did we hit it?" Lamech asked, elated.

"Bullseye!"

"Let's see what it is," he urged his son. "They think your father is too old to be a mighty hunter. We will show them today!" Laughed Lamech, clapping his son on the shoulder, as the latter led him to the spot.

"What is it? What kind of animal is it?" Lamech joyously asked his son as Tubal-Cain approached their quarry. Lamech felt the tension in his son's shoulder, felt his body tremble. "Do not tell me we missed..." Lamech muttered in disappointment.

"If only we had..." Tubal-Cain whispered with trepidation.

"Tell me, what is it?" Lamech impotently stumbled over his son's words. "What did we hit?"

"It is a man, a man with a horn coming out of his forehead, Father," Tubal-Cain's voice trembled. "I fear that we have killed Grandfather Cain," he whispered.

Lamech clapped his massive hands together, heartbroken at the realization that Abel had been avenged by him. His powerful hands smashed into the head of his son, who was turning to embrace and console him, fracturing the boy's skull in an inadvertently tragic act. Tubal-Cain fell, onto a bed of leaves and twigs, on the floor of the forest. An awful moan issued from his throat, as Lamech sensed that he had crushed his son's head between his fingers. "Tubal-Cain!" He cried, falling to his knees alongside the lifeless bodies of his son and grandfather.

"Lamech! Tubal-Cain!" Lamech, prone on the ground over the bodies and weeping, could hear the calls in the distance. "Lamech! Tubal-Cain!"

Lamech raised his head from the ground, recognizing the voices of his wives. "What can I tell them?" He thought apprehensively. "Even without this tragedy, they despise me; what will happen now?" A rush of emotions hit him. "Maybe it's better for me not to answer, to lie here among the trees, to be preyed on by the beasts of the forest…" The thought of the forest animals chewing on his flesh while he was still alive sent chills through his body. "But what will they do when they see what I have done…?" He sat for a few moments, trying to decide whether to answer his wives' call. He felt the cold of the coming night stealing into his bones. "I cannot stay here!" He decided.

The wives heard the bitter cry in the distance. "Listen, it sounds like Lamech's voice," Adah told Zillah. "Apparently, the old man's hunting trip was unsuccessful, so he sits pathetically and weeps bitterly."

"Tubal-Cain… Where are you?" Zillah called out loudly to the place from which the crying was heard. "Tubal-Cain! Lamech! Answer me…"

"Over here…" Lamech's voice could be heard in the distance. The women looked in the direction of the voice, watching as their husband rose from the undergrowth.

"Stop playing games, hiding from us like you're some kid!" Adah rebuked her husband as she approached him. "Where is Tubal-Cain hiding?" She asked angrily. "Have you not noticed that it will soon be night?!" The women advanced rapidly towards Lamech, searching for the mischievous Tubal-Cain, expecting him to come out of nowhere and scare them. "Where's Tubal-Cain?!" Zillah screamed, seeing her husband's crestfallen face.

Lamech, his gaze downcast, sensed that his wives were very close to him. "Tubal-Cain was killed…" He whispered and burst into tears.

Zillah and Adah ran quickly towards the place he pointed to, staring in horror at the lifeless body sprawled on the damp forest floor.

"Tubal-Cain! " The cries burst forth from the heartbroken mother, who rushed to hug her dead son's body. For a long time, Zillah and Adah held Tubal-Cain's body in their hands, weeping over the glimmer of youth extinguished so swiftly. "You…" Zillah whispered to her husband with hatred. "You murdered our son!"

Lamech twisted inwardly, searching for some way to explain the tragedy, realizing that his wives had not yet noticed the body of the slain Cain. "I did not murder him! It was by mistake! I did not mean it!" He tried to explain himself. "We went out hunting and then Tubal-Cain told me to shoot an animal that was in the distance. I hit it, and we went to see what kind of animal it was, and Tubal-Cain saw that it was my grandfather Cain…" Lamech paused to motion his wives in the direction of Cain's body. The women's cries were renewed when they saw the patriarch of the family lying dead, an arrow piercing his throat. "So, when Tubal-Cain told me that the beast was not an animal but Cain, I slapped my hands together, accidentally striking poor Tubal-Cain in the head, and he died on the spot," he said tearfully.

"These poor souls must be buried," Adah whispered to Zillah, seeing that the sun was about to set. "There's nothing to do. It's going to get dark soon, and if we stay here in the heart of the forest, we'll be prey for the animals. Let's hurry up, my dear sister," she said sadly, as she began to dig graves for the child and the old man. The women dug for a long time, burying the bodies in the heart of the forest with weeping eyes. Then, stumbling their way out of the heart of the forest to their home, guiding their husband.

"What did I do?" Lamech sadly asked his wives. "Did I kill them on purpose? You know I did not mean it. It was an accident!"

Zillah and Adah refused to continue living with Lamech. "We do not need you!" They said angrily to their tormented husband.

"I will summon you to the court of Adam!" He yelled at them. "He'll tell you that you cannot do this!"

"Do what you want…" The women laughed, knowing that Adam had separated from his wife after the sin with the tree of knowledge.

Lamech and his two wives entered Adam's room with reverence. They recognized that they were entering into the chamber of a being who was the direct handiwork of the Creator. Adam sat on the ground, face veiled in mourning. For years, he had sat in that chamber, suffering, separated from all other human beings, in exile from his wife and offspring, a self-imposed exile. Lamech cleared his throat, drawing Adam's attention to him.

"My lord," Lamech said in awe. "Unfortunately, I have committed a sin by my own hand. Inadvertently, I killed your son Cain, and my son Tubal-Cain." Adam raised his face to Lamech, and Lamech could feel the grief in Adam's heart, hearing that his firstborn son had also died violently. His intellect told him that the matter had been foreseen. Adam stared at Lamech, thinking about what he could say to him. He sympathized with Lamech, who had killed his own son as well. Shaking his head, he spoke, "tell me what happened."

Lamech began to tell Adam the story of his life, his wives, his children, and the unfortunate incident which had resulted in two deaths. "Since the incident happened, my wives have been refusing to live with me! I've come to ask you to order them not to defy me," Lamech concluded.

"Have you repented?" Adam asked.

Lamech nodded affirmatively. "For a year in total, I have been alone, regretting the horrible crime done by my hand."

"If so, wives of Lamech, you must not separate from your husband! The man has repented for the crime he committed. You must go back and live with him!" This was his definitive verdict.

The peals of laughter coming from the two women surprised Adam and Lamech. "You must be kidding! It's true, he repented for a year. He's barely eaten and drunk all these months but does that seem enough to you?! You have been sitting in the same place for one hundred and thirty years. Fungi has begun to grow on you because you are as still as a corpse! You cut yourself off from your wife and all your descendants, for a sin you committed inadvertently. You have been sitting in your room, meeting almost no one for years, trying to atone for your sin! And you say that his single year of penitence for killing two people is enough?! If so, apply this rule to yourself first. Stop cutting yourself off from your family through this self-imposed decree!"

Adam looked in amazement at the two women, realizing that there was truth in their words. "You are right," he said after a few moments of silence. "I took it upon myself!" Said Adam and rose from the dirt in which he had sat for many years. The fungi on his flesh began to flake off one by one, onto the uncultivated ground.

Lamech and his wives watched as the great Adam stood up to his full stature, amazed at his beauty and perfection. "I took it upon myself," he repeated with a smile, "you too have taken it upon yourselves!"

The three bowed to the ground before Adam in reverence. "We took it upon ourselves," the women murmured.

Nine months passed, and Adam and Eve had a baby. "Seth," Eve gently named her newborn, "the appointed one. *For God has appointed me another seed instead of Abel; for Cain slew him.* Perhaps he will be the one who will allow us to repair our world."

Adam and Eve went on to have many more sons and daughters over the years. When Seth was one hundred and five years old, his firstborn Enosh was born.

"Have you seen her?!" Uzza asked Azael in astonishment.

"How could you not?" Azael answered, trying to keep his eyes from jumping out of their sockets.

Uzza sighed, "She looks even more perfect than our mother. I must try to talk to her," he said and started walking towards Naamah, enthralled.

"I'm coming with you," Azael chuckled, hurriedly trying to catch up to his brother running towards the woman.

Naama looked at the two individuals running towards her, "these are not ordinary people," she thought with a self-confident smile. "They look like the sons of God. With them, it seems worthwhile to bring children into the world." Naamah stood up and eagerly awaited her suitors.

The two men stood in front of her, their eyes straining to escape their skulls. "Are you…?" They asked in unison.

Naama smiled ingratiatingly. "Happily," she replied to the two of them.

Nine months passed and Naama bore a son, a strange and powerful boy. "Asmodeus will be his name," she said with a smile when she saw her child, "the king of all demons and spirits he shall be."

After Uzza and Azael had been with Naamah they began to take from the daughters of Adam as they desired, ignoring the words they had spoken to their Creator. Their lust waxed ever hotter, yielding giants who filled the earth with their progeny. Uzza and Azael were banished beyond the mountains of darkness by the Creator so that they would not completely corrupt the face of the earth.

CHAPTER FIVE

The Generation of Enosh

I t was late afternoon. The sun was inching westward, as if bowing to its Creator before setting. Migratory birds flapped as they made their way through a sky painted in shades of yellowish purple, a pastoral scene. A gentle wind wafted past, blowing leaves high in the air.

A large group of people gathered around their youthful leader, a brave man who had developed quite a reputation since he had been a little boy. His audacity and brazenness were widely renowned. He showed no fear or trepidation before any man or beast. He was always eager to commit acts of mischief and malice, a thief who gathered bands of miscreants who devoted their time to pursuing their pleasures and whims of the heart.

"Enosh," came the call from the ranks. "Please tell us your history. Who are your ancestors?"

Enosh smiled happily at the question, which had been asked at his behest. "My father's name is Seth," he said proudly, anticipating the second question.

"And what was his father's name?" Asked the questioner.

"Adam," he replied with a smile.

"And what was Adam's father's name?" Here came the long-awaited question.

"My father's father had no father! The Creator himself made him," said Enosh, longing for the next question.

"How did He do it?" He was asked.

He smiled lightheartedly. "It's no problem! I can do the same! My power is equal to that of the Creator, and I can make human beings, as He did!" The sounds of astonishment and wonder arose from the crowd, causing a tremor of joy throughout Enosh's body. "I'll show you!" he said, piling up dirt and shaping it into human form. Enosh, who was familiar with magic and spells, began to whisper over the lump of dirt all manner of bizarre and weird incantations and chants. The people assembled, looked at their leader, and started to fill with fear and excitement when they saw the earthen body jolt into movement. The mass of dirt, into which Enosh had inserted a demon's soul with his spells, rose to its feet.

"Bow before the creation of my hand!" Commanded Enosh.

The exhilarated crowd bowed down to the image made by Enosh, ready to surrender their lives at the command of their revered leader.

"I am the son of God!" Declared Enosh before his people, who looked upon him with veneration.

"Now, back to your dust!" Cried Enosh. The earthen body collapsed in its place, merging with the dirt.

"There is no power but me!" Enosh shouted happily as he watched his people bowing before him.

"What shall we do, our lord?" Asked the people, bowing before their glorious leader. "How may we serve you?"

"There is no king without ministers, and a king is honored when his ministers are honored," he began, delivering his doctrine. "I am the son of God, and I am the greatest of all His ministers. The

Creator's desire is that you honor and pay tribute to His ministers. The host of heaven, the stars, and the constellations are also the ministers of the Creator, and you must honor them. You are insignificant, deficient creatures when compared to me or to the host of heaven, so it is inappropriate for you to turn directly to the Creator. In order to connect to the Creator, you must worship His ministers."

"How are we to worship His ministers?" One of the people wondered.

"You shall worship the host of heaven by making statues and graven images that will remind you of the mighty powers the Creator wrought. You shall offer sacrifices to them, and you shall turn to them in your time of need," Enosh instructed.

"However, you must worship me differently. I do not need sacrifices, nor do I desire a statue in my image. In order for you to have a relationship with me, you will bring me your young daughters so that we can mate and have important sons like me. In addition, one-fourth of whatever you own you must bring to me, and I will protect and keep you."

The gathered crowd quickly ran to fulfill Enosh's will, crafting graven images, statues of stone, iron, and wood. They brought sacrifices to the heavenly powers, and they turned over their daughters to Enosh.

Seth sat, struggling with the sorrow that filled his heart at the growing rumors regarding Enosh's exploits. Over the years, the tales of his son Enosh had come knocking at the door of his humble domicile, depressing his spirit. His son employed various pretexts to avoid meeting him, even though Seth desperately sought to return Enosh to the path of good.

Seth had undergone decades of fasting and weeping before the Creator to help in an effort to reform his son. However, the scuttlebutt only grew louder and louder. Immorality and idolatry filled the earth, abominations that seemed to be indulged solely for the sake of angering and rebelling against the Creator. Depravity and desecration had become commonplace; prostration, libation, and immolation were sacrifices before every idol and image. Robbery, thuggery, and bribery took place along every street in every city, any vice trumping every virtue.

After receiving a prophecy, Seth decided to go in search of his son to return him to the path of decency. Discovering the whereabouts of Enosh was not a complicated task. From everywhere, pilgrims loaded up their young daughters on their animals, heading towards the ivory palace built by Enosh's command. Seth joined the wayfarers, towards the residence of his wayward son

"Father, what are you doing here?!" Enosh jumped out of bed when he saw his father standing there in tears.

Seth's initial reply was a bout of weeping, as he witnessed the profligacy of his firstborn.

"Why did you come here?!" Enosh asked emphatically.

"Woe is me, woe is me!" His father whimpered. "Is this why you were created? To descend to the lowest depths?! To be like an animal that constantly pursues its lusts?!"

"What are you looking for?!" Enosh shrieked helplessly as he looked at his father.

His father could not stop crying. "I am looking for my son, scion of Adam, the grandson of the Creator's own handiwork," cried Seth from the depths of his heart. "But I find a creature worse than a filthy animal, leading himself and his entire generation to sin!"

Enosh looked at his aged father angrily, removing from his heart every glimmer of respect for his parent. "Get out of here, old man, before I order my servants to kill you."

"My son, please, you can control your passions," Seth tried to dissuade his son. "You can improve your ways and behave properly as the scion of Adam."

A peal of laughter burst forth from Enosh. "Control my passions? Why? I have everything I desire! Why should I act according to the laws dictated by your morals? And what is wrong with the laws I have enacted?

"Believe me, I really do not understand you and Grandfather; you lot are wholly illogical. All your laws are against nature, trying to carve out a path for yourself that you perversely think is moral and superior. But think about it: if an animal does not devour the weak, the weak will remain alive, and their weaknesses and flaws will be passed on to the next generation. Does the Creator of the universe not want us to perfect and correct His world?

"Now, as most people are fools and dupes, it is not possible for them to worship the Creator directly, so I focused them on worshipping statues and idols. And because they are so inferior, I sacrifice too, mating with their daughters, impregnating them with wise and powerful offspring. You call them children of Adam, while I call them children of Enosh. Future generations should come from me, Enosh the Great!" Enosh laughed at his agitated father, "If you want, you too can join me. I assure you, you will enjoy every moment."

Enosh stopped laughing for a moment, as if remembering something. "At last, I understand how my firstborn, Kenan, turned out so odd-- he's just like his grandfather. Abstaining from everything, lonely and praying all day. He is already forty, and has never seen a woman. I invite him to join me in the festivities, but that fool refuses every time. Maybe you ought to take him with you; he drives all the people here crazy. Unfortunately, I ended up with an idiot son, who fails to understand the pleasures of life."

Seth looked at his lustful son and realized he could not change his ignorant mind. "I have a prophecy to deliver to you!" He said firmly. "Soon the Lord will cleanse the world with water. He does not want to wipe away all of Creation, just those like you! Either you repent for your deviant ways and influence your people to return to the path of good, or the greater part of you will die!"

Seth turned his back on his son, leaving the room knowing that his words would not affect a man so immersed in his lusts. In his heart, the one remaining hope was that he could save his grandson Kenan and take him along. The sound of derisive laughter accompanied him as he left. "Foolish old man, you threaten me with death, but you do not understand what it is to live! Do not forget to take my idiot son Kenan with you..."

A tremor passed through the ground. The people, who a moment earlier had been kneeling in front of their idols on the tranquil seashore, looked up in horror. Their deafening screams and shouts filled the air, as they saw water towering high above them. The ocean had gathered itself into a soaring wave, rushing toward the shore on which the people had brought sacrifices to the host of heaven. The people began to run amok, trying to escape from the beach, which only a few minutes earlier had seemed quiet and idyllic. They tried to flee from certain death, even as they realized a slight distance from the waterline would not save them.

The tsunami surge progressed rapidly, crossing the shoreline, washing over every crevice in its path, picking up whoever stood in its way, carrying them hundreds of feet and slamming them into the lofty buildings. The bodies of the children of Enosh were smashed by the heavy rocks, as the wave shattered stones like clods of dry dirt. Trees were uprooted along with the altars built beneath them, erasing the deviant path that the people had chosen to walk.

The wave lifted everything. Effortlessly overturning the earth on which, a few moments earlier, crooked and devious people had walked. For long minutes, the wave continued to surge, sweeping away everything in its path, laying waste to the corrupted universe. A third of the world was washed away, leaving tens of thousands of sodden corpses lying on the earth with no one to bury them.

The report of a natural disaster reached the door of Enosh's palace. Crowds pounded on the gates, demanding to hear why he was angry with his children and drowning them by the thousands. Enosh locked himself in his chambers, afraid to go out and face his people, feeling that they might harm him, and blame him for the vast destruction.

Then the great doors to the ivory palace opened, and a young man stood there to face the raucous crowd. His frail body, clad in simple, white linen surprised those standing at the gates. His compassionate eyes stared at the rioters seeking to hold Enosh responsible for the disaster that had befallen the land. Gentleness and love radiated from his face, restraining the wave of people. They halted in their tracks, like a bloodthirsty warrior suddenly discovering an infant on the battlefield, given pause by its very helplessness. Tears welled up in the eyes of the young man standing before the people.

"Where's Enosh?!" Someone called out to the young man.

"Enosh? That unfortunate man is hiding in his chambers, frightened by your rage." The young man smiled at the people.

The mob began to surge forward to try and enter the palace and take revenge on the man whose actions had led to the death of one third of the world's population.

"But what good will it do you if you kill him?" Asked the young man. "My father, Enosh, made the same mistake you made!" The powerful voice of the frail young man stopped the rioters' advance. "My father thought that his ability to control demons and devils gave him superiority over other human beings and made him a god. You too, mistakenly thought that of him! The truth is that controlling demons and devils is a very simplistic science that any human being can learn. You turned away from the Lord and regarded this power as divine, but this is not true at all. Every human being was created with psychic powers by which to control these lesser beings!" The young man smiled at the crowd standing in front of him. "Understand, if a person can control other humans who have free will, then surely a person can control demons, who have no free will."

"Who says you're right?" Shouted a man from the crowd.

The man laughed. "They do," he said, pointing behind him.

A sound of fear and terror erupted from the large crowd standing in front of the youth, as tens of thousands of horrible demons and devils appeared from behind him, bowing to him. The people fell on their faces, genuflecting to the new god they had encountered.

"Get up, you fools!" The youth commanded those who bowed down to him. "Are you so unthinking as to understand not one word of what I have said?! I am no different from you. I am merely an ordinary person who learned these simple vanities almost by accident, as I learned the will of the Lord from the children of Adam. You must not bow or worship me or any other creature in the world. We must all worship only God, the Creator of the Universe!

"Will you teach us how to worship?"

"I will learn and I will teach too," Kenan reassured them.

For many years, Kenan taught his contemporaries wisdom and knowledge, ruling over the earth. Some human beings had begun to walk the path desired and outlined for them, while others persisted in their foolishness. Kenan strove to bring his contemporaries back to the path of truth and to undo the decrees he envisioned falling upon the human race. He warned his contemporaries that the seas would flood the land again as a result of their actions. Due to the ignorance of the generation, the oceans would once again arise, as they had erased a third of Creation; but Kenan's warnings of a global flood that would erase all humanity were considered dubious.

Kenan's eldest son, Mahalalel, was born to him at the age of seventy. Mahalalel begat Jared when he was sixty-five years old. Enoch was born to Jared at the age of one hundred and sixty-two years.

"Enough, Father, I cannot go on like this." Enoch sat on the ground of his room, crying before his Father in Heaven. "I try to teach your sons the right way. As long as I hid in my room, worshipping you alone, I was not susceptible to their spirit of arrogance. Since You commanded me to go out to the people and teach them Your laws, I have felt overwhelmed by the sin of pride. I know that I am nothing, and I have no true understanding or intelligence, but whenever I speak to your people, they bow to me and look at me as if I were God. Their unsophisticated minds are unable to understand, that my own merit is only by virtue of Your grace. No longer can I live among them; I'm scared to death of the feelings of haughtiness that bubble up within me."

Enoch's voice broke as he wept, "I stopped appearing before them every day, instead meeting them once a week, so that I could spend more time with you, but this only increased their dependence and admiration for me. Since the age of sixty-five, I have been teaching Your children Your ways. For two hundred and forty-four years, I have been trying to bring Your sons back to You. True, many of Your sons walk the path of truth today, perhaps nearly all, but I feel I have no more strength to endure the honor people pay me. I cannot remain a simple man, if they continue to treat me like this..."

There was a quiet knock at the door. Enoch wiped away his tears, and with great sorrow he went to open the door which was infrequently disturbed. His son Methuselah stood in the doorway, his eyes watering, sorrow and grief covering his face.

"What happened?" Enoch asked apprehensively.

"He died..." cried Methuselah. "Adam has departed from the world, the perfection of Creation has returned his soul to the Creator." Enoch burst into tears, sadly embracing his eldest son, feeling the pain at the passing of the righteous man.

A massive funeral was organized, as people from all over the world came to pay their last respects to the forebear of humanity.

Enoch stood on a small hill, in front of the people, to mourn the handiwork of the Creator, the first man.

"Brethren, beloved children, our righteous patriarch has passed away. The handiwork of the Creator of the Universe is gone. The sun shines less brightly as the provender of the world has been taken from us, at the age of nine hundred and thirty. He sinned once in his life, and for this he sat fasting for one hundred and thirty years. We are all the children of this most wonderful creation of God.

"He was supposed to live a full millennium, but in his love for us he gave up seventy years of his life to the savior all mankind is waiting for. A man who will return our hearts, without exception, to our Father in Heaven. When I studied with him, he once told me that the Lord showed him all his descendants, until the end of all generations. He revealed to him all that they would learn and innovate in the world, showed him how long each of them would live, and when each would depart from the world.

"Our patriarch told me that while God was showing him everything, he saw a beautiful baby in a crib. 'Who is this?' he asked. The Lord answered, 'this is the savior of your descendants, the messianic King David, who will be born many years from now. However, he is destined to die in infancy.' Adam told me that he started crying and begging for the Creator to take years from his own life and give them to this baby. The Creator willingly agreed to take seventy years from Adam and give them to the messianic king in days to come." Enoch wiped tears from his face.

"This is our dear patriarch, who gave his life for us. Blessed be the True Judge. May his memory be a blessing."

The people took their patriarch's bier to the Machpelah Cave in Hebron. The bier was swallowed up into the depths of the earth so that fools would not come to worship the created in the place of the Creator.

Fifty-six years after the death of Adam, Enoch faced his own demise. Sequestered in his room, he emerged annually to see the people. One day a year, the crowds celebrated as their revered. holy man revealed himself to them.

"Whatever shall I do?" He whispered in fear, knowing that in the next hour he would have to fight the passions that threatened to overwhelm him, seeing the absolute adulation and awe that all the inhabitants of the world had for him.

"In a few days, the trial will be over," Enoch heard a heavenly voice say. "You will depart this world shortly. Until then, try to teach them as much as you can."

Enoch smiled happily at the thought that the yoke of this trial would soon be lifted off his shoulders. Quickly, he got to his feet, then went out to his people.

"In a few days, I will leave you," he said to the crowd, his face glowing. "Now I must teach you ..."

For hours upon hours, tirelessly, Enoch laid out, before the people, laws and judgments which they had to obey. The crowd thronged before him, some sleeping, some listening, while time passed in the unceasing sermon.

Late at night, a noise came from the sky. The frightened people looked up to behold a huge fiery horse descending from the sky. Enoch smiled happily, ran towards the steed, joyously waving farewell to the shocked people. Enoch jumped lightly onto the back of the mount, which began galloping. A great multitude ran after the revered man, refusing to leave him, refusing to part with him.

The horse halted. Enoch begged the people to leave him alone and let him die, but the people refused. Eight hundred thousand people were running after the man who had led his generation for the last three hundred years. Eight hundred thousand people were trying to catch the fiery horse. For a whole week, Enoch warned his loved ones that if they did not leave him, they would die too.

On the seventh day, snow fell, making it difficult for those who trailed resolutely behind the mounted Enoch. In the evening, the horse rose above the ground and soared upwards towards the gray sky, leaving the people who saw the spectacle lifeless. A delegation, later sent out to search for the leader of the generation, found all these people buried under the freezing snow.

Methuselah, son of Enoch, was crowned king over all human beings. A righteous and honest man, he was dedicated to teaching his contemporaries the way of God. Morality and decency were his watchwords.

However, despite Methuselah's remonstrations, lusts of the flesh and lewdness overshadowed righteousness and chastity; robbery and violence were incited by people greedy for ill-gotten gain. Idolatry, which was far less demanding, quickly overtook the worship of God. The people descend into the abyss of oblivion, towards all imaginable abominations and lusts.

Methuselah's son, Lamech, also tried to teach the people, but his efforts were for naught. Hunger and famine came to the land, in order to persuade human beings to correct their evil ways but instead, the wicked used it as a pretext to plunder and loot the land.

At the age of one hundred and eighty-one, he married Ashmua, daughter of his uncle Elishua, son of Enoch. A year later, their son was born. Lamech named the child *Menachem* (comforter), but Grandfather Methuselah told Lamech he ought to be named *Noah* (rest), as he had been born circumcised.

He knew, as Adam had taught him, that the birth of a circumcised child would signal the end of famine in the world. "Do not call him Noah, even though this is his true name. Call him Menachem, so the sorcerers cannot harm him."

CHAPTER SIX

Noah

The day was drenched in sun. There was discernible joy on the faces of the people thronging the streets. Music and song filled the air, raising the sprits of the men and women on hedonistic outings in the heart of the town. It was a tumultuous scene, men and women strolling and intermingling licentiously and without shame.

A shout arose from the edge of the market, drawing the attention of the bystanders to the source of the screams. An old widow, selling her wares wept as a young man, son of one of the city councilors, leaned down from his horse to seize some of her produce without paying. The spectators burst out laughing at the scene. The brazen youth approached the howling old woman, who was dressed in rags, and slapped her across the face. "Madwoman, you're interrupting my fun!" He rebuked her. "I penalize you twenty apples!" He declared, as he reached into her stall to collect the fine.

Voices were heard from all sides, "he's right!"

"I've been harassed by this madwoman too." Within a few minutes, the old woman was left desolate in the market, with no fruit and no stall, crying over her fate.

"Apparently, this crone finds that her life has grown tedious," laughed a middle-aged man, revealing his rotten teeth. The middle-aged man approached the old woman, dragged her to the street corner, and beat her to death.

The sound of hurried footfalls rang out as people rushed to the market square. Two men, one older and one younger, stood on a small stage, addressing the crowd. They were covered from head to toe in white, their heads bowed earthward, with white hoods obscuring their faces. Their pale hands peeked out from the edges of their long sleeves. Their charcoal-black beards protruded below their hoods, contrasting with their snowy attire.

"People!" The younger of the white-clad men shouted. "How long will you persist in committing evil? How long will you continue to do beastly deeds and anger your Creator? Don't you know that God, Creator of heaven and earth, will make you pay for your corrupt ways? Do you think that there is no justice and no judgement? Do you think there is no true judge?"

"There are judges, that's true!" A young woman cried out. "They come to us so we can show them a good time!" Wild laughter arose from the crowd at the young woman's response.

The laughter subsided after a few moments. The white-clad man resumed as if he had never been interrupted. "You must know that the Creator of the world hates lewdness! To fix the world and raise it to a higher level, He created us, human beings! If we fulfill His word, He will reward us abundantly and bless us. Yet, you rebel against him and choose the path of perversion. The Creator wants to give you the best, but you reject Him!"

"The best? What could be better than what we have?" A man in the audience laughed. "We have to plow and reap only once every forty years. The land is bountiful with everything good. Even the act of plowing itself has become a trifle, since you, Menachem, invented the plow. The truth is that you are a genius! How did no one think of that before?! Apparently, every genius is a little crazy, so now you're telling us to stop enjoying life. Thanks to you, we have plenty of fruits, vegetables, bread, and wine, almost without working. Our women give birth to healthy, whole, strong, and beautiful sons and daughters. Although we are not sure they are our children," he said with a leer. "But what does it matter? We are all one big family, who needs more than that?" Voices were raised in agreement throughout the large crowd.

"God wants to give you much more than that!" The second, older white-clad man explained. "Material wealth and pleasures of this world are not the purpose! The Creator wants to shower you with good in the world to come, if you follow His will in this world!"

"The world to come?! Who said there is a next world? Have you been there? Has anyone come back from there?" The audience teemed with questions and challenges.

"Certainly it exists," the younger speaker insisted.

"Menachem, stop trying to confuse us!" A man at the end of the row shouted. "It is only because you are unable to have children that you are talking like that, thinking up all kinds of nonsense! So what if you cannot father children? You can still live it up!" The crowd burst out laughing again. "I'm sure a lot of the girls here will agree to 'marry' you and your grandfather Methuselah. Stop being shy. They're good girls…"

"God will bring upon you a deluge, and He will destroy the whole world!" Menachem shouted before the laughing people.

"We'll deal with it. We have boats and ships to weather any flood," someone in the crowd chortled.

"Repent, and God will forgive you," Methuselah exclaimed in a pleading voice.

"You can forgive me yourself," a man called out from the crowd, "but I have more pleasurable things to do…" He walked away.

"Come on," giggled a young woman. "We've had enough of this show for today. I'm sure there will be another performance tomorrow." The crowd dispersed, leaving Methuselah and Menachem alone in the bustling market square.

"The end of all flesh is come before Me; for the earth is filled with violence through them; and, behold, I will destroy them with the earth."

This was the shocking prophecy Noah had received. Noah sat in his room; his teary eyes downcast. Speaking to his contemporaries for one hundred and eighty years had made no impression at all. Not a single person had changed their deeds due to the rebuke he and his grandfather had offered. A feeling of utter failure filled his heart as he thought about the abuse he and his grandfather had experienced in their dealings with the people, who had seen them as a joke, an amusing circus act put on in front of them for free.

The knowledge of the impending destruction of the earth, sooner or later, had discouraged Noah from marrying, from being fruitful and multiplying. Then God had corrected his misapprehension. "You must marry a woman and have sons with her," he was commanded.

As for the looming catastrophe, he was told: "*make you an ark of gopher wood; with rooms shall you make the ark, and place pitch upon it, inside and outside. And this is how you shall make it: the length of the ark three hundred cubits, the breadth of it fifty cubits, and the height of it thirty cubits. A skylight shall you make for the ark, and to a cubit shall you finish it upward; and the hatch of the ark shall you set in the side thereof; with lower, second, and third decks shall you make it.*

Noah married Naamah, who was eighty-two years older than he; the daughter of the righteous Enoch who had been taken up to heaven in a storm. She was a righteous woman who walked in her father's ways and was disgusted by the deeds of her generation.

Noah began preparations for the of building the ark. After twenty years of marriage, the couple had three sons in a row: Japheth, Ham and Shem.

A group of people gathered around Noah, seeing him diligently tending the full forest of cedar trees he had planted. Noah tended to his grove meticulously, making sure that the cedars would grow straight and tall.

"Noah, what are you doing? Is our life too tedious for you?" They laughed at him.

Noah stopped his work, looking at the assembled people mocking him. "The Lord is destined to bring a deluge upon the earth, so I am building an ark which my family and I will enter when the floodwaters come," he said, then continued his work.

"He's really lost his sanity, poor thing," sniggered one from the contemptuous crowd.

"Noah! Why not take some of our cedars? Why do you have to grow so many trees? Ask nicely, and we will give you ready-made cedars!" They roared with laughter, anticipating an entertaining response.

"God commanded me to build an ark in order for you to see what I'm doing, to understand that my words are not uttered in vain. I am willing to invest all my energy to prove to you that what I'm saying is genuine. And God does not want the ark to be contaminated by impure hands," Noah said.

"So when will this deluge take place?" One of them demanded.

Noah looked at the questioner, trying to make up his mind as to whether he was serious or not. "Eighty years from now! Forty years ago I planted this forest by God's command, when I was four hundred and eighty years old, now I am five hundred and twenty years old. Forty years ago, God told me that he would give you another one hundred and twenty years to repent before the deluge. So," Noah concluded soberly, "that means there are only eighty years left until the flood!"

"Eighty years?" His interlocutor repeated, his face displaying fear.

"Indeed!" Noah said with the hope that his questioner might repent.

The serious man concluded with a broad grin, "if so, my dear friends, even if this madman's words are worth something, we still have eight full decades to enjoy ourselves!"

The peals of laughter bursting from the crowd made Noah's face fall. He felt the cynical laughter of his contemporaries cut through his very soul.

When the cedars had grown magnificent and tall, Noah and his sons chopped them down. They sawed them, crafting gigantic, wooden planks to build the ark their father had commanded them to build. It was difficult, heavy labor, which began one hundred and fifteen years after Noah had first planted the forest.

People gathered around the construction site where the massive ark was being assembled. From all over the region, the curious came to see the four madmen — and to mock and deride them. They ridiculed the eccentrics who were diligently engaged in their craft. The four men continue their work without paying attention to the scorners.

Finally, the ark was completed, a meticulously planned and artfully constructed vessel. There were three decks, each divided into rooms and compartments. The bottom deck was for the storage of food, fresh water, and refuse which the weeks of being sealed in the ark would produce.

The second deck, which was narrower, housed the animals. The top deck, tapering to a one-cubit wide skylight at the top, contained the living quarters for Noah and his family.

This was the product of five years of intensive construction; but it was not only the ark that Noah built during those years. He also married off his sons, to the daughters of Eliakim the son of Methuselah. However, their marriages would not be consummated until the deluge was over and they left the ark.

On the tenth day of the month of Marcheshvan, one thousand, six hundred and fifty-six years after the Creation of Adam, heavy grief descended on the world, as the long-lived Methuselah passed away at nine hundred and sixty-nine years old. People gathered to accompany the oldest of men on his final journey. Although he had been mocked and ridiculed during his final years, many came to accompany the man who was a living monument to the Adam of yore, seven generations earlier.

Noah wiped the tears from his eyes, understanding that his grandfather had died so that he would not witness the punishment about to befall mankind. He understood that God, in His compassion, had taken his grandfather from the earth before the apocalypse.

The divine command came to Noah: "go and sit by the hatch of the ark, you and your household. I will send you all the living things upon the earth, so that they may enter the ark with you. They will be male and female, beasts and animals which are uncorrupted, in mated pairs."

"But how will I know which animals to admit into the ark? How will I know which are uncorrupted?"

"Whichever animal comes and crouches before you are the ones you shall bring into the ark."

Noah hurried to the hatch of the ark to greet the animals, on whose behalf he and his family had been laboring for one hundred and twenty years. He could hear noise and commotion outside, as the bystanders fled in terror from predators reaching the site of the ark — where people had gathered to watch the eccentric shipbuilding family. Thousands of spectators had been observing the giant, pitch-covered ark; now they scattered everywhere, seeing that all the beasts of the forest were on their way to the ark.

"Noah! What is the meaning of this menagerie?" Shouted a man from atop a tall tree toward Noah, sitting peacefully at the hatch of the ark.

"As I told you, God is bringing a deluge upon the earth. In a week's time, it will begin! I will shelter the animals in the ark because God does not want to completely destroy His world, but to rebuild it in holiness and purity," Noah explained as he watched the animals coming and crouching before him.

Noah nodded his head at a pair of prostrating pachyderms, and the elephants entered the ark. Entry was granted only to those animals which bowed and scraped before Noah; those who refused were angrily removed by a ring of ferocious beasts which now circled the ark. Thousands of pairs of animals, birds, reptiles, and insects entered the ark in perfect order. They formed a long double line, the end of which, could not even be seen from the hatch of the ark.

"How will we fit them all?" Shem asked his father in bewilderment. "The ark may be enormous, but it does not have space to accommodate all these animals."

Noah smiled. "My dear son, have I not taught you that 'space' is an illusion? God fills all space, and we exist within Him. He can do anything."

"If so," Shem reasoned, "why build such a large barge? We could have made do with a dinghy!"

"You are correct, but the Lord commanded us to make a great ark, so that everyone would come to marvel at it and ask us why we build it. Now, we can tell them what is destined to happen, perhaps motivating them to repent." Noah's face fell. "Unfortunately, that was not the case."

Hours passed, then days. The zoological caravan continued to embark upon the ark. The human spectators around the massive shop, now numbered in the tens of thousands, wondering at the marvelous scene.

An older man, the disbelief clear on his face, demanded, "Noah, in all seriousness, what is going on here?"

"The animals are entering, and tomorrow my family and I will join them on the ark. We will seal the hatch behind us. As for you…" Noah wiped away a tear.

"What, do you think that you and your family will live, while we all perish?!" The older man laughed at Noah. "If the floodwaters come, you too will die, I promise you that!" He seemed panicked by the thought of torrential rains drowning the earth but still enthralled in the lusts and abominations he so enjoyed. He could not break his shackles. "We will take our hatchets and axes, and we will breach your vessel. If there is to be a deluge, then you and your family will drown too!" He impotently shouted, gazing at the thousands upon thousands behind him.

Noah looked at the crowd pityingly. "Why will you not repent instead? If you express regret and return to God, then there will be no deluge. Then we may all live."

"Live?! You call that living? You have your endless list of restrictions and prohibitions that we are supposed to abide by! What sort of life is that?" He screamed powerlessly. "Also, if we do as you say and there is no flood, how will we ever know if you were telling the truth? Perhaps, it is all fantasy! Are we to live the rest of our lives according to your delusions? No thank you! If there is a deluge, then you and your family will drown alongside us all!"

Dismayed, Noah replied, "we shall see tomorrow."

CHAPTER SEVEN

The Deluge

A week has passed since the animals began to embark. God's words were being fulfilled. *"Of every clean beast you shall take to yourself seven and seven, each with his mate; and of the beasts that are not clean two and two each with his mate; of the fowl also of the air, seven and seven, male and female; to keep seed alive upon the face of all the earth."*

Noah and his household stood with their backs to the ark. The ramp, which the last of the animal had just mounted, was now standing empty, as if it were waiting for its last passengers, the humans, to ascend it. The heavens turned gloomy, a darkness at midday. Lightning and thunder tore through the murky sky, and drizzle began to fall, creating a fine mist on the assembled horde surrounding the ark on all sides, wielding axes and hatchets.

"Is this your deluge, Noah?!" exclaimed one of the men with a laugh, trying to raise his voice over the booms of thunder.

"You can still repent," Noah shouted to the crowd, half in despair.

"Noah, be careful, your hair's getting wet. Watch yourself, you might drown!" Laughed a young woman.

The rain intensified. Noah felt he had to enter the ark with his household, but he was reluctant to abandon the huge crowds around the ark. He fervently wished that the precipitation would turn into rains of blessing, refusing to believe that God would truly annihilate everyone left outside.

"My husband, we must go in and seal the hatch!" Naamah said to Noah as she saw he was hesitant to enter, understanding his look and the struggle in his heart. "This is the will of God ..." She whispered consolingly to her husband.

Noah and his family entered the ark, pulling in the ramp as the rainwater rose unnaturally. Boiling hot springs began to erupt from the ground beneath the feet of the people shouting frantically. Noah and his family heard screams of desperation and death; they watched as tens of thousands of people ran to try and breach the ark, being stopped by the beasts of prey, which kept them from entering the rescue ship. His sons pulled in the ramp, sealing the hatch in front of everyone. They could hear the pain and pleading of the people who finally realized their end was nigh, calling out for mercy and repentance.

The deluge lasted forty days and forty nights, a time that seemed, to Noah and his family, like an eternity. They could still hear screams and pleas as the ark was lifted by the tide of the tempest. The air was filled with the sound of rushing water, along with heartbreaking and jaw-rattling thunder and lightning. The ark was shaken by the roiling waves, its hull creaking as if it were about to shatter. The animals within voiced their terror, from howling canines to lowing cattle to birds squawking in fear of imminent death. Noah, Naamah, their sons, and their daughters-in-law were tossed like meat in a cauldron, pitched from one end of the ark to the other, screaming and crying at the top of the lungs. Noah, bruised and battered, used the last of his strength to look to the heavens and supplicate his Creator. "*We beseech You, Lord, save now.* We have no strength to withstand the threats which surround us. *The breakers of death surged round about me; the menacing floods terrified me. The cords of the netherworld tightened; the snares of death lay in wait for me.* Answer us, Lord, answer us. Redeem us, turn to us, and show us favor; redeem us and rescue us!"

Gradually, the water calmed down, and the ark began to float slowly over the subsiding waves.

Right away, Noah and his family found their chores to be back-breaking and grueling. They had to feed the animals, birds, reptiles, and insects' day and night, going to the trouble of feeding each in its proper time. Their eyes were swollen from the lack of sleep and awful stress, their arms heavy from the burden of distributing copious amounts of food. The stench was unbearable, as they were sealed inside the ark with the dampness, the animals, their food, and their waste.

One day, Noah slowly approached the lion, which was eagerly awaiting its food. Hours had passed since Noah's appointed time to feed the hungry lion and provide something that would satisfy its voracious appetite. Noah, with great apprehension, presented the starving predator a heap of hay and leaves, knowing that such a vegetarian repast would never satisfy the hunger of the carnivore; even if it consented to eat, it would not be sated. The big cat looked angrily at Noah, rebuking him for presenting such objectionable victuals. It stuck out its massive paw, claws slashing at Noah's leg with great force, slicing his flesh to the bone. Noah screamed in pain, escaping in terror from the chamber of the frustrated beast.

"What am I to give this chameleon to eat?" Japheth thought to himself. "It doesn't eat anything. It will just starve to death." He was concerned at the sight of the skinny lizard. He peeled a juicy pomegranate, recoiling in revulsion at the little worm wriggling inside the fruit. In disgust, he shook the worm out of the pomegranate, dropping it on the floor. The chameleon darted over and happily snagged the worm with its tongue. Japheth smiled happily, understanding God's providence over all His creatures.

For forty days and forty nights, the rains continued to fall. Afterwards, for a hundred and fifty days, water covered the entire earth. There were no trees, no mountains, nothing aside from water. The ark floated above it all, a small leaf on an infinite sea, the last refuge for all of earth's animals and birds, a rescue ship for the last remnant of humanity.

Noah went to open the skylight at the top of the ark to see the world of infinite water. He anxiously chipped away at the pitch covering the window fasteners. Finally, he opened the skylight, allowing a refreshing breeze to blow into the miasma of the ark. Noah inhaled the fresh air gratefully.

Suddenly, he recoiled in panic. A huge human eye peeked at him through the skylight. "Please, give me something to eat," the titan said in a weepy voice.

"Og?" Noah called in astonishment.

"I'm hungry," the giant whispered pleadingly.

Noah climbed down to the lowest deck of the ark to fill a box with fruits and vegetables, though he knew that such an amount of food would not suffice to satisfy the titan.

Og gulped the food down eagerly, "thank you. I'm still hungry, but at least that's something."

"How did you survive the boiling water?" Noah asked in amazement.

Og smiled happily, "I just clung to your ark; the water around it remained cool. Apparently God did not want the pitch on the ark to melt."

Noah looked at the titan who had escaped the deluge, realizing that he was now responsible for the giant as well. "I'll go get you something more to eat," Noah said thoughtfully, once again descending to the bowls of the massive ship.

Ham drifted through the ark, annoyed. He watched his wife, who was feeding the animals under her care with dedication. His lusts overpowered him. "Come here!" He demanded of his wife, ordering her around as she looked at him in alarm and fear. Ham wildly grabbed her hand, dragging her to their private stateroom.

A wind passed over the great waters, as they began to subside. The ark rumbled, as the people and animals inside it felt the keel strike something solid and come to rest atop it. Their seemingly endless cruise had come to a halt. Noah opened the skylight, and the sunlight dazzled the eyes of his family. They could breathe freely, fresh air rushing into their nostrils.

Noah stuck his head out of the ark savoring the refreshing breeze. "Hurry!" God commanded him. "Send out the raven, so you may know if the waters have retreated from the face of the earth."

"Why the raven?" Ham asked his father.

Noah looked at his wayward son angrily, "the raven is the cleverest of all birds, so I will send it out." Shem returned eagerly with the raven, which peered contemptuously at Noah and his son who carried it. Noah reached out, picked up the raven, and placed it in the open air above his head. However, the raven merely circled the ship, refusing to go anywhere, squawking in protest over the skylight.

Ham audaciously declared: "I think you had best retrieve it."

Noah responded derisively, "you are birds of a feather, aren't you? You, the raven, and the dog — all three of you have violated the prohibition upon us all in the ark! That's why you have such sympathy for him."

Ham looked down angrily, knowing that his disgrace was obvious to all, now that his wife's pregnancy was visible. "So what if we did that? That's not a reason to let the raven die. You want to exterminate its species from the face of the earth because of this act it committed? You just hate it!" He responded aggressively to his father.

"And what good will it do you?" Noah replied with disgust. "It is not a clean bird; you can neither eat nor sacrifice it!"

Ham grinned in his father's face. "In your opinion, did the Creator make something unnecessary in His world?" Ham's grin widened as he saw his father's discombobulation. "And if you do not loathe and want to destroy it, why did you not send one of the clean birds, of which there are seven of every species?" A peal of laughter erupted from his throat. "Perhaps you are attracted to the raveness?"

Noah raised his hand and slapped it across his son's face. "Only a twisted mind like yours could come up with such things! You show your true face! I am ashamed to call you my son!" He denounced him angrily.

He thought sadly, "the root of evil is in this son."

Ham turned away from his father, contemning him for his actions

The days went by. Noah sent the dove to see if the waters had dried up. The dove returned with nothing.

Waiting another week, Noah sent the dove again, and by evening it had returned with an olive branch in its mouth. Noah rejoiced at the sight of the olive branch — this was incontrovertible proof that the trees had begun to grow again. His heart skipped a beat as he realized what this meant-- they could leave the ark and find food. It was as if it said: "may my food be as bitter as an olive, but from God's hands; rather than sweet as honey, but from human hands."

Another week passed and Noah sent the dove out again. This time, it did not return.

Now it was the first day of the month of Marcheshvan, and Noah pulled back the ark's cover. He could see that the world was all mud and mire. Witnessing the boggy scene, Noah realized that he could not leave the ark without an explicit directive.

Twenty-seven more days passed, and the long-awaited command was issued: "*go forth from the ark, you, and your wife, and your sons, and your sons' wives with you. Bring forth with you every living thing that is with you of all flesh, both fowl and cattle, and every creeping thing that creeps upon the earth; that they may swarm in the earth, and be fruitful and multiply upon the earth.*"

Noah, his family, and all the animals came out of the ark. They found themselves in the Ararat Mountains, northeast of where the family had begun their compulsory cruise. The land was desolate, the heavy rains having consumed everything. Trees, plants, flowers, and herbs had been completely obliterated by the flood that swept over the land. The precipitation had penetrated into the topsoil, turning up the dirt and ripping out all the vegetation. Corpses littered the landscape as the family began their long journey back to their previous homestead. In the absence of predators, all the bodies had been left to putrefy, causing noisome stench and decay. Four couples and the newborn, Cush, made their way, witnessing the destruction and devastation that covered the face of the earth. Tears flowed from the eyes of the adults as they encountered the omnipresent death filling the land.

Noah cried as he went, howling and mourning his generation, wiped off the face of the earth, dismayed by the destruction and death. Within him arose a feeling against the Creator who had destroyed His entire world wrathfully. However, in his heart he sensed a voice, "foolish shepherd! You ought to have cried like this when I informed you that I would destroy My world! What's the point of crying now? You are not the person mankind has been waiting for!"

Noah and his family spent many days walking to where the first man was created, in order to reach the place where he had built his altar and brought his sacrifice. Birds, animals, and beasts accompanied the clan, sustaining themselves on any bit or morsel of something worth eating, barely surviving until they came to their destination. Noah and his sons carried loads on their backs, as did those animals who could bear burdens. They had sacks full of seeds and countless shoots, species of trees, plants, vegetables, and fruits that had been carefully kept out of reach from animals. The journey was long, the burden was heavy, the road seemed endless.

"Ugh! I'm tired! Where are we going? What's wrong with this spot? What does that place in the middle of nowhere have that this place in the middle of nowhere doesn't?" Ham sat down where he found himself, setting Cush down on the ground. "I'm staying here!

What does it matter where we bring the sacrifices? For that matter, what do offerings have to do with me? Who needs them at all?"

Noah looked at his son in disgust, loathing Ham in his heart. "We are going on! With or without you!"

Noah continued on his way with Naamah, Shem and Japheth following him with their wives. Ham's wife hurriedly picked up Cush, running to catch up to Noah. Having no choice, Ham picked himself up off the ground and trailed behind the rest of his family, glad that, at least, he no longer had to carry his son in his arms.

As the mountain towered before Noah, a smile of joy arose on his face. He reverently approached the site of the altar built by Adam one thousand, six hundred and fifty-seven years earlier. His hands longingly caressed the stones, which had been battered by the passage of centuries and all of the privations of the intervening years. Quickly, he restored the ancient altar, putting the stones back together.

"I must offer a sacrifice, to thank God for the good He has bestowed upon me and my family," he thought jubilantly as he built the altar. Still, the chronic pain in his lame leg obscured his joy. "I cannot offer the sacrifice, because I have a blemish. My sons Shem and Japheth will present the offering instead."

Noah looked happily at the pillar of smoke rising upwards, feeling a scent penetrating his nose, blinding the rest of his senses. His eyes closed languidly, and a voice was sensed in his heart: *"I will not again curse the ground anymore for man's sake; for the imagination of man's heart is evil from his youth; neither will I again smite anymore everything living, as I have done. While the earth remains, seedtime and harvest, and cold and heat, and summer and winter, and day and night shall not cease."*

Noah was relieved to hear God's promise not to bring another deluge.

Then he heard God's blessing. *"Be fruitful and multiply, and replenish the earth. And the fear of you and the dread of you shall be upon every beast of the earth, and upon every fowl of the air, and upon all wherewith the ground teems, and upon all the fishes of the sea — into your hand are they delivered. Every moving thing that lives shall be for food for you; as the green herb have I given you all. Only flesh with the life thereof, which is the blood thereof, shall you not eat. And surely your blood of your lives will I require; at the hand of every beast will I require it; and at the hand of man, even at the hand of every man's brother, will I require the life of man. Whoever sheds man's blood, even within a man, his blood shall be shed; for in the image of God made He man. And you, be fruitful and multiply; swarm in the earth, and multiply therein."*

He shook at the very thought of the severe punishment brought upon the world due to lusts of the flesh, and the retribution which had destroyed the earth.

"This is the sign of the covenant which I make between Me and you and every living creature that is with you, for perpetual generations: I have set My rainbow in the cloud, and it shall be for a sign of a covenant between Me and the earth. And it shall come to pass, when I bring clouds over the earth, and the rainbow is seen in the cloud, that I will remember My covenant, which is between Me and you and every living creature of all flesh; and the waters shall nevermore become a deluge to destroy all flesh."

Light drops began to descend, while the sun was still shining. Noah tried to understand what the rainbow was, what the Creator meant. Then it appeared in the sky, bands of every spectacular color climbed from the ground to the highest heaven. Noah was enchanted by the sight. This then, was the rainbow. It warmed his heart to consider the wonderful phenomenon of the sun's rays being refracted in water droplets.

God explained: "if your children follow the path of good, then it will rain only at night, when precipitation neither disturbs nor troubles people; but if your children diverge from the path, then it will rain during the daytime as well. Then you will know that it is because of your sins that the rain falls when it is inconvenient — it is only My covenant with you that keeps me from destroying the world again."

Noah was lying in his tent, undressed and stark naked, inebriated thanks to the strong wine he had prepared, now that the vineyard he had planted had finally produced its vintage. His intoxicated snores sawed through the silence of the camp set up by his clan. Canaan, Ham's youngest son, approached his grandfather's tent, peeked out of the opening of the tent and saw his inebriated patriarch.

"Father! Come and see Grandpa, he is completely drunk," Canaan laughed as he told his father about what he saw. Ham approached the tent silently, hearing his aged father's snoring, watching the naked old man. Behind him, Canaan snuck in, longing to see what his father planned to do.

"Why is he naked?" The thought popped into Ham's mind. "He must have been with Mother." It was the obvious conclusion. "This fool has not learned his history!" Anger filled Ham's heart. "When Adam had two children, one killed the other for the inheritance! We are three brothers, and this drunk wants to have more children?"

Ham entered the tent, pulled out his knife, and castrated his father. Out of the corner of his eye, he saw, in the back of the tent, the garment his father had inherited from Methuselah his grandfather.

It had been passed down from Enoch, who had received it from Adam himself. It was the leather garment God had prepared for him when He expelled him from heaven. Ham went to the back of the tent, quietly stole the coveted garment, and slowly left the tent to hide his loot.

"Did you see the drunken old man?!" Ham asked his brother jokingly. "He's lying in his tent, completely naked! That ancient fool drank so much wine, it was coming out of his ears. The old man thought he would bring more children into the world? As if it weren't enough for the three of us to share the inheritance of the world!" He saw the uncomfortable look his brothers exchanged. "Don't worry, I have taken care of him, he will never again be fruitful and multiply!"

Japheth and Shem considered their brother in shock, speechless. Finally, Shem screamed at him, "you wicked bastard!" With a tear glistening in the corner of his eye. "Come on," he said in a whisper to Jephthah, "We will go and conceal the dishonor of our righteous father."

Shem and Japheth entered their father's tent, with their eyes closed, covering their father with a robe. Tears flowed from their tightly closed eyelids, as they felt their father's pain.

A few hours passed, and Noah finally awoke, in intense pain from his genitals. He saw his robe, soiled with blood. A vague memory flooded his mind as he recalled the agony he had undergone while intoxicated-- the recollection of Ham's face leaning over him. Ham had been holding his knife, which was dripping blood. Noah would never forget the demonic leers of his son and his grandson Canaan; they were etched in his mind as he had struggled to awake in excruciating pain, rolling around in his intoxication. Then he had lost consciousness because of the pain or the wine; now, the fog lifted, replaced by the consciousness of what his son and grandson had done to him.

"*Cursed be Canaan!*" Noah said in anguish, recognizing that his grandson had been the initiator of the catastrophe which had befallen him, realizing that he could not curse Ham, someone who had been blessed by the very mouth of God along with his brothers, he directed his imprecation to Ham's son. Noah condemned Canaan to slavery. *"A servant of servants shall he be unto his brethren."* He also felt gratitude to his other two sons, who had concealed his dishonor. *"Blessed be the Lord, the God of Shem; and let Canaan be their servant. God enlarge Japheth, and he shall dwell in the tents of Shem; and let Canaan be their servant!"*

As the years passed, the sons of Noah multiplied, as Shem and Japheth continued in the way of their father. Ham and his sons, on the other hand, persevered their infuriating wickedness.

CHAPTER EIGHT

Nimrod

The flowering field was filled with the scent of spring flowers, as the sun caressed the colorful meadow. Butterflies, in a variety of spectacular shades, danced playfully, sucking the juicy nectar pleasurably. A little doe walked among the blooming vegetation, frolicking carefree among the fresh flora.

Its eyes encountered the strange sight of a human figure standing in the heart of the field, communing with nature. A primal urge commanded it to flee from the person who might endanger it, but a feeling of kindness and tenderness emanating from him, compelled it to approach the putative foe. Its legs led it reluctantly toward this person, who seemed to radiate endless love and compassion.

It bent its head to bow down before the man dressed in resplendent attire, radiating equanimity and tranquility. Its nose rubbed against the man, enjoying the scent that the garment exuded. Then strong hands gripped its fragile body as if in a vise. Its legs tried to escape the sweetness that had become a death trap. The twinkle of a ray of sunshine reflected on the tip of the knife's blade as it suddenly came into view. The doe's eyes opened wide with the horror of its impending death. A cruel smile etched itself in the doe's heart as it felt the knife slicing through its outstretched neck.

Nimrod son of Cush son of Ham arose, his face beaming with triumph at the fresh trophy. He wiped away some of the blood on his dripping hem, then cleaned his hand by running it through the luxuriant vegetation. He left the carcass behind him, the torn body left for the beasts of the field, after sating his hunger with raw flesh. The tall and swarthy Nimrod began to make his way toward his father's house, anger flooding his heart, knowing that his family was subservient to the family of Japheth, due to the curse of Grandfather Noah.

A slight smile tugged at the corner of his lip at the playful thought that came to his heart. "Just as I hunt the beasts of the field effortlessly and all the animals surrender before me, so be it with my family members; and all the more so with our enemies, the Japhetite's." His scheme was beginning to take shape, seeming more realistic and feasible as there was much to think about. His fleet feet carried his sturdy body in a brisk run toward the hiding place where he had left his everyday clothing. He neatly put on his tattered robe, as he took the trouble to hide Adam's garment from any observer's eye by putting on a mundane outfit.

"Don't you think it's high time we abandon this course of perverse weakness?!" Nimrod turned to his father Cush and his uncles Mizraim, Put, and Canaan.

Mizraim looked at his nephew sadly, "and what would you have us do? Noah, our grandfather, cursed us to become the slaves of Shem and Japheth. Unfortunately, this curse is the command of God. We cannot do anything about it."

Nimrod surveyed, with his penetrating eyes, the four old men sitting in front of him. A feeling of contempt and disgust filled his heart, seeing the people accepting the curse as a destiny that could never be changed. "Unfortunately, this curse is the command of God. We cannot do anything about it." He mockingly mimicked his uncle's broken tone. "Who said there is nothing to be done about it? Who is Noah that you submit to a few words he said? Who is this God whom you bow and enslave yourselves to?" His loud voice struck the elders in astonishment. "I am telling you that I do not intend to live as a slave, and I inform you emphatically that soon, I intend to go to war against the sons of Japheth, and then we will see who will be slaves."

"But, dear Nimrod, how will you fight them?" Asked his uncle Put, fearing for the lives of his enthusiastic nephew and the rest of the family. "They outnumber and overpower us, moreover they are carrying out the command of the king of the world."

Nimrod rushed to his feet, opened up his cloak, and tore off the old robe which shrouded his body, revealing Adam's garment beneath it. "From now on, I am king of the world!" He declared audaciously, looking at his three uncles, who fell on their faces in terror. "The younger generation of our family is with me already! Will you join us or not?" He skewered his uncles with his gaze, making clear that refusing to join him was not an option. The old men nodded in fright, accepting the young man as their new master.

Nimrod turned to his shocked father. "Henceforth, I am the ruler! You will see, today, who is the true king of the world!"

Nimrod left the room, leaving the old men behind. A number of swarthy and sober young men waited for Nimrod outside the door of the room, looking reverently at their cousin, who proceeded to announce the beginning of the carefully planned revolt. "There is nothing to wait for! The revolution begins now!" He said with characteristic determination.

The young people looked at each other jubilantly, ready to carry out the plot they had been brewing in recent weeks. Their hands longingly caressed the blades secreted under their clothes. They started walking, innocently as it were, toward their hated masters' houses, gesturing to the young men working in the fields and homes that the uprising was at hand.

A few minutes after Nimrod left the elders, screams and shouts began to fill the camp, women and children scattering in every direction, their clothes stained with the blood of their husbands and parents, slaughtered in their homes.

An old man who broke out of his house in an attempt to escape the abattoir was easily hunted down by Nimrod, who happily directed the scene.

The loud echo of his laughter cut the captured women to the quick; they knew that they would soon be crushed beneath Nimrod and his men.

A few hours later, the smoke of the roasted meat began to fill the celebrating camp. Nimrod and his allies from his family relished the quick victory and their release from their bondage to the Japhetite's. Peals of laughter rang out from the victors, intoxicated by wine and the exhilaration of freedom, the sweetness of vengeance against their oppressors rejuvenating their hearts. Weeping and keening were heard from the rooms where the women and children mourned their husbands and fathers.

The new army of Nimrod numbered five hundred and forty warriors — most of them Hamites, along with some of his friends and companions from among the Semites and Japhetite's. The campaign of conquest began as Nimrod and his soldiers, determined to impose his rule on all human beings, started to move from city to city and from region to region as they accepted those who were willing to surrender to them, and mercilessly slaughtered their opponents.

In every city and town, a ruler was stationed over the inhabitants. The people feared for the lives of their children who might be taken to serve in the army of the new autocrat, knowing that if they did not fulfill his will, their conscripted sons would pay for it with their lives. Decade would follow decade of unchallenged rule over all humanity. A reign that trampled the lives of the inhabitants under the heel of new power, a rule compelled and purported to replace the sovereignty of the Creator over all human beings. Laws, invented anew by Nimrod and his advisers, would be imposed on his disenfranchised subjects. With draconian and arbitrary legislation, these leaders would undermine any idea of justice and truth. By the time Nimrod was done, a century of cruel rule would destroy every spark of desire to challenge the dictatorial system of government.

A great call rang throughout the civilized world, heralding a change in the character of authority and leadership. People gathered from all over the world for the great ceremony, the coronation of the new king of the world. Nimrod stood on a raised platform, clad in the resplendent attire of Adam. At his feet stood his courtiers and bodyguards, dressed in the finest robes, embroidered with gold and precious stones. A hush fell over the crowd, a tremor passed through every heart which knew the fickle spirit of the one who ruled over the whole earth. Nimrod looked down from his place, at the little people who gazed at him in terror, a slight smile passing over his lips, knowing that he had reached a sublime status which could be surpassed by no man. His sturdy hands rested on his waist, expressing his determination; his gaze scanned and penetrated into the eyes of his subjects trying to escape his glare.

"People!" He said in a condescending and contemptuous voice towards the small and frightened creatures. "Today is a day of good tidings! A day when I, Nimrod, become king of the world! There is no other king but me! Neither in earth, nor in heaven!" The resounding voice shocked the people, who were trying to figure out where he was heading. "From now on you must know that there is no one else but me! I am the monarch! I am the high king! And it is me, only me, whom you must worship! Offer your sacrifices to my name! Tender your prayers to me! From now on, I and only I, am the king of heaven and earth!" His hands were raised high. "Nimrod is the king!"

The sound of stormy applause was heard from Nimrod's courtiers and bodyguards shouting, "Nimrod is the king! Long live the king!" The stern glances directed at those standing in front of them made it clear that it was advisable — indeed required — for the crowd to join in celebrating the coronation.

The sound began to swell, sweeping up all those who lived their lives unwittingly, merely hoping to survive until the morrow. From among the ministers strode a young man, his bold and clever face shining with joy and jubilation at the sublime ceremony. His pale skin and bright eyes indicated that he was not a Hamite. His powerful body and confident demeanor indicated that he was a warrior who recognized his high status. Terah son of Nahor, a close friend and confidante of Nimrod, approached his master, his hands carrying a large gold crown inlaid with precious gems, glistening in the bright warm light. Images of the stars and constellations were engraved on the crown, with Nimrod's own face positioned above them. Terah approached his master, placed the crown on his head in reverence, and bowed before the man who had made him his minister and lord commander of his army.

The crowd bowed their faces to the ground as they witnessed the ceremony, wallowing in the dirt, shaking and sweating before their monarch. The sound of trumpets and the beating of drums arose from all sides, pulling the people to their feet, dancing and gyrating in the presence of their new god. Sacrifices were slaughtered and immolated in front of Nimrod, who stood proudly on his stage, looking with contemptuous joy at the creatures who worshipped him.

CHAPTER NINE

Terah

"Congratulations! Congratulations, my dear friend!" said Maradon, son of Nimrod, to Terah. "Another little boy for Terah our friend. You are more than a little naughty," he winked at Terah. "Already seventy years old, you have a toddler Nahor, baby Haran, and now a newborn! You are very active for your age. I am overjoyed for you and for your fecund wife Amathlai, who has borne you three sons in three years." Maradon embraced Terah, as his eyes surveyed Terah's wife greedily.

Maradon's name was a source of fear for all the inhabitants of the earth. The knowledge that the king's son was wont to do whatever he pleased with arrogance and pridefulness made all people approach him with trepidation — and if they could, they would do everything to avoid the capricious and rotten prince. Any depraved or abominable act seemed to him amusing or exciting. His body shook with delight when he saw how people kept their distance and evaded him, knowing that whatever he felt like doing would be allowed.

Terah, feeling Maradon's gaze upon his wife, Amathlai daughter of Karnebo, wriggled out of the embrace with the distasteful man who still clasped his shoulder. "Come, my dear friend, the courtiers and mages are waiting for us to join them at the banquet. Your dear father, in his great generosity, sent us a royal feast straight from his table!"

All the ministers, wise men, and mages stood up in honor of Terah and Maradon, wishing good luck and congratulations, through mouths full of food and drink.

"Terah! What do you call your infant?" One of the participants shouted.

"Abram," Terah said joyfully. "Abram, for Nimrod who is like my father (*av*), has lifted and raised me high (*ram*)," he explained.

"Long live Abram!" The blessing rang out from people eagerly raising the glasses of fine wine, sipping the splendid vintage to satiety. Then, they extended the empty glasses towards the servants to refill their goblets. The feast lasted for many hours, the sounds of singing and chanting echoed from the house, flooded with brilliant light and joy over the newborn.

Many hours later, the door of the house opened, the moon and the stars in the sky lighting the way for the people leaving Terah's stately home. Heartfelt greetings and words of farewell accompanied the cheerful group that staggered towards their homes, which were not far from Terah's in their thriving city, Harran. The sound of mirth and conviviality was suddenly interrupted by a strange humming sound heard above their heads. The partygoers raised their heads towards the heavens, looking in amazement at the strange sight. An enormous shooting star cut across the sky from east to west at incredible speed, swallowing four stars from the four directions of the compass. The crowds' breath was taken away by the puzzling sight, their eyes looking at the scene disbelievingly, hoping it was all a drunken delusion. Their gaze downcast, they wended their way home, each one hoping that when the wine wore off, his companions would tell him it was only his imagination that had manufactured such a bizarre phenomenon.

"Good morning!" Whispered one of the ministers to another as they met the next afternoon at the king's palace.

His companion shook his head gingerly. "What good and what morning? My head is exploding after last night's feast. I'm afraid I drank too much yesterday. I couldn't sleep all night, even though I was completely exhausted."

"Why? What happened to you?" The first minister asked, his puffy eyes betraying that he, too, had not slept at all the previous night.

"I don't know, but when we left Terah's house I thought I saw a strange scene. I'm sure it was just an alcoholic delusion, but still, all through the night I kept replaying it, and I could not sleep for a moment."

"What did you see?"

His companion shifted uncomfortably as he brought the memory to the forefront of his mind. "I saw a huge star rise from the east and swallow four stars from four directions. I know I did not really see it…" The man mused as the first man blanched. "Why are you so pale?"

"If that's true, it was not a drunken mirage…" The man whispered in horror. "I saw it too!"

The ministers fell silent, pondering their next move. "Let's go ask everyone else who was at Terah's party, maybe they saw it too…"

Ten of Nimrod's ministers and sages knocked on his door, waiting for their master's approval to appear before him. The heavy door rumbled open, and the ministers entered the king's palace. The splendor and opulence of the room did not move them as always, their fearful hearts insensitive to the wealth radiating from the very walls of the mansion.

Nimrod, dressed in his wondrous raiment and with a crown on his head, greeted his loyal men with a smile. A slight glance at their sagging faces made it clear to him that something was going on. "What happened? Why do you look like that?!" He asked grimly, feeling that the displeasure of his men was bringing his mood down. His servants were silent, quailing at the king's frown.

"Confound it! Are any of you willing to open your mouths and tell me what's going on?" Nimrod screamed at his men who usually chattered non-stop, but now were as hushed as the cliffs on the coast.

One of the ministers decided that he would be the one to convey the terrible message to his master. "Your Majesty, last night we were all at Terah's house. He had another son, and he invited us all to celebrate the birth of his thirdborn…"

"Yes… So what happened? He had a son! Well…?"

"Forgive me, Your Majesty," the minister stammered. "When we left the house of Terah, in the middle of the night, we saw a frightening spectacle. A huge star rising from the east crossed the sky at great speed and swallowed four stars from four directions." The minister was silent, looking in fright at the darkening face of his king.

"Yes…" Nimrod whispered, and his voice trembled.

"We remember that in the past, Your Majesty told us that one day a child would be born, who would endanger Your Majesty's kingship, who would try to conquer the world for himself. We all think," the minister said, indicating his colleagues, "that Your Majesty's prophecy is true, and that this child born to Terah is the child who imperils the kingdom." The minister looked at his king, choosing his words carefully. "We think that Your Majesty should take Terah's son and kill him, the sooner the better! We know that Terah is a close friend to the king, and that this will make it difficult for the king, but for the king's sake, Your Majesty must do so. Terah is a faithful minister and servant of the king. He will not shirk his duty, if Your Majesty explains the danger inherent in his thirdborn. "

Nimrod nodded, knowing that it would not be easy to convince Terah to kill his newborn son. He pondered the gifts and prestige he would have to give Terah so that the lord commander could reconcile his mind to such an awful duty. "Summon Terah! But tell him not a word of what we have discussed."

Nimrod paced back and forth in his large room. More than an hour had passed since he sent for his beloved servant, Terah. His mind worked feverishly, trying to resolve what things he would say to his favorite among all of his subjects.

The door opened slightly, and Terah, dressed in his uniform, entered before his beloved king, prostrating himself in submission to his best friend, with a loving smile on his face. "Hello, my liege and king," he said happily. "I am glad my dear lord has called his servant to come and see the gleam of his divine face."

"Arise, my dear friend," Nimrod demanded. "There is something that oppresses my heart, and I know that it is you alone whom I may consult to settle this distressing matter."

Terah got up quickly, approached his king and kissed his hand humbly. "Tell me what weighs on Your Majesty's heart, my lord."

"Do you remember what I told you? How I saw that one day there would be a man who would endanger my kingdom?" The king said casually, as he directed the lord commander of his army to sit. Terah nodded in silence, looking at his king. "I know who this man is. My advisers and sorcerers witnessed an ominous scene yesterday which removed any doubt as to who the person is," Nimrod continued, a bit more pensively.

Terah's face shone with joy, "if so, my lord, what is the problem? Kill the man and eliminate this threat to the monarchy! Tell me, who he is, and I will do it happily!"

Nimrod tut-tutted. "It's not that simple, because this person is the son of one of my dearest subjects," the king said dejectedly.

Terah looked at his master, "I understand, my lord, the difficulty, but we have no choice! We cannot leave the threat to Your Majesty's kingship! As hard as it is, it must be done!"

Nimrod lowered his eyes, hoping that the feelings his boon companion was describing wouldn't change once Terah learned who the putative threat was. "You do not understand, my beloved friend, how difficult it is for me," Nimrod said as he considered Terah's face. "The man who is destined to decimate my kingdom is your newborn son. Yesterday, you celebrated his birth with your colleagues, but he is the person of whom I speak!" A tear rolled from the corner of Nimrod's eye as he saw the falling face of his best friend.

"This... This is nonsense!" fumed Terah, rising to his feet in fury. "The courtiers and mages are probably jealous of the love that we share. That is why they are trying to make you hurt my son, in order to bring us into conflict."

Nimrod shook his head in regret over the futility of the argument. "I thought so too at first, but, unfortunately, after researching and examining it, I realized this is not case. To my dismay, my loyal comrade, your son is the man foretold, and there is not one shadow of a doubt about it."

"But, my lord..." Terah tried to beg for his son's life. "Your Majesty knows me. I will give him a good education, and even if he is augured to be such a man, when I teach him the way of truth, he will be a faithful and obedient subject to the king."

"Enough, my comrade, you cannot change the decree."

"We'll wait for him to grow up, and if it seems like he's heading down the wrong path, I will volunteer to execute him myself!" Terah attempted.

"No, my comrade, I simply cannot take that risk. Give me your son, and I will fill your house with treasures of gold and gems." Nimrod tried to appease the father, who was mourning his son while he still lived.

Terah lowered his face in sorrow. A few minutes passed while the two companions sat in silence, facing each other and pondering in pain what had to be done. "My king," said Terah as he regained his composure after hearing the awful decree, recalling other matters he needed to discuss with the monarch. "There are more important things on the agenda right now that we need to discuss...".

Nimrod looked at his faithful companion, concluding from Terah's gaze that he had made his peace with the harsh sentence. "Yes, my friend," Nimrod smiled happily, realizing that the lord commander of his army had come to terms with the difficult decree and was trying to banish the thought of his son about to be slaughtered. Nimrod and Terah went on to discuss, for another two hours, the affairs of the kingdom and the wars being waged in remote places; the search for a new place to build the royal capital; and the construction of the tower that Nimrod so longed for. The two friends sat comfortably, drinking fine wine and eating to their hearts' content the sumptuous feast presented to them.

"I have another matter to ask..." Terah said as he cleaned his mustache from the drops of wine that adhered to it. "Does my lord remember the wonderful horse he brought me about a year ago?"

"Indeed, I remember; it is hard to forget such a horse, perfect in its appearance and ability, a worthy gift for my beloved friend." Nimrod reclined in his chair, relishing the memory of the noble steed, which he had bestowed upon his friend after Terah had emerged victorious from a long campaign, thanks to his brilliant strategizing.

"A few days ago, a man came to me with a business proposition; he asked me to sell him the horse, and in return he would fill my house with barley," Terah said as he gazed into Nimrod's wide-open eyes. "I told him that I must address my king before I give him an answer, because I do nothing without consulting the patron of the world."

Nimrod rose angrily to his feet. "What is there to ask at all? To trade a noble and wonderful horse, which I bestowed upon you as a gift, in exchange for barleycorns? This is how you want to lead my kingdom?! Do you have doubts about such a simple thing?! Even if he were to fill your house with silver and gold, it would still be an idiotic question! Are you that desperate for fodder?"

Terah also got to his feet and stood before his king, his eyes lowered, "Am I that desperate for gold and gems? If you are angry about swapping a horse for silver and gold, what should I feel about trading my son for gold and gems? What will gold and gems give me? What does a man long for, if not that his sons will succeed him after he dies?"

Nimrod's face flushed with rage, his hand angrily pulling out the large sword resting on his thigh, with the intention of decapitating the man standing in front of him.

Terah fell on his face in tears, "I was just joking, Your Majesty! You know that I will do whatever you ask of me; but see that it is unbearable for me. I will bring my son to my king, and he will do with him as he pleases."

Nimrod returned his sword to its sheath, understanding the heart of the lord commander of his army. "I understand your grief, my friend, but you know I have no other choice."

"May I ask my lord that he give me three days for the sake of convincing my wife, that I may appease her with gifts and words of wisdom so that her spirit will not collapse when I bring my son to you?"

"Of course, my beloved friend," Nimrod said, as he went to hug his friend in reconciliation and affection.

Terah knocked lightly on the door of his house before entering. Nahor, his two-year-old son, ran towards the door, identifying his father by his knock, and one-year-old Haran clapped his hands happily when he saw his father enter the house.

Amathlai, his wife, contentedly laboring in the kitchen, deftly wiped her hands and walked over with a smile to greet her husband.

"Has something happened?" She asked apprehensively as she saw Terah's tense face.

"We'll talk about that later," he whispered to his wife, as he leaned over to lift Nahor by his arms.

"Father, you must see Abram! Little Abram smiled at me today," Nahor laughed happily, gesturing with his hand toward the small crib next to the main room. Terah walked over to the crib looking compassionately at his infant son sentenced to die.

Night had come, the big house was quiet, the roar of the wood in the fireplace merging with the sound of the little ones' peaceful slumber. Terah and Amathlai were sitting opposite each other, at their heavy dining room table, wrought of fine wood and inlaid with gold. Amathlai gazed into her husband's miserable eyes, afraid to start the conversation. "What happened?" She asked in a whisper after long minutes of silence.

Terah sighed from the bottom of his heart, pondering how to inform his wife of the terrible decree. "I was at Nimrod's today," he said, stalling for time. "He told me that there is a person who threatens to destroy his kingdom, and that person must be killed…"

Amathlai nodded her head, as she understood that her husband would soon need to go to war again, compelled to leave her and her children to deal with this potential rebellion. "I see…" She whispered sadly, knowing that Terah had no desire to leave them.

"No, you do not see!" He said firmly, trying to stifle the scream which wanted to burst forth from his throat. Amathlai looked at her husband's agitated face in shock. She had never seen him on the verge of losing his temper. The tear that flowed from the corner of his eye splashed on the table, sending a vibration through his wife's body, who for a moment, saw how her husband, her rock, was about to be shattered to pieces.

A choked cry came from her throat as she realized that she had miscalculated; what Terah had to tell her was far more bitter than another military campaign he had to lead. "What do I not see?" She whispered as a torrent of tears washed over her face.

"Abram…" Terah whispered as he glanced at the crib from which the regular, rhythmic breathing of the newborn could be heard.

"What happened to Abram?" Said the mother apprehensively, hurrying to get up to see if she had failed to notice something amiss with her infant son.

Terah grabbed his wife's hand, urging her to go back to her seat. "Nothing has happened to Abram yet," he whispered, still trying to keep things quiet.

"What do you mean by 'yet?'" Amathlai cried out, trying to stifle her voice and not to disturb her sleeping infant.

"What I mean is…" His decisive voice sounded defeated.

Amathlai felt that she was about to go mad from the silence that followed. She grabbed Terah's hand and as he felt her fingernails digging into his palm absentmindedly, he knew that he had to come clean. "Nimrod told me that the person who will ultimately destroy his kingdom is our son Abram," he said, suppressing his own emotions and feelings. "Nimrod told me that I must bring Abram to him, and he will execute him. And if not, he will come here and kill our whole family!"

A cry erupted out of Terah's mouth as he clutched his hand, the flesh cut to ribbons by his wife's fingernails. The blood from his hand and his tears mixed on the gleaming surface of their ornate table. Amathlai, in the meantime, slumped to the floor, racked by sobs. The young children were awoken from their peaceful slumber, their cries mingling with those of their broken parents.

Loud knocks were heard on the heavy door, sturdy fists broke their way into the house of the army chief. "Lord Commander, by order of our divine King Nimrod, you must come with me to him, together with your newborn son!" Said the officer in charge to his superior.

"Our king has stated that the three days you requested are over, and you must now accompany me with your thirdborn son," the officer declared, unable to meet Terah's gaze.

"Sir," he pleaded, "there is no choice! King Nimrod said that if you refuse to come, we must burn you, your household, and all that you have!"

The officer looked up at Terah, "please sir, I know that if you engage in combat, I have no chance of surviving. But His Majesty the King sent with me thousands of soldiers to carry out the mission. Against such a force even you, Lord Commander, will not be able to win. I know that this matter is very difficult, but it's better to save your other two sons and your wife than lose everything."

Terah nodded in silence, going to the corner of the room where his wife and three children were huddled. "There is no choice, my dear," said Terah, taking the child from her hands. The mother hugged her two remaining sons to her heart, a huge cry bursting from her chest.

"I am sorry, sir," the officer whispered to Terah. "We have no other choice." Terah took the newborn in his hands, and the long line of soldiers escorted him to the palace.

"Sir, I did what you asked me to do," Terah said to Nimrod with a downcast face. "Here is my youngest son, whom my wife gave birth to only four days ago." A tear flashed in the corner of his eye. "All I ask, my lord, is that I may leave the room while my lord will do what he will do."

Nimrod looked proudly at the commander of his army, admiring the loyalty of his best friend. "Certainly, my dear friend," he said, in a voice demonstrating understanding of the father's distress, "I did not think to ask you to be present at such a time."

Terah handed the king the crying baby and hurried out of the room. His shoulders were hunched and his legs were in a hurry to escape the abattoir. He could hear the baby's wail after he slammed the door behind him. A few seconds passed, and the sound of crying stopped. His heart skipped a beat, thinking of the murdered baby beyond the closed door.

Nimrod sat down happily on his throne. On the ground, lay the body of the enemy who had endangered his kingdom.

With a broad smile, he turned to the guard standing by, "bring me water to wash my hands," he commanded with a smile, "and provide me with a good meal and a jug of fine wine. I must celebrate today. And cast this carcass out of here!"

CHAPTER TEN

The Cave

Darkness enveloped the cool stone walls, thin drops trailing their way along the rock crevices. Silence hovered over the gloomy reality that refused banish by the light of one measly candle. Perpetual quietude reigned, disturbed only from time to time when the noblewoman would enter through one of the walls, bringing food and drink to the little boy isolated from all the other people. This was a brief opportunity for the mother to speak to her youngest son, persuading him not to leave through the secret passage. In the cave, there was no day, no night, but an ongoing monotonous reality of a feeble flicker in the heart of perpetual darkness.

"Mother, I want to come with you," the boy begs the woman. "Why do I have to stay here alone?"

The mother wipes a tear from her face, hugging her little son tightly to her lap. "My love, it's dangerous for you to go out. Bad people will want to hurt you."

"But, Mother, why would anyone want to hurt me?" The boy cried, as on previous occasions. "I haven't hurt anyone. I haven't harmed a soul."

The mother tightened her hug, knowing that she would be unable to continue to hide, from the child, the reason for his gloomy, separate existence. "Abram, I know it's hard for you to be left here alone, and I cannot stay with you here. But if I do not return home, people will start looking for me; and if they start looking, heaven forfend, they may discover you here. And then…"

"So what if they find me? What will happen?" The boy pressed his crying mother.

"He will kill you," she whispered in fear.

"Who is he? Why would he kill me?" Her son was amazed.

With an expression of devout awe, his mother replied. "Why, God Himself!"

"Who is that?" Abram wondered.

"Divine King Nimrod, and the statues and idols made in his image," his mother naïvely replied, believing that her three-year-old son was ignorant to the existence of the Creator.

Abram parted from his mother's fierce embrace, recognizing that there were many things he did not know about the world outside the walls of the cave. Abram sat down in front of his mother with a pensive look. "What is God?" He asked after a few minutes of silence.

The mother smiled understandingly at her son's obliviousness. "God is the one who created the whole world. The land and the sea, the trees, the stones, and all other creatures. God is the Creator of everything."

"Is He like us? Man?" The child probed.

"Yes and no; He is, like us, flesh and blood, but He is not an ordinary person, He is God!" His mother answered in confusion.

"And how old is He?" He asked with a smile.

Amathlai thought for a few moments. "As far as I know, He is one hundred and seventy-three years old," she replied.

"Is He the oldest thing in the world?" The interrogation continued.

"No, certainly not," his mother laughed aloud. "There are many people older than him. For example, there is Grandfather Noah; he is already close to nine hundred years old."

Abram burst into mischievous laughter. "So how did He create everything, if Noah was here before him. How could the Creator create before He, Himself existed?"

Amathlai looked at her son in astonishment. "How am I to know such things? That's what I was told when I was little, and I do not ask too many questions!" She chided, in a storm of emotions.

Abram looked at his agitated mother, "and what are these statues and idols that are also God?" He asked simply.

"There are all kinds," said the mother in an attempt to put her son's mind at ease. "Some are large, and some are small; some are made of stone, others of metal or wood; some look like humans, and some look like animals."

"And what do you do with them?"

"Bring sacrifices to them and pray to them," Amathlai replied. "Do you want me to bring you one next time I come?"

Abram ignored the suggestion. "Who makes them?" He asked with a smile.

The mother shrugged proudly, "your father has one of the best workshops in the whole world." She told her son, intending to prove to him his high pedigree. "People wait in line for years for your father, Terah, to prepare gods for them."

Abram burst out laughing, to the surprise of his alarmed mother. "If my father creates gods, then maybe he is God; and maybe I am God too, because he created me!"

Amathlai got up off the rock she had been sitting on, looking at her son as if he were crazy. "Apparently, the solitude and isolation from the world has driven you mad," she lamented, distancing herself from the amiable child who had exposed himself as a heretic.

Abram looked at his terrified mother, realizing that she could not understand what he was saying; but he tried to get his mother to stay put so she could answer some questions that still perturbed him. "Sorry, Mother, if I upset you. It's probably because I'm so alone and don't have any friends," he said with a shamed look, apologized to Amathlai. "But, Mother, I still do not understand why they would want to kill me? I'm just a little boy, three years old. What could I have possibly done wrong?"

Amathlai looked at her unfortunate son in pain and settled down. "Truly, I fear that the only reason King Nimrod seeks your life is the wickedness of narrow-minded and jealous people. You do not know, but your father Terah is the most beloved person to King Nimrod. Although your father is a hundred years younger, King Nimrod drew your father close and gave him the highest position in His kingdom, lord commander of the army." She sounded proud of her husband's status. "On the day you were born, your father made a feast for his colleagues, the King's courtiers and magicians. The next day, they told the King that when they left our house, they saw a big star piercing the sky and swallowing four stars from four directions. These drunks were very frightened. They saw it as a sign that you were destined to dethrone the King. So, His Majesty ordered your father to bring you to Him for execution." The mother was silent for a moment, letting her son digest all the new information.

Abram grinned happily. "But Father refused!"

"Yes and no," Amathlai replied. "He did not want to take you to our lord, but the King declared that if he failed to do so, our entire family would be burned."

Abram laughed. "Some beloved friend! But how are you and I still alive then?"

"One of the maidservants had a boy at the same time I did. That was the baby your father brought to King Nimrod and identified as his son," as if confiding a terrible secret to him. Were Nimrod to learn of it, she and her husband would be executed forthwith.

"Did he believe it?" Abram was astonished.

Amathlai nodded affirmatively. "He murdered that child and forgot the matter completely. He even showered your father with endless gifts to repay him for his loyalty and dedication to the kingdom.

Abram chuckled aloud. "Your god is a dumb and foolish one!"

"Quiet!" Amathlai said, with an expression of devout awe. "He is our God. How can you say such things about Him?"

Abram's continued chortling made his mother tremble.

"If your god can be deceived in this way, then he is nothing more than a fool. Where have all his divine powers gone, if he cannot accomplish such a simple thing?"

"Stop talking like that!" Amathlai shrieked helplessly. "What do I know about such matters? How am I to know how God's powers work?"

Abram stood up and hugged his mother, "Mother, I don't want to upset or sadden you, but you know I have been sitting here in this cave for three years. I have no one to talk to; I have no one to ask questions of; I just sit here all day alone and think. Maybe my thoughts are strange, but I have to find out, especially when I know there is a god who wants to kill me."

The mother looked at her little son compassionately, sorry for the madness that gripped her child due to the loneliness in which he was confined.

"Mother, may I ask another small question?" Abram whispered. "It's a little hard for me to understand why all the gods want to kill me. It must be, that everyone decided to end my life, because if not, how can one want this and another not? If all the gods are omnipotent, what if one wants me to die and another does not?"

The mother shook off her troubled son's hug, "I'm leaving now! I'll come back in a few days!" She said anxiously. "Perhaps…"

Abram crouched in the corner of the cave, leaning his back against the bare stone wall. Feeling the drops of water creeping down his lower back, resting his head on his knees with a sore heart. "If she doesn't come anymore, what will happen to me? I must have talked too much! What should I do?"

Thoughts ran through the little boy's head as it became clear to him that he was being persecuted by the king of the whole earth. "What did I do that cost me my life? How am I different from the other children my age who play in their homes with their siblings? How long will I have to hide here…" Tears flowed from the boy's eyes, wetting his only garment.

Minutes, hours, days slipped by as Abram was absorbed in thought. The food began to ran out as more and more time passed. Hunger began to gnaw at him; a fear that his mother did not intend to return metastasized into the knowledge that he had been left alone in the world. Feelings of starvation and exhaustion filled the child's heart. He determined that he must get out of the cave; whatever would be, would be.

On shaking knees, he made his way to the spot his mother would come to visit him at. He was frightened by the idea of seeing the world beyond the cool stone walls. He put his hands on the heavy rock covering the opening, but he could not budge the stone.

Thoughts of despair and sorrow rushed into the child's heart, but he chased them back to the dank corners they lurked in.

"No, there must be a Creator of the world!" The boy thought defiantly. "Creator, if you exist, please help me open the door so I can worship you alone!" Abram prayed to the unknown. His little hands pushed the rock again, and this time the stone door moved, as if surrendering to the child's prayer. Dazzling sunlight poured in, overwhelming the vision used to darkness broken only by feeble candlelight, blinding the eyes accustomed to a life of gloom. The illumination was stunning, filling the world with warmth and pleasantness. Abram shaded his eyes with his hands, feeling a burning in the dilated pupils shrinking in the face of the abundant light. Abram knelt, bowing to the sun that enlightened the whole of existence. "Now I know who God is!" The thought passed through his heart. "This great light is the Creator!"

Abram stood at the entrance of the cave, his eyes growing accustomed to the immense light, his heart filling with prayer and praise towards the sun animating the world with its abundant rays. He picked fruit and vegetation from the surrounding field, restoring his hungry soul. His heart rejoiced at the revelation of the Creator to him in His abundant light. For several hours, he watched the new Creator, observing His movement from far away. However, his mouth, filled with song and exultation, fell mute as he saw the light disappearing from his eyes in the foothills to the west.

A new light appeared, smaller and softer, chasing the great light away. It gave off a pleasant white light, soothing, relaxing, and calming his eyes. "This little light is surely the Creator! Even though it is smaller, the great light flees before it, so it must be the Creator, not the other!" Little Abram prostrated himself before the moon that shone over the land, marveling at the army of gleaming warriors who accompanied and served it. Hours of prayer and thanksgiving to the Creator of the world illuminated the darkness of his life.

However, a waxing light then rose in the east, obscuring the moonlight, eliminating the army of stars.

Abram stood up and laughed at his foolishness. "Maybe you two are great, but you are not God!" He concluded confidently that the sun and moon simply play their roles in the sky. "Like me, you too are puny servants of the Creator of all existence!"

For Abram, the days passed in solitude, and the silence was disturbed only by the wild animals and the forces of nature. Epistemologies and philosophies were propounded and dismissed in the fertile mind of the growing child.

He spent long nights observing the lunar phases and the movements of the planets, stars, and constellations, with a discerning and curious eye. The moon's orbit and the changes it underwent were engraved in the heart of the excited Abram. He memorized the changing positions of the celestial bodies, seeking to discover the logic of their revolutions and rotations.

He would also sit silently, in an attempt to feel the flow of life within his own growing body. He plunged into the depths of thought with the expectation of examining the mysteries of the soul pulsating within the mysteries of physicality. A slight movement of the ear brought a smile to his serene face, concentrating on the possibility of controlling matter. Years of exploration of self and nature, of the hidden and the revealed, filled the dimensions of creeping time.

It was now no trouble for Abram to push open the cave door confidently. He took one last look at the only home he had ever known, making the fateful decision that he could no longer remain hidden amid the desolation of the cave and the field.

He was a child, about nine years old, living and growing up alone. A child whose only companion had been his own thought and reason.

"Hello, Mother," the familiar voice from the depths of the past struck Amathlai. The earthenware plate in her hand shattered on the ground, the remains of food scattering on the ornate marble-tiled floor. Amathlai looked up to find a boy who was growing up to be a handsome, broad-shouldered lad. A broad smile revealed white, healthy teeth and greeted the stricken face.

A few seconds passed, the son and mother faced each other, unable to contend with the onslaught of opposing emotions. For long moments, she reviewed the distant past, the loving heart of a mother for her youngest child.

Amathlai knelt, reaching out to welcome the son she had been forced to abandon, at her husband's behest. At last she could release the secret, hidden tears she had been so careful to conceal so as not to shatter her husband's noble façade.

The mother wholeheartedly embraced her young son. For half-a-dozen years, the concern for his wellbeing had been replaced by grief and mourning, believing that the cave had become his crypt. Now she sobbed and gasped with relief. "Abram!"

Night arrived, the warm sunlight disappeared, moonlight took its place. Sounds of laughter and joy rose from the two adolescents returning with their father from the workday in the idol workshop. This urged Amathlai to hide her youngest son in a room at the back of the spacious house. Amathlai hugged her returning sons, washing the feet of her smiling husband, happy after another busy workday. Dinner was served to the three of them, who spoke loudly.

"Mother, did you know? Today, I finished the new god I made," Haran proudly told his mother. "He's so strong! He has three heads: one of a lion, one of an eagle, and one of a cat…"

"Oh, is that what it's supposed to be? The pussycat looks just like you!" Nahor said mockingly to his brother.

Haran rose angrily to hit his brother.

"I was just joking," Nahor defended himself.

Haran returned to his seat with a proud smile on his face.

"So it seems today was very successful," Amathlai said with a face that betrayed a bit of her sadness.

Terah looked at his wife, realizing that something had happened. A brief meeting of glances made it clear to Terah that it would be worthwhile to postpone conversation to a later time. When the meal was over, the boys quickly went to their bedroom to sleep, after a long day of swinging hammers and chisels. Soon, the rhythmic sound of breathing filled the space, and their parents could talk freely.

"My dear, what happened?" Terah interrogated his wife, as she placed a steaming mug in front of him. "You've seemed upset and uneasy all evening. Does something bother you? Is it one of the manservants or maidservants?"

Amathlai looked down, trying to gauge what her husband's reaction would be to their little boy's return. There was concern for her son's life if Terah were to discover him, but she could not hide Abram's return from his father.

Still the silence stretched out, as Terah considered how his wife avoided complaining about servants who did not do their jobs faithfully. "She's too compassionate," the thought arose in Terah's heart. "She treats manservants and maidservants as if they are ordinary human beings. Every time I hit one of them, tears well up in her eyes as if I had beaten her. But what can I do? They are slaves, and such animals must not be allowed to grow prideful!"

Terah waited, the conviction that one of the slaves would soon be dealt a harsh sentence growing in his heart. His sturdy hands played with his staff, lying on the table, as if to ready it for its imminent task.

Amathlai raised her glance a bit. She whispered, as if revealing a terrible secret, "he has returned…"

Terah looked at his wife in amazement. What was the source of the fear in her voice? "Who is 'he?'" He asked in the authoritative voice of a man who was never afraid to speak, threatening to shake the walls of the house.

In a faint voice, Amathlai responded, "'he' is our son!"

Terah jumped up as if snakebit, spilling the steaming mug with the hand holding the staff. "Abram?!" He shouted, immediately trying to take back the name, lest some nearby servant overhear it.

Amathlai nodded in silence, letting her husband fall into his chair, understanding the consequences of the news that had been delivered to him.

"Are you sure it is him?" He inquired. Hoping against hope that it was not true.

Amathlai shook her head, with a half-sad grin, "a mother knows her own child."

"But you told me you sealed the cave behind him! How could he have survived?!"

"I do not know, but this is the situation, as it stands."

"How does he look?"

Amathlai smiled maternally. "He looks handsome and healthy, he resembles you …"

Terah buried his head in his hands, his fondest wish was that it might be a mere nightmare. "Where is he?" He finally managed to ask, realizing he could not wake himself from this scene.

"I put him in the back room, so he could not hear what we were talking about." Amathlai got up to pour her husband another mug.

Terah drew inward, thinking feverishly about some stratagem to extricate himself from the danger he had thought dead and gone for years. "What are we to do with him?" He whispered, as if to himself.

Amathlai took the initiative and answered the question she had anticipated, "I have thought about it. We must talk to him, explain the situation, present him the two options he has: either he may stay with us and learn our trade, or he must strike out on his own."

"Do you think he will learn our trade? The last time I allowed you to visit him in the cave, you gave me the impression that he was a little madman. He believes in nonsense and rubbish, and he defies everything which we hold dear! Why would you think he has changed?!" Terah felt he was about to lose his own mind.

"I think he will agree to at least pretend that he is a believer..."

"Perhaps the simplest thing is to kill him? He will not be the first or last person I kill. It's inconceivable that he remain here alongside Nahor and Haran. He is still capable of ruining them with his apostasy."

Terah heard Amathlai burst into tears at the thought of her third-born being condemned to death for a third time, and he knew she could not bear it. The woman cried and sobbed, begging her husband not to touch the boy. Terah felt a rebellious tear seek to burst from his own eye at his wife's weeping.

"I have an idea ..." She whispered as she wiped the tears from her eyes. "We will send him to Grandfather Noah and Father Shem! They are very far away from here. There is nothing for him here. He may live with them, and we may have peace. My youngest child may grow up far away from me, but at least I will know that his death was not at my hands."

Terah got up quickly, happy with the creative solution his wife had come up with. He dispatched one of the slaves, secretly ordering him to harness a horse to the cart and take the boy to Noah and Shem, dwelling in the land of Canaan. He decided that the slave would pay with his life for the mission, so that no one would remain to reveal his dark secret.

It took two weeks of riding from Harran to the land of Canaan. On his return, the slave was murdered, and Abram the heretic was forgotten.

CHAPTER ELEVEN

Abram

oah sighed from the bottom of his heart.

Abram, who attended to Noah in his study hall, ran to find out the meaning of this deep moan, worried about the health of his elderly mentor, who had just passed the unimaginable milestone of nine hundred and forty years of age. "Master, what troubles you so?" Abram asked his progenitor with concern.

Noah looked at the vital young man who stood before him, who had served him faithfully for thirty-nine years. He lovingly caressed Abram's smooth, strong hands with his own careworn fingers; the pain was visible in the eyes which had seen so many revolutions and upheavals in the world. He teared up.

"I have failed in my mission!" The elder lamented, sobbing like a young child. "Everyone on earth is my descendant, but of my offspring only three have remained faithful: my loyal son Shem; his great-grandson Eber; and you, Abram, great- grandson of Eber's great- grandson. Every other person in the world has gone astray. What then was the purpose of the deluge, if three centuries later, we are back where we started?! The Lord wiped out every living thing on land, except those with me on the ark; but the world has returned to its former state…" The ancient man dissolved into tears, broken by the generation's depravity.

Abram embraced the man who had been the only father he'd known since coming to Canaan, the only father he'd had in all his life, the mentor who taught him of the Creator and the ways of faith and worship. "I know, master, the sorrow that fills your heart, but this has been the case for hundreds of years. It was only a short time after you left the ark that your children, throughout the world, began worshipping statues and idols. What has happened now that so weighs upon your heart?" Abram tried to understand the meaning of the crying.

"Woe is me!" Groaned Noah, from the depths of his being. "Even to utter these words tries my soul." The tears were soaking his long snowy beard. "What is new? The wicked Nimrod is building something in the land of Shinar. This arrogant fool wants to build a tower that reaches the heavens, in order to engage the Lord Himself in combat!" His face fell.

"What of it?"

"Don't you see, Abram? As long as the people worshipped idols and were oblivious to the reality of the Creator, it was possible to give them the benefit of the doubt and say that they were mistaken. But now that they are building this tower, they reveal that they are aware of the Creator's existence — and that they want to revolt against Him and battle Him!

"Nimrod is the root of this great evil, a manifestation of the Other Side. He is the force which the human race must overcome, to be worthy of the name it bears. The battle is not between God and Nimrod. Were it His will, He could wipe him from existence in an instant. Instead, the struggle must be between humanity and

Nimrod; the people must seek to establish the sovereignty of good over them and to eliminate the forces which oppose such a goal.

"However, most people are enthralled by Nimrod and those like him, ensorcelled by the opportunity to follow their every whim. To live like an animal is a simplistic existence, with no demands; to most people, it seems far more worthwhile than the alternative.

"That is why I say that I have failed in my mission. I did not have the courage to fight evil, so the punishment for this crime is about to befall the entire human race," he concluded miserably.

"So what?!" Abram replied firmly. "It is Nimrod and his allies who made their bed, and it is they who will be forced to lie in it!"

"Don't you understand?!" The old man looked angrily at his disciple. "That Nimrod and his friends lie in the bed they made is good and well, but the problem is that all the other people, the little people, the unseeing sheep led by the cruel shepherd, will also share his fate. You must understand, the overwhelming majority of people do not know their own minds; they do not have the ability to think and decide for themselves. The poor fools are drawn to powerful, charismatic figures. Most of the people have always been thoughtless and indecisive. The fools are dragged after those who seem strong and in control. Most of them are preoccupied with the vanities of this world; they are caught up in the race of daily life, unable to pause to consider the essence of reality.

"That is why you have been so fortunate. The isolation of your young life gave you the opportunity to ponder the great truths of the universe. Your time in the cave was the greatest gift your father could have given you. If only he had been aware of the power of disconnecting from mundane pursuits and dedicating oneself to delving into philosophy, he would have pulled you out of the cave and thrown you into the workshop alongside your brothers, so you might labor day and night instead of reaching the insights you have acquired.

"Do you comprehend? This is no sublime science. No discipline or brilliant mind is required in order to grasp it. Any human being is capable of reaching this level, regardless of intellectual capacity. All it requires is that one extricate oneself from the unending current of daily life, pausing to reflect for just a few moments. Every person is capable of this feat, but so few endeavor to take advantage of the opportunity!"

Abram silently acknowledged the words of wisdom, experiencing the feeling of exaltation in recognizing that he had to give thanks for being uniquely able to understand the reality of God, due to his background. "So what will happen?" He hesitantly asked after a few minutes of silence.

"Most likely, a great calamity will befall the world," Noah whispered with teary eyes.

"My lord, be careful!" Viceroy Terah cried apprehensively as he pulled King Nimrod, who was standing at the bottom of the tower, to the side. A swarm of people carried the bricks they had made hastily, like tiny ants climbing up the mountain to infinity. A few stories up, they were no longer discernible as people. The huge distance yawned between the ground and the vault of heaven.

Moments after Terah pulled his master away, a huge brick shattered on the ground with a thunderous sound. Nimrod looked at the small crater left by the brick's impact, right where his feet had been seconds earlier. A smile of gratitude came over his face as he realized that his best friend had saved his life again.

"Dunderheads!" Terah fumed. "It takes months for each stone to reach its place at the top of the tower and these idiots are not careful at the most important moment. You can see here that this brick was smeared with clay to cement it in place! A few more seconds of attention, and we would not have lost it."

Nimrod placed his hand on his friend's shoulder, consoling him over the waste. "How long will it be until you finish the tower? Until we reach... Him?" He asked Terah, who was in charge of the project.

"To tell the truth, I don't think we're far off... I know I said something similar two months ago, but this time the end is within reach." Terah looked at the tower with admiration. The huge bricks were beautifully arranged, measuring a cubit on each side; a feeling of nostalgia gripped his heart as he remembered the first brick he had baked. His brilliant innovation had been to form uniform bricks, rather than chiseling stones to facilitate the construction of the wonderful tower.

A thumping sound behind him disturbed his thoughts. Terah turned around, fearing that another brick had fallen from the hands of one of the workers. However, the sight which greeted him was that of a crushed human body, one of the workers who had fallen from the top of the tower. "What a numskull!" Terah said with a smile to Nimrod.

The two friends walked away from the tower, sharing the unspoken fear that they might be crushed under the next thing to fall. "You must come to my workshop," Terah said happily to the king. "The statue I prepared to place at the apex of the tower is ready."

Nimrod walked happily with his friend, eagerly anticipating seeing his wonderful work. Terah opened the door of the workshop, his two sons Haran and Nahor, bowing before their monarch and their patriarch. Terah walked over to a huge statue covered in white cloth. There was pride and cheerfulness on his face. Nimrod stood in front of the sheet. He could see that at the top, it was draped over something sharp, and from that point it swelled to ensconce the body of the statue, all the way to its feet. With one dramatic gesture, Terah pulled the cloth off. In front of Nimrod stood a statue that was a perfect replica of him, holding his sword aloft. The high king looked longingly at the statue, which seemed ready to spring to life. He felt like he was looking into a mirror. "Bravo, brother, you are a consummate artist!" He declared approvingly.

A young man stood in the heart of Shinar's bustling market, his garb at odds with that of the large crowd. This unfashionable youth attracted the attention of passersby. People stood up, examining the fellow covered from head to toe in thick and broad clothing. The young man's body seemed to disappear under the cloak of brown clothes. His long fingers protruded from the hems of his long sleeves. He stood erect and steady, like a sturdy cedar defying a hurricane. The men and women around him wore clothing which revealed more than it concealed, and they regarded him with derision.

"What bizarre creature is this?"

"Where did he come from?"

"Why does he dress as if it were snowing?"

"Doubtless, another madman!"

The gathering crowd pointed scornfully.

"World-class idiots!" The man roared suddenly, shocking the crowd before him. "Do you not know that *the earth is the Lord's, and the fulness thereof; the world, and they that dwell therein*?! Do you want to fight with the one who spoke and brought the world into beginning?!"

A peal of laughter burst from the crowd. One of the men addressed the speaker, "so another clown has come to entertain us! Yes, friend, what do you have to say?"

"My dear brothers, do not rebel against the Holy King! A terrible punishment will befall you if you do so!" He pleaded.

"Who rebels against the king? We all worship the holy King Nimrod with devotion! Have you seen the tower we are building?!"

"People, I tell you that the Lord is God, He is one and His name is one! He is the God of heaven and earth — and the God of Nimrod as well. I am Abram, servant of the Supreme Lord, and all of you must acknowledge this, so that you may be spared!" The voice of the speaker carried far and wide, like a man who expects his words to make an impression on the hearts of his audience.

"Abram? Where did you come from? I say you're just some crazy person trying to rebel against our king! Go back to where you came from or come help us at work! You're just messing with our minds!" The bystanders nodded, turning their backs on the speaker, who was left alone in the middle of the market, save one hunched figure.

A lonely old woman stood in front of the young man, looking excitedly at the child she has not seen for thirty-nine years. "Abram, my son!" she cried — whether it was in joy or grief was impossible to tell.

Abram took off his hood, looked at his mother, and saw the tears streaming down her face, the tears of a mother whose son had always remained in her heart.

CHAPTER TWELVE

The Tower of Babel

The mother and son were seated by the antique table, which Abram remembered from his previous meeting with his mother. Amathlai held her son's hand, trying to formulate a plan as to what to do with the rebellious boy who has returned to his hometown. The light of the dancing candles illuminated the room from which her son had been sent far away from, so many years earlier.

"Son, you cannot continue to behave in this way! I understand that your years of loneliness and being in the company of the two elders have made you think in a distorted way. But you must take yourself in hand; you cannot stand against the whole world. Your father is one of the most respected people in the country. You must not shame him!" She lectured, her eyes boring into him.

"Even if you do not believe that Nimrod is a god, at least do not come out against him! You do not know him; he will kill you without batting an eyelash! Believe me, Abrami, I am your mother who loves you! Even when I was far from you all these years, I was always your mother, interested only in your benefit! Do not believe him, but at least do not talk about it. Your father is supposed to come back tomorrow night to take me to the ceremony for erecting the statue, which he has made to place at the pinnacle of the tower he designed. I do not want him to meet you before this big day; he has too much to deal with as is. You will stay in the room where I left you last time. I will bring you food and water, I will give the servants a day off tomorrow in honor of the event, so that no one will run into you by accident."

Abram looked at his mother compassionately. "Mother, do you really believe that Nimrod created the world?"

Amathlai looked down. "What difference does it make what I believe? Why should I delve into matters far beyond my ken? I am the wife of the viceroy. What else could a woman want in life?"

"But what does it matter that you are his wife? If he is on the wrong path, you must find the way to the truth yourself!" He said emphatically. "I too could hide beneath the mantle of Terah and say that I am the son of the viceroy. I could live a life of opulence and magnificence like my brothers and deny the truth! I too, could be a blind lunatic, following Terah the fool as he kisses the hem of evil Nimrod's robes."

Amathlai rose angrily to her feet. "You will not speak of your father that way, do you hear me? You have no right to speak thus of your father! The man you call a fool endangered his life and the lives of his whole family to save you! Because he saved your life, you are still breathing! This is what Noah taught you over these past few decades? Where is your gratitude? The debt you owe your father ought to be infinite! That man imperiled his honor, his status, and the life of his family just for you!" Amathlai's eyes blazed with fury. "I very much hope you will internalize what I've told you. If not for your father's love, you would have been dead long ago!"

Abram looked down, taking it upon himself to be silent for the time being. "Well, Mother, I shall go to the room. But please, do not stand too close to the tower tomorrow..."

The great day of triumph and rejoicing had arrived! All the people gathered at the foot of the tower whose top disappeared, into the heights of heaven. The news had spread like wildfire throughout the country. The statue would reach the top of the tower today, to be stationed on the divine battlefield. Millions of people had counted down the days until the long-anticipated event, an occasion they had been working towards for many years. Now, it had finally arrived.

Thousands of musicians serenaded the sublime ceremony. Drums, trumpets, harps, organs, and sundry instruments filled the space with their tunes and melodies.

Then the music abruptly stopped, except for the thunder of the drums. The people bowed and prostrated at the appearance of their god ascending the stage, which stood tall at the foot of the tower.

Then the drums too, fell silent, as Nimrod raised his hands. "My people, my creations!" He shouted. "The time has come!" The sound of applause from the crowd rising to its feet reached its crescendo. "Now my image will stand atop this tower and wage war against the one who dares to believes He is fit to rule over us!"

The applause rang out even louder this time, overpowering the drumbeats and the trumpet blasts.

It was a sun-drenched day, filled with the smell of blooming flowers. The pleasant sunbeams fueled the hearts of the people who had so long awaited this sublime day.

Nimrod raised his hand, signaling the people to hold their applause. "In a few moments, the cloth will be cast from the top of the tower, unveiling the statue in my image. This is the sign that my effigy has reached the pinnacle of the tower. When the cloth reaches the earth, the battle has been joined!"

Nimrod looked up at the tower. There was utter silence as the people raised their eyes up to see the discarded veil flutter down. Terah stood next to his wife, looking proudly at the fruit of his labors, as sculptor and architect, which formed the basis of the historic event taking place before their very eyes.

Then a tremor went through the crowd as the people realized that something unexpected was happening. Their eyes gaped wide in horror at the dreadful spectacle. The tower which they had spent so many years building seemed to be crushed from above by an invisible force, as if a great unseen foot was stomping on an anthill, smashing it to the ground. The people screamed, shouted, and shrieked as the splendor of their work was trampled.

The lower third sank into the ground, while the upper third shattered into pieces, shrapnel flying far off to slice and smash the heads of the attendees. Fire broke out in the heart of the tower as the middle third went up in smoke, extinguishing their long-awaited hope.

The people ran everywhere, trying to escape from impending death. The sound of horrible cries arose from some as they felt their bodies mutating, twisting, and transforming into elephantine or simian forms. The land, which had been reveling in its revolt, was now shaking with a tumultuous noise. The survivors scattered in every direction, as the newly transmogrified beasts fled into the wild to hide their shame.

The earth shook as the Creator trampled it underfoot, causing a tsunami to surge from the sea and drown a third of human civilization, wiping out the buildings and all who were within them. Destruction, devastation, and the silence of death filled the world.

The survivors in Shinar had no choice but to try to rebuild their shattered lives. As they wandered through the debris of their homes, trying to rebuild the structures that had collapsed from the devastating earthquake, tsunami, and fire, two brothers stood surveying the wreck of their family home.

"Bring me that board," said the older to the younger, who stared at him, dumbfounded.

The younger brother was attempting to decipher the elder's seemingly random assortment of syllables. "He must have gone crazy," the younger brother thought, trying to figure out what his older brother wanted.

"Why are you standing there like you're made of stone? Bring me the board already!" The older brother shouted at his younger brother, who continued to stare at him. Finally, the older brother pointed at a pile of planks lying haphazardly next to his axe.

The younger brother walked sadly towards the axe, surmising that the trauma had addled his brother's mind. "He is so far gone..." He thought sadly as he handed the axe to his glaring older brother.

"This imbecile wants to make fun of me!" The older brother thought. "He's acting like an idiot, like I don't get that he refuses to help me! He just stares at me as if he cannot grasp what I am saying! Handing an axe to me instead of a plank?!"

The anger merged with grief and sorrow over the loss of their loved ones and property; this brought a cruel smile to the face of the older brother, who received the anticipated axe with diabolical joy.

"Now you'll stop being an idiot!" The older brother said as he split his younger brother's skull open with a swing of the axe.

"Now you'll understand what's being said to you!" He shouted in the face of the corpse.

People all over began talking to each other in an incomprehensible salad of syllables. Seventy different languages sprang up simultaneously, as people were so frustrated that they could not understand each other, they began to quarrel and beat each other — even to death!

Terah and Amathlai entered their half-destroyed house with their two older sons, surveying the damage. The patriarch sat down at his beloved dining room table, caressing the crack in the wood where a rafter from the ceiling had snapped his pride and joy in twain.

"Starting over will require all of our strength," he mused. "The situation out there is horrific. Even though the hodgepodge of languages is driving people insane, my family and I have escaped this strain of madness." Terah looked at his wife making her way to the back of the house, wondering, "where is she rushing off to..."

Amathlai hurried to her youngest son's room, to check that nothing had happened to him and to prevent him from venturing out to confront his troubled father.

Abram greeted her with a thin smile.

"Are you all right?" She whispered to her son, with amazement on her face. The room where Abram was concealed looked perfect, as if nothing had happened in the few hours since she'd left him.

"I'm fine," Abram grinned. "How was the inauguration?"

Amathlai looked at her son, clearly realizing that he had been proven right. "It was awful," she murmured, wiping away a stray tear. "Luckily, nothing happened to us! Stones passed over us. People next to us were killed and injured, while we are whole and healthy. How fortunate we are to have survived."

Abram glared at his mother. "Fortunate? This is not luck, this is divine providence! The Lord did not want you to be harmed; therefore nothing happened to you."

"If it is as you say, why would He want nothing to happen to us? After all, we rebelled against him too!" Amathlai challenged him.

Abram smiled broadly, "maybe He is showing the gratitude which I have failed to; maybe He rewarded you for saving me."

"And why would He thank us for that? After all, you are our son, and it is human nature for parents to protect their children."

A mischievous spark ignited in Abram's eyes, "because the truth is that He is my father, and it is the way of a father to have gratitude towards those who help his son, even if they do so out of a sense of obligation."

Amathlai scratched her head, trying to figure out what her son was trying to say. Suddenly, she heard a voice close to the door, which brought her back to the reality of the ruined house. "I have to run. It's Haran, he must not see you! Tomorrow or the day after tomorrow I will talk to your father and brothers, and I will explain the story to them. I fear this will be too hard a blow for them now."

Amathlai did not wait for her youngest son's response, and hurried out of the room shouting, "Haran, I'm coming!"

The door of the room opened, and Amathlai led Abram to the room where his father and brothers were waiting. Terah's face looked tense, his black eyes fixed on his youngest son entering the room accompanied by his wife. He drummed his fingers restlessly on the surface of the wrecked table.

"Well Abram, you have grown and become a man," Terah said, trying to break the silence in the room.

Abram smiled at his father, trying to recall the man he remembered from many years before. He gazed at his brothers, who looked almost like mirror images of him. "Hello, father," he said in a gentle but firm voice, "and hello to you, Nahor and Haran."

Terah got to his feet, wrestling with himself. "How should he treat his son, who according to his wife, denied everything that was sacred to him?"

Abram also found himself struggling internally.

"Should I go and hug him? The man is a complete heretic! He makes idols and bows to them! Still, he is my biological father, and the will of God is that we honor our parents. Perhaps if I show him affection, he will repent for his evil ways!"

Abram walked confidently toward the father he had never really known, embracing him lovingly. He warmly shook his brother's outstretched hands. The reunited family sat around the table, exchanging life experiences, trying to make up for Abram's long absence. For a long time, Abram told his brothers about his days in the cave and with Noah, attempting to avoid the topic of the faith he adhered to.

Nahor and Haran told their younger brother about their lives, their work, their families, their wives, and their children. Nahor had married Milcah, older daughter of Haran. However, Haran lamented that his younger daughter, the beautiful Iscah, had already grown up and matured. She was almost forty and still unmarried. "It's because she has all kinds of nonsense in her head ..." Haran grumbled.

Abram smiled a little, remembering the only time he had left Noah's academy in all his time there. He was about twenty-five years old then, filled with the passion of his beliefs and determined to seek out his older brothers and teach them the true faith. So, he had headed to his brother Haran's house to try to convince him of his wrong ways.

When he came to Haran's house, he found no one there but Haran's daughter, Iscah. Abram's face turned slightly red. A slight tremor passed through his body as he brought up the memory of Iscah in his heart. She was a teenager then.

There was a surprised look on her face when she saw a young man she did not know knocking on her father's door. The stranger looked very much like her father. Iscah welcomed the guest warmly, offering him food and drink, after realizing that he had come a long way. A casual conversation between the two made it clear to them that they had to marry each other. Iscah was already weary of the vanities of the world and recognized that every man of her generation was obsessed with them — which established for Abram that she was the young woman for him. After a few minutes of conversation, Abram broached the topic of matrimony to Iscah.

"I am ready to marry you," she replied, "but only if you go back to Noah's academy, to complete your studies with him, until Noah tells you that you are ready to go out into the world. I will wait for you until you return..."

The couple married secretly, swearing to be faithful. Then Abram returned to Noah's academy to continue his studies.

Terah snorted derisively, ripping Abram from his memories, as if he were about to tell his family something important. The brothers' conversation was halted.

"Tomorrow, I intend to move back to Cuthah, I have nothing to do here, as King Nimrod returns to his capital. To my dismay, the gods, apparently, found some defect in the tower we built, so they destroyed it. In Cuthah, we have the finest selection of sculptures, so my lord Nimrod and I mean to offer sacrifices there to please the gods."

A burst of strangled laughter escaped from Abram, who clamped his hand over his mouth to stifle the sound.

Terah stared penetratingly at Abram, and Amathlai jumped up trying to save the situation. "I think it's time for us to go to bed! We're all very tired!"

Terah continued to stare at Abram. "What's so funny?"

"I just remembered something, Father," Abram lied.

"Well, we need to go to bed! We have a busy day tomorrow," Amathlai concluded the family reunion abruptly.

"You, be careful not to do or speak nonsense!" Terah spat at his son in anger. Abram nodded in agreement.

CHAPTER THIRTEEN

The Rebel

Dear Father,

I know that not long has passed since you left our home to accompany our lord King Nimrod on his mission to appease the gods. We arrived in our city of Harran in peace.

However, to my great dismay, I must inform you of what Abram is doing around the city. He found a dog and named him Nimrod. He walks the streets and asks the people to bow to the dog. The cheeky brat tries to convince the people that the dog is a higher creature than the trees and stones from which we make the statues! He drives the people crazy by telling them that there is a dog in Shinar and there is a dog in Harran, and they are both named Nimrod.

Mother, Haran, and I tried to reprove him and stop him, but he refuses to listen to us. I'm sorry if hearing this disturbs you, but you asked me to let you know if Abram did anything unusual.

With love,
Your son,
Nahor

erah tore up the letter angrily, fuming at his rebellious son. "Nimrod will kill me and my whole family because of this child! He does not accept authority. He thinks he can do whatever he wants" The anger in his heart increased, "this boy is endangering everything; because of his nonsense, I will lose everything I have achieved in my life. I must inform Nimrod before the news reaches him from another source, and then…"

Terah got up hastily, turning toward his master's house. In his heart, he began devising a scheme to save his himself.

"Your divine majesty, my liege, lord King Nimrod," said Terah as he bowed and prostrated to Nimrod.

Nimrod raised his scepter, motioning for Terah to sit down next to him, seeing the desperate look in his friend's eyes. "What is it, my friend?"

"My lord knows that there is no one in the world more faithful than my family and I," his voice trembled. "But a terrible thing happened to me at home!"

Nimrod looked at his friend, hoping that no disaster had befallen the family. Terah resumed, "my lord remembers the baby who was born to me many years ago, the boy whom my lord's advisers said would want to destroy Your Majesty's kingdom."

Nimrod nodded, but to his surprise, he found himself annoyed. Why did his friend remind him of those horrible forgotten times? Why did his friend recall, again, a child killed by him? "The baby who died, you mean?" He whispered with a sigh, recalling the devotion of his best friend.

"Ah, yes… The baby that was supposed to die…" Terah looked out of the corner of his eye at Nimrod, hoping that his king would accept his words. "The baby I presented years ago for Your Majesty to dispatch, so he might no longer pose a risk to my lord's kingdom... I want to say that the child I brought, which I thought was my child... But Your Majesty must understand... I do not know exactly how it happened, maybe my wife misled me... but the baby I brought to my lord was not the right child..."

Nimrod rose to his feet in frustration, towering over his friend, who cowered before his throne. "What exactly do you mean?" He boomed, his eyes threatening to burst out of his skull.

"I mean, sir, the boy is still alive. I do not understand how it happened, but the boy is still alive and in Shinar. I do not know where he came from, but he appeared a few days ago at my house in Shinar and started speaking and doing nonsense."

"What is he doing?" Nimrod sat down in his chair, trying to hide the trembling in his knees, feeling anxious and fearful, emotions he was unfamiliar with.

"He goes through the city streets and says that there is only one true God, while Your Majesty and the idols are lies and fictions." Terah hoped desperately to conclude the conversation, "it might be worthwhile to consult the advisers and councilors."

"Summon them!" Nimrod said tightly, trying to hide the alarm stealing into his heart.

"Your Majesty," suggested one of the advisers, "what is the problem? Send a battalion of soldiers there, and execute this audacious rebel! Shall one man, who is not even capable of raising a sword, be allowed to denigrate Your Majesty's divinity?! A battalion of warriors will do the work!"

Nimrod smirked, chagrined that he had not thought to take such obvious action in the first place.

However, a few days later, King Nimrod found that he had more than one rebellion on his hand.

"That upstart!" Nimrod jumped up from his throne, his face flushed with rage. The messenger standing in front of him paled in fear of his monarch, vibrating with fury.

"Chedorlaomer? This nobody is rebelling against me?! I will show this rotten servant the back of my hand! This miscreant is taking advantage of the destruction of my tower to establish a kingdom for himself!" His arm went to his scabbard, ready to draw his blade on the spot.

The messenger, who had just informed his sovereign about the new power raising an army and conquering settlements in Canaan, was terrified, trying to devise a way to get out of the throne room without further enraging the monarch, who now had a new crisis to deal with, in the aftermath of the fall of his grand tower.

Maradon, Nimrod's son, looked at his wrathful father, "Do you know why he rebelled? It's all because of Abram son of Terah! Because you have not killed him yet, the people begin to doubt your divinity. Now all sorts of riffraff dare to challenge you. The real war is not with Chedorlaomer, but with Abram! We will destroy Chedorlaomer, but if we do not destroy Abram, it will not be long before the next nonentity has the audacity to try to seize your throne."

Nimrod frowned angrily, knowing that his son was in the right. "Perhaps we ought to start with Chedorlaomer, and from there we will continue straight on to Abram."

He passed a few seconds in thought, planning the necessary military operation. "On second thought, let's settle the score with Abram, then move on to Chedorlaomer. It seems to me that we will need several days to mobilize our troops, who are busy restoring order after the fall of the tower. Only once we have set things right can we deal with this rebel."

The call went out to the warriors to go out and catch the youth who derided their god-king. Thousands of armed fighters gathered by royal decree, eager to bring the rebel to justice.

"Stop your nonsense! Do you hear me? You had better stop if you want your head to remain on your shoulders!" Nahor roared at Abram, who was tranquilly feeding his dog.

Abram grinned, "Dear Nimrod, do not listen to him, he is just an infidel, he does not understand how big and important you are. Do not be angry with him and do not kill him, he still does not understand that he should bow to you." Abram handed the little street dog another piece of meat. "Nahor, perhaps you ought to offer him tribute so he doesn't get mad at you..."

Nahor looked angrily at Abram, "You're crazy! Completely crazy! Offer tribute to this ugly mongrel?!"

"Ah... Sorry... Why don't you offer a tribute to the statue you made? Does it seem more divine to you than my cute Nimrod...?"

"Stop calling him Nimrod!"

"Why, isn't it a pretty name?"

Nahor turned away, furiously leaving Abram and his dog. "Don't be offended, cutie, he's really not a nice guy." Abram's laughter accompanied Nahor's departure.

The army advanced toward Harran, on a mission to bring the rebel to justice. Ten days of hard riding from Harran in Babylon to the town of the same name situated just north of the land of Canaan. "The border of the land of Harran," the commander observed. He turned to his soldiers, ordering them to seize the rebel and bring him to the king alive. "I want our king to have the pleasure of be-heading him!"

The fierce warriors slowed their place, as a heavy, black cloud enveloped the warriors' camp. An incomprehensible and unfamiliar feeling of fear seeped into them. The warriors turned their mounts around, fleeing before something unknown.

"Abram," the voice called out from behind him in surprise. Abram turned on his heels, seeing in front of him an awe-inspiring and unfamiliar figure, a figure he had never seen before.

"Sir, who are you?" He asked respectfully.

"My name is Gabriel. I was sent to tell you that a great army has come out of Cuthah to catch you and bring you to Nimrod." The voice sounded peaceful and calm. Abram recoiled, realizing that the one speaking to him was no ordinary man. "What should I do?" He asked, somewhat apprehensively.

"If Nimrod wants to see you, you should go to him right away!"

Shock gripped Abram. "Shall I go to Nimrod?! What shall I do with him? He will try to kill me, and I am not a man of war!"

"Abram...?!" The voice sounded like a teacher rebuking his student for forgetting what he had learned.

"I see, but how do I get there? It's a distance of more than forty days by foot!"

"I'll see to that..."

Abram felt himself pulled through the dimensions of time and place. It felt as if the physicality of his body was being stripped from him. Moments later, he was then reincarnated in another place, far away. Abram shut his eyes, joyfully recognizing that there was noth-ing beyond the abilities of God.

Suddenly, he heard shouts and screams, people recoiling in terror. His eyes opened as if awakening from a good dream. A big smile appeared on his face. "Did you want to see me?" He asked Nimrod, who was surprised to see his nemesis materialize before him.

"How did you get here?!" Nimrod demanded as he fell back into his throne.

Abram laughed dismissively. "This is no question for a god like you!"

"Tell me how you got here!" Nimrod was infuriated by his lack of control or understanding of the situation.

"Calm down, sweetheart, you need to understand that if my God wants to do something, it just happens. He wanted me to come to you, so I came. Do not tell me you cannot do the same... What kind of God are you if you cannot do such simple things...?"

"I am God!!!" Screamed Nimrod. "Kill him!!!" Nimrod's body-guards stood in their place, uncomfortable but unmoving. Their eyes were riveted to the fragments of their idols, smashed on the ground at the periphery of the room at the instant of Abram's manifestation.

Abram felt the anger rising inside him, as he considered the lowly man on the throne pretending to be what he was not. In anger, he approached Nimrod, who was sitting in his chair with his own face blazing with rage. Abram grabbed the collar of Nimrod's royal cloak and upbraided him. "Listen to me well! You are no more than a pathetic man, a servant defying his master!"

Nimrod curled up on his throne unwittingly, looking like a rebuked child.

"Now, I must depart. If you want to see me again, summon me... Perhaps I will come."

Terah's door shook with a loud rapping. He got up reluctantly, considering the unexpected knock. "I wonder who it could be at a time like this! It must be a solider coming to tell me about Abram's death." An unpleasant feeling passed through his body, as he realized that he was actually looking forward to the death of his son.

Terah opened the door slowly. "Hello, Father! Do not tell me you are not happy to see me..." The ominous smile almost overwhelmed Terah.

"What are you doing here...?"

"I just came to visit you, Father. Do not worry, I have already visited Nimrod. It was actually an interesting visit; he will surely tell you about it when you meet."

"Listen to me carefully! You must restrain your son! If he continues down this path he's on, he will die! I will kill him myself!"

Terah stood before his distressed master. Nimrod had sent messengers to his house to fetch him shortly after Abram came to visit. "You'll take care of the house and the store until I get back!" Terah had ordered Abram without alerting the king's men. "And be careful not to do anything foolish!"

"Your Majesty, I do not know what to say... I told my lord that it would be better for him to kill Abram. I do not know how to take control of him, he does not listen to me! The boy is completely crazy! I have not much to do except tell my lord to kill him!" Terah felt that Abram's next outrage might cost him his head. Horror enveloped his being as he saw Nimrod's furious face. "Why did my lord not command his brave warriors to kill the boy?"

"Brave warriors? They stood there, like statues, when Abram was here! They were paralyzed by fear before your son!" Nimrod scowled at his shamefaced guards, with loathing.

"And why did Your Majesty not slay him?" Terah asked naïvely.

Nimrod leapt to his feet, raising his hand as if readying to slap his best friend in the face. "Stop asking questions! You must restrain your son, or I will have to kill you along with him!" His voice rose to an impotent shriek. "Now get out of here!"

As Terah left, his face fell. His heart was gripped by grief and agony, as he was banished by his best friend. His ire grew as he plotted to destroy his son.

"Gods for sale! Gods for sale! Today only, what a deal! Buy two, get one free!" Abram made his way through the streets of the city, dragging the idols his father had made to sell. "Gods from Terah's workshop! They cannot see, they cannot hear! Gods who will allow you to live it up! Gods who don't speak, for people who don't think!"

People watched the young man, dragging behind him beautiful and artfully wrought sculptures by a rough rope tied around their necks. An old woman approached Abram, "how much do they cost?"

"The little one, six gold coins; the big one, eight; for that ugly one, I'll only take five," Abram said mockingly. The woman rummaged in her pockets, searching for coins to buy her gods.

"So which one do you want? The ugly one who can do nothing, the little one who can do nothing, or the big one who can do nothing? The three of them are puppets, all exactly the same!"

The woman looked up in amazement at the bizarre merchant.

"If they upset you, you can just break them or throw them in the trash," Abram grinned, "Actually, why are you wasting money? Take a rock from the ground and bow to it!"

"What are you trying to say...?"

Abram looked at the woman in pity. "Do you not understand? This statue is just a piece of stone or wood carved by a man. It can do nothing, and certainly it cannot save you from your troubles. Moreover, you are already many years old, and it is only a few days old. Think, ma'am, is a piece of stone worth bowing down to?"

"So what am I supposed to do? I have many misfortunes and problems! Whom will I pray to?!" The woman looked as if she were about to burst into tears, feeling that she had no one to blame for her pain. Abram began to explain his faith to the unfortunate woman.

Hours passed, the sun was about to set, leaving the streets desolate. The horizon went gray and purple, birds chirping and cattle lowing, the atmosphere disturbed by the sound of the half-broken sculptures being dragged through the dirt. Abram entered his father's workshop, looking in disgust at the idols placed in every corner of the large hall. Anger gripped his heart at how the experience of idol worship blinded people, preventing them from believing in the Creator. He knew that fools would always prefer to hold on to something solid and tangible, as long as no demands were made of them. The great sledgehammer, with which his father would begin carving the statues, sparkled before his eyes in the light of the last rays of the sun at dusk. A wide smile bloomed across his face. "Let's see what he says about it…" His hands gripping the sledgehammer, he smashed the statues. The sounds of shattering and splintering were as sweet in his ears as the finest melodies and symphonies. Then he turned to the logs designated for carving, whose destruction gave him a sense of pleasure. Abram smiled contentedly, feeling the sweat covering his entire body from the effort to destroy the idols. One large statue remained, the last in the hall. "Statue, I wonder what my father will do to you after I tell him that you made all this mess." Abram laughed uproariously as he bound the sledgehammer to the hands of the great sculpture.

"Abram!!!" The sound of shouting awakened Abram from his sleep. A smile rose on his lips, as he realized that his father had returned home. "Abram!!! Where are you?"

Abram wore a worried look on his face, "What happened...?" He asked his father, who looked like he was going to lose his temper. Terah took hold of his son, dragging him to the workshop. Abram looked at the destruction and devastation in his father's workspace, and could scarcely keep a smile from his face.

"What happened? I'll show you soon what happens!" His father screamed in anger. "What have you done to all my gods!"

"Me? How can I do something to God?" Abram innocently asked.

"Who did it, if not you?!" Terah screamed, almost deafening Abram.

Abram pointed an accusatory finger at the giant statue with the sledgehammer. "It was him! He did it!"

Terah looked at his son, spittle forming on his lips. "You will not drive me crazy; you understand?! Do not tell me that is the one! It's just a lump of stone that cannot move or speak! So do not tell me 'He did it!'"

Abram smiled at his father beatifically. "I will explain it to you. An old woman came here and brought him a plate of food as a tribute. The other idols wanted to eat his food, so he got mad at them and broke them... If you do not believe me, ask him..."

"Enough!!!" The scream was deafening. "Stop confounding my mind! They do not eat or walk or do anything!!!"

Abram met his father's gaze. "If so, why are you bowing and worshipping these puppets! Whom are you trying to convince? Stop lying to yourself!" Abram turned his back on his father and left the hall, leaving his father with the fragments of his gods.

Abram walked the streets of the town, talking to whoever was willing to listen, defying the idols without fear. He laughed at the fools presenting offerings to the statues standing in the streets. "Sir, do not forget to clean his head. It seems to me that one of the pigeons thought his head was a nice place to deposit its droppings."

"Excuse me," an old man addressed Abram. "Do you know if your father's shop is open?"

Abram looked at the old man and recognized him as having bought a large statue from his father a few days ago. "And why do you need my father's shop?"

The man lamented, "two days ago, I bought a god from your father's shop, and then thieves came and stole it in the middle of the night." He wiped away a tear. "Now what will I do?"

Abram sighed, looking at the old man's eyes, which seemed to display intelligence. "Do you not understand that there is nothing in these statues? If they cannot protect themselves, how can they protect you? The statues are not God! Nimrod is not God! There is only one God, who created the earth, who sustains the living. There is no one else but He!"

"What are you really saying? What should I do?" He asked helplessly.

"You must worship your Creator! To publicize that there is only one God!"

The man seemed doubtful, "and how will I know that this is the truth?"

"If you do so, I assure you that everything stolen from you — except the statue — will be returned to you, and that you will have life in the world to come."

"If that happens, what am I to do?"

Abram put his hand on the man's shoulder. "When what I told you has come to fruition, you will have the privilege of teaching the other people you meet, because the Lord is God in heaven and on earth, there is no other but He. He is one, and there is no second; He brings death and life; and Abram is his faithful servant."

Two days after this encounter, all the property stolen from the man was miraculously returned. The man walked the streets of the city announcing the miracle that had happened to him, teaching all present what Abram had instructed him. Nimrod's guards caught the rebellious man defying their lord and brought him before the king for trial. The man was executed by Nimrod, as he continued shouting aloud what Abram had instructed him.

CHAPTER FOURTEEN

Ur Kasdim

Then there came a day of feasting and rejoicing in the palace of Nimrod; all the ministers and friends of the king had come to celebrate the anniversary of Nimrod becoming God. Tables were laden with meat and fattened poultry, to be devoured by the drunken invitees. Musicians, singers, and songstresses entertained the audience, filling the atmosphere with rhythmic melodies. Lewdness and licentiousness prevailed in the room, which was adorned with statues as debauched as the masters. Shouts and drunken cries merged with mutual curses and insults.

The doors of Nimrod's feasting room were pushed open noisily and forcefully. Abram entered the room with a confident step, turning his face toward Nimrod, sitting on his glorious throne. The people pushed into the corners of the room, awed by the presence of the young man who was not afraid of them.

Nimrod looked straight into Abram's eyes, seeing the boldness that characterized his father Terah. "What do you want?!" He demanded with restrained anger, gritting his teeth when he saw his nemesis standing before him on his joyful day.

Abram reached out, grabbing Nimrod's collar as if he were a foolish brat. "Woe unto you, wicked one who rebels against his God! Woe unto all of you who rebel against the Creator of heaven and earth!" Abram's hands shook Nimrod like a leaf. Nimrod tried to conceal his embarrassment from his ministers and servants as they watched their god's being manhandled by this youth. "Stop your nonsense before you die!" Abram shouted as he smacked Nimrod in the face.

"Kill him!!!" A helpless shriek emerged from Nimrod's throat. Several servants approached Abram, trying to strike him with their swords, but the blades seemed to be feathers caressing Abram's body. "Catch him! Imprison him! Let him die of starvation in the dungeon!"

The guards approached, with apprehension, the man they had failed to kill.

"Of course, where do you want to put me?" Asked Abram, as he presented himself to the guards with a smile.

"I can no longer deal with this," Nimrod's voice sounded shattered. His face was pale from lack of sleep; his eyes swollen, black circles surrounding them. "I have hardly slept for a year," he complained to Terah. "All the time, I hear your son's voice, laughing and joking at my expense. Even though he is in a dungeon far from here, I keep hearing his laughter echoing in my head. For a year, I have withheld food and water, but he is still alive. The guards who come to see what is happening with him go crazy and talk about the Creator of the world as if it were not me. I must destroy him, and quickly…"

Nimrod's face fell, and Terah looked at his friend with sympathy for the pain and grief his wayward son was continuing to visit upon his king.

"I think I have an idea," said one of the bodyguards suddenly. Nimrod and Terah looked up in amazement, considering a man whose name they didn't even know, one who dared to listen in on and interrupt their conversation. The helplessness they felt compelled them to acknowledge the man's words. Nimrod nodded, giving him permission to speak. "We cannot kill him, neither by sword nor by starvation, but if we make a great conflagration and throw him into it, he certainly will not be able to withstand it. He may be a great sorcerer, but against the fire he will be powerless."

Nimrod and Terah shared a satisfied smile.

The slaves dug a large pit to form a furnace, in which a great fire was ignited. It was stoked for forty days and forty nights; the glowing stones forming the floor of the furnace began to melt from the intense heat. A large catapult was prepared to throw the rebel into the fire. A platform was built for the purpose of accommodating the thousands of the king's dignitaries who were invited to see the dénouement of the rebellion against their god-king.

Terah and Nimrod waited impatiently to see Abram thrown into the fire. Haran, Abram's brother, standing next to his father, smiled happily.

"We shall call this place Ur Kasdim," Nimrod laughed arrogantly. "Only demons (*shedim*) could withstand this fire (*ur*)."

The voice of the bloodthirsty crowd rose to a fever pitch. Abram, in manacles and iron chains, was brought towards the catapult. "Very well, is this where I am to sit?" Abram asked the guards, who were ready to place him in the bucket of the trebuchet.

One of the guards showed Abram his place. "Sir, it's not too late to recant," he remonstrated, a tear rolling from his eye merging with the streams of sweat washing over him from the distant furnace. "All you have to do is bow to him…"

Abram smiled at the young man, "never give up on your true faith, even if it costs you your life! If God wills it, nothing will happen to me." Abram winked at the guard, "flying sounds interesting…"

The catapult was released, Abram was thrown into the fire, and the crowd roared with applause.

Haran remarked to Nimrod and Terah, "it's hard for me to believe it will help…"

The sound of applause grew louder, the emotions of the crowd enflamed at the sight of the heretic getting his what he deserves.

Abram felt the waves of heat as he flew through the air, but he kept his eyes closed in prayer, totally immersed in his relationship with his Creator. His body landed in the blazing fire, the flames rising high above his head. A pleasant feeling of warmth passed through his hands, as his manacles and shackles melted away. His clothes remained intact, the fire seemed to refuse to hold on to them. Abram laughed with pleasure as he realized the miracle done on his behalf by his Beloved; his euphoria was unbridled as he realized how he had been emancipated from the chains and plans of human beings.

From within the flames came a shout, "Nimrod, won't you come in? It's so nice and pleasant in your little furnace. Do not be afraid; surely the fire will not be able to harm one like you!"

Horror and trembling seized Nimrod when he heard the voice of Abram. A slight chuckle from nearby distracted him. Nimrod looked at Haran, brother of Abram, who was giggling. "What's so funny?!" A shriek of despair escaped from Nimrod. "Are you mocking me?! Now you'll see what happens to you!"

Fear and trepidation dawned on Haran's face, "but…"

A devilish smirk accompanied Nimrod's next decree, "guards, cast Abram's brother into the furnace. Apparently, he's made of the same stuff as his brother. We'll see if he too can withstand the fire…"

Guards held the weeping Haran, who pleaded for his life; but sturdy hands bound him, and he was lifted into the bucket of the trebuchet by his legs. Haran was launched into the fire, burnt to ashes even before he hit the bottom.

"More fuel!" Nimrod screamed at his servants.

Frightened, they tried to approach the furnace, but the flames consumed them before they could get close to the pyre.

The inferno continued to rage for three days and nights. The blazing fire could not be extinguished, but Nimrod and his men stood in shock at what their eyes beheld. Abram was walking around in the furnace, laughing and singing, praising and exalting his Creator.

"Abram, get out!" Declared Nimrod finally, his eyes swollen from lack of sleep and constantly gazing into the brilliant flames.

Laughter rang out from the furnace, "maybe you will come and help me out, Nimrod?"

"Stop your nonsense already, and get out… Please."

Abram came out of the fire and approached Nimrod and his astonished men. The people looked at the man coming out clean and unruffled from the blazing fire and bowed before him. Nimrod felt a tremor pass through his legs, which refused to hold his body up in front of the man who emerged unscathed from the fiery pit of death. Nimrod fell and prostrated himself before Abram.

"Why do you bow down to me? I am not God. I am a man like you! Bow down to the One who created you and me, the heavens and the earth," Abram said to the people kneeling before him.

Nimrod stood up, though his face remained downcast, "your God is true, and you are true," he whispered in a weak voice.

The people hurried to bring Abram gifts and presents. Each minister brought Abram his son. "Please, teach him what he needs to know," they begged anxiously.

Nimrod stood before Abram, presenting his son to him. "This is my son Eliezer; please teach him your faith."

Nimrod and his men stood in front of the furnace, while Abram stood across from them, a sword in his hand. Abram ran toward Nimrod, who fled as quickly as he could. Abram took an egg out of his pocket and threw it at Nimrod's head. Nimrod saw the egg fly towards him and shatter on his head, becoming a large river drowning all those with him — except for three. Nimrod looked at their faces — or rather their face, as they all shared his own face. The river drained to a single point, becoming an egg again. The egg hatched, and a chicken came out of it, flying at his face, knocking him over and beginning to peck his eyes out...

Cold sweat washed over Nimrod's body, as he woke in horror, in his bed. "It's just a dream!" He tried, in vain, to comfort himself.

When Nimrod shared his dream with his councilors, the treasurer looked at Nimrod in shock, "Sir, this dream does not bode well. Only two years have passed since Abram emerged from Ur Kasdim, and the man is getting stronger. Not only are there almost no people who still believe that you are a god; the people are no longer willing to accept you as king. The taxes paid by your subjects have dropped by a third. They say they will pay their taxes to 'King Abram,' not you." The minister lowered his eyes, "there are also brats who mock Your Majesty. Moreover, this upstart, Abram, has come out against the important practice which appeases the gods, offering our sons and daughters as sacrifices. He walks among the people and tells them that this is despicable and forbidden. He teaches them that the Creator of the world would never agree that a parent should slaughter his child."

Nimrod looked at his men, their heads bowed. If only Terah were still with me, but he said he wanted to retire, to focus on his art, he thought sadly. "Does anyone have an idea?" He asked.

"Your Majesty," Enoki, the new lord commander of the army, confidently opened, "I do not understand what the problem is! We will gather our army, and we will go and destroy Abram and the gang of weaklings associating with him! We are men of war, while they are soft and studious. Your son Eliezer, who is among us today, has shared with me that Abram and his disciples do not even practice the art of war; they only listen to Abram's lectures all day and study the books he writes. There is no such thing as an invincible man! There is no man who is not mortal! I promise, my lord, just say the word, and I will bring Abram's head back to Your Majesty!"

Nimrod looked at the young minister, feeling empowered by the man's boldness. "Then do it!"

Eliezer son of Nimrod waited for the assembly to end, and left the room with swift steps, escaping the palace as quickly as possible.

CHAPTER FIFTEEN

The Return

On the banks of a river in the land of Shinar, the sound of the rushing waters was tranquil and calming. Abram's tent was packed, cheek by jowl, with the tones of rhythmic chanting and scholarly debate coming from the students sitting on the colorful mats. Outside the tent, horses neighed, sheep bleated, and cattle lowed.

Boys and girls were playing in the wide meadow, chasing chickens and ducks. The women's tent, which was set apart, was full of the din of many hands preparing food and drink for the students and their families. Every day, the camp grew, as more and more families came to take refuge under the aegis of the man who had emerged from the inferno of Ur Kasdim hale and hearty.

Eliezer, the son of Nimrod, entered the tent, looking for Abram. His eye went straight to his master in the center, who was sitting next to his young nephew Lot.

"Why is he investing so much in Lot son of Haran? The fellow is fundamentally corrupt!" The thought pierced Eliezer 's heart, as he made his way to his master, who greeted him with a smile.

"Hello, my friend, welcome back. Is something amiss?" Abram hugged Eliezer, who looked worried.

"Sir, I must speak to you alone."

Abram kept his arm around Eliezer's shoulder, feeling love for his devoted disciple, scion of his nemesis. "Come, my friend, tell me what's bothering you..."

Abram and Eliezer exited the tent, facing the wide field. The pleasant sunlight imbued the idyllic scene with the feeling that nothing could be better.

"What is happening, Eliezer?" Abram asked his faithful student. "Why do you look worried?"

"My lord knows that every day the size of our camp increases..."

Abram smiled beatifically. "Yes, there are more people who approach to learn about the true faith."

"That's exactly the problem, sir! Our camp is getting too big! Every day our numbers swell!"

"What of it, my dear friend? Why worry? We have more than enough food and drink for everyone." Abram looked at Eliezer, unable to understand his apprehension.

"Food and drink are not the problem. The problem is that Nimrod views us negatively. He is starting to feel threatened by the large number of people in our camp."

Abram's laughter brought Eliezer to a halt. "And what about that? Let him feel threatened! I am not afraid of him, and you should not be afraid either!"

Eliezer sounded stressed, his voice trembling because he did not know what move to make. "My lord knows that my father Nimrod is unaware of the truth." His voice trembled, as he loathed mentioning that Nimrod was his father. "He thinks I come to him to give him information about what is happening in our camp. He gave me to you as a slave in order to spy on your house, then tell him what is happening in my lord's camp. He does not know that I am faithful to my lord, and that I am disgusted with him and his ways." Eliezer looked at Abram in humility, "I hope my lord knows my loyalty..."

Abram hugged Eliezer, like a father embracing his beloved son, "of course, my dearest friend..."

"Today, I was at Nimrod's palace; he gathered all his ministers and told them about a dream he had. He interpreted the dream to indicate that you were going to kill him and all his people. He was so afraid of the dream that he ordered all his soldiers to attack our camp. He is going to bring tens of thousands of trained and armed soldiers against us in order to destroy this sacred congregation." Eliezer burst into tears as he spoke. "He is utterly committed to killing my lord."

Abram looked at Eliezer seriously. "You know full well that he can do nothing against the will of the Creator. If the Creator wills, He will save us, as He saved me from the fires of Ur Kasdim."

"I know, sir, but in any case, if a war breaks out, even if we win, there will be tens of thousands of casualties; and unfortunately, I do not think our camp will be spared. Many of the newcomers have not yet become strong in the true faith. They still have not abandoned their idols," Eliezer explained his concerns.

"I see," Abram said after a long pause. "Let me think about it a little."

"I do not think that there is much time to think, my lord," Eliezer sounded very anxious and insistent. "I am afraid that we have a few hours at most until the army comes here and wipes out the entire congregation."

Abram looked at his dedicated servant, worried about the people who could be hurt because of him. "Saddle my horse. I need to go to Noah's academy. Nimrod will not hurt these people if he knows I am elsewhere. I will send you a message in a few days about our next move."

Eliezer rushed to fulfill Abram's command.

The time at Noah's academy proved to be a sublime pleasure for Abram, who thirstily imbibed the teachings of his erstwhile master. It was a delight to sit tranquilly and engage in the study of wisdom without the heavy burden of leading the people; for the fugitive from the king's justice, it was refreshing and restorative.

The emissary sent back from Eliezer informed him that Nimrod's soldiers, who had arrived at the camp, had returned as they had come after Eliezer had taken care to convey the news that Abram had fled the camp. Abram instructed Eliezer to guard the camp for the time being, until the king's rage subsided.

"Sir, there's an old man who wants to see you," said one of the slaves to Abram, leaning over his books. Abram nodded, finding it hard to tear himself away from his studies. The door opened, and Abram looked up from the book; for a moment he thought he was hallucinating.

Abram jumped to his feet, seeing Terah, his father, standing before him, "Father?!"

Terah advanced towards his son, his arm outstretched in peace. Their long handshake was full of apprehension. "It's good to see you, my son," said Terah slowly, fearing the reaction of the son he had sought to get rid of.

However, Abram hugged Terah, "it is good to see you, dear father, what are you doing here?" Abram sensed in the way his father stood how humbled and ashamed he was.

"Your mother and I always sought your wellbeing," Terah retreated slightly, looking at his son, the once-firm voice sounding shattered. "We were afraid that something would happen to you." Abram looked at his father, trying to understand his motives and actions.

"Look, my son, I will understand if you say that you do not want to see me anymore, if you refuse to listen to my words." Abram thought he saw a tear in the corner of his father's normally harsh eyes.

"Since my retirement from King Nimrod's service, I have had a lot of time to think. When a person has nothing to occupy his body, then his mind is free to reflect. I thought a lot about you, your words, my life, and my faith; and the more I thought about it, the more I saw that I had played the fool. The constant demands of daily life, coupled with my elevated status, gave me a feeling of omniscience — that I knew everything, and that my path was the only correct path. It is not easy for me, but I must say it, because it seems to me that you are in the right, I was on the wrong track all along." Terah's shoulders trembled a little, his voice sounding like he was about to burst into tears.

"I do not know if you can ever forgive me, and I will understand if you tell me to turn on my heel and leave you forever. I do not know how I dare to come before you today and beg your forgiveness, but…" Terah dissolved into weeping from the bottom of his heart, regretting his misdeeds over benighted decades, what he had done and what he had tried to do.

Abram approach his father, who fell into his embrace. He felt Terah slump, trying to find refuge with his son. "Dear father, it's all right. You do not need my forgiveness."

Abram embraced his father with true affection, rejoicing from the depths of his being over his father's epiphany. Terah was now on the right path, at last.

A few days had passed since the reconciliation of father and son. Abram and Terah sat in front of Noah to learn wisdom and morals, relishing the wisdom of the elder who had known the contemporaries of Adam, the first man.

"Father, it seems to me that it would be better for us to return to Shinar; Nimrod has probably given up on finding me there. In my opinion, it would be best to go back there and take our family and allies with us and emigrate to the land of Canaan. I think we ought to send a messenger there to order all our people to gather our possessions and prepare to set off."

The father nodded in agreement, ready to follow his son and teacher, wherever he took him.

The journey from Shinar to a foreign land was massive, both in terms of distance and the number of participants. Thousands of people followed their leader into the unknown. Many days on a journey through desolation and wilderness, to a place where they could practice their faith without the danger of enmity and violence. The land of Harran, Abram's birthplace. When they arrived at their long-awaited destination, the locals warmly welcome them. Tens of thousands of people, who knew the distinguished family of Terah, came to visit the large encampment on the outskirts of the city.

Three years had passed since Abram and his men came to Harran. Three years of constant study for the newcomers who frequented the growing camp every day. A big tent city had arisen on the outskirts of the metropolis, which seemed to shrink by contrast. Abram sat in the tent, the latest new class of students had just left the tent.

There was a soft footstep behind him, and Abram felt his heart rejoice at the beloved sound. Iscah, his wife, slowly entered the tent, the steaming food spreading a pleasant aroma through the space as she approached and served her husband.

"Sarai, my dear, sit down a bit," Abram asked of his wife. Sarai was the name that Abram gave to Iscah after their marriage.

The woman sat down in front of her husband, happy for the precious moments she had to spend with him.

"Yesterday, the Lord revealed Himself to me," he told Sarai, as if revealing a secret. "He commanded me to get out of here — but only you, I, and some of our slaves and property. We are to go to the land of Canaan. All the other people will have to stay here in Harran in the meantime."

Sarai nodded, even though she knew her husband was not looking at her.

"I will tell Eliezer to gather the necessary equipment and a few slaves. In two days, we will set out on the journey toward the land of Canaan," Abram said, knowing that his wife would do whatever he told her.

"Of course, my lord," Sarai whispered. "Whatever you say…"

Dawn broke, and soon fresh sunlight began to caress the vast expanse of the meadow.

Eliezer stood at the door of his master's tent and was displeased. "My lord, Lot your nephew showed up as I was saddling the donkeys, he says he insists on his right to join you on the journey to the land of Canaan. I told him you said only you, your wife, I, and some of the slaves would go on the journey, but he said nothing would stop him from joining you." Eliezer spoke angrily, hoping that his master would refuse to let Lot accompany them.

Abram sighed weakly, recognizing the distaste his servant had for his nephew. "Eliezer, my friend, I understand what is in your heart, but perhaps if Lot comes with us there is a chance that he will change his ways a little. It is possible that being with us will cause him to abandon the lusts he indulges in."

Eliezer pursed his lips with a grimace, "will Lot change? Unfortunately, I do not believe it is possible, sir."

"Nevertheless, my friend, there is always some chance that something will penetrate through the shell of gross materialism and allow the boy to improve himself. Allow him to accompany us."

CHAPTER SIXTEEN

The War of the Kings

From Cuthah, King Nimrod and Prince Maradon led thousands upon thousands of armed cavalrymen, ready for merciless combat against King Chedorlaomer of Elam. Chedorlaomer had taken over vast regions, putting intense pressure on their former master, Nimrod. Most of the former Cuthean empire had already come under the control of the forces led by Chedorlaomer. For twelve years, Elamite sovereignty had gone unchallenged; but over the next five years, the rulers of the local city-states launched their own revolution against the new king. In particular, the kings of the five great Canaanite cities of the Jordan Plain, led by Bera of Sodom, had rebelled against Chedorlaomer, trying to escape the subjugation and taxation of the upstart monarch. Nimrod decided to seize the opportunity and try to regain the empire he had unquestionably ruled for many years. What better time could there be for Chedorlaomer's erstwhile sovereign to challenge him than when he was being challenged by his own unruly subjects?

The vale spread out before Nimrod, who was at the head of his army, alongside his heir. The warriors looked out over the vast valley, in which the great hosts filled the earth. The glow of the spearheads appeared like so many stars, glinting across the multi-colored glade. The battle was already raging between the Elamites and the Plainsmen; tens of thousands of cavalrymen engaged each other across the valley.

"I expect you to destroy these rebels quickly. We do not want to stay here long! You know warcraft; go down and destroy these rebels! It is time to repay Chedorlaomer for rebelling against me seventeen years ago." Nimrod waved his hand, signaling to his army to attack the enemy Elamites.

Whinnying horses and whooping men poured from the hilltops into the dell, their sounds echoing among the warriors already engaged in battle upon the valley soil. Undaunted, Chedorlaomer waved his hand at the additional army that was rising over him, encouraging his soldiers, confident of his victory. "Now we will show them what we are made of!"

Soon, the space was filled with the sounds of clanging swords and screaming men as enemies rushed to face each other — instilling hope in the hearts of the Plainsmen who had been slowly falling to the Elamite forces.

Chedorlaomer signaled to one of his officers to take his men and outflank the Cuthean cavalry galloping down the slopes into the valley. The Elamite fighters began launching spears and arrows at the descending forces of Nimrod. The horses slipped and stumbled on the steep descent, crushing their riders under their bodies.

Prince Maradon caught sight of the rebellious Chedorlaomer. He deftly leapt off his horse like an eagle attacking its quarry, clearing a path through the Cutheans with his sword, advancing towards his father's nemesis.

Out of the corner of his eye, Chedorlaomer saw Maradon's relentless approach. He thought of all the years he had known the prince and fought alongside him; he recognized all too well the fighting ability of the son of his former master. The two warriors eventually stood facing each other at the edge of the battlefield, just outside the commotion. The heat of the sun revealed beads of sweat emerging from the combatants' foreheads.

"I haven't seen you in a long time, traitor," Maradon hissed in hatred.

A slight smile appeared on Chedorlaomer's face. "I didn't think you had missed me so much."

"I treasure your visage so much, today I will take your head off your shoulders and bring it to my royal storehouse."

"I'd rather you not. I prefer it where it is, so I can watch you bow to me."

"Not a chance!" Said Maradon, leaping to attack him with youthful exuberance. The prince's sword sailed at the rebel king's head, but the latter blocked it with his iron shield. Chedorlaomer then raised his own blade; and for the next few minutes, they exchanged blows. The swords clanged dreadfully, with terrible force, neither able to seize an advantage.

Maradon suddenly had an idea and threw himself to the ground, knowing that his enemy would have to approach him; then the prince could cut his legs out from under him and defeat him. Chedorlaomer warily approached his fallen foe, trying to press his advantage. A slight smile arose within Maradon, seeing his ploy about to succeed. As if wielding a tremendous sickle, he swept his sword towards Chedorlaomer's leg as the rebel stood above him. The Elamite upstart wasn't quite quick enough; he leapt out of the way, but Maradon's blade still slashed open his heel.

However, Maradon then lost his balance, and the split second was all Chedorlaomer needed to bury his blade deep in the prince's prone body. As Chedorlaomer looked at the corpse sprawled at his feet, he felt that it was only a stroke of luck which had allowed him to emerge victorious over his enemy.

Nimrod and a few of his soldiers began to flee for their lives, leaving behind the bodies of Maradon and many other Cutheans and Plainsmen, who soaked the soil of the valley with their blood.

The army of Chedorlaomer continued to control broad swathes of territory, routing the Cuthean forces and subjugating the residents, who were required to pay exorbitant taxes to the new king. Nimrod, humiliated and defeated, had no choice but to accept the Elamite superpower.

The rippling murmur of the slowly flowing stream water could be heard well through the open tent. The light breeze whispered, the playful rusting of the leaves of the fruit trees joining the symphony of nature. Still, the noise of the dough being kneaded sowed sorrow in Abram's heart, as the muted sounds indicated how little bread was being made.

Their encampment was so much smaller than before, housing just the childless Abram and Sarai, Eliezer his manservant, and the limited number of male and female slaves she needed for the household. The camp was often abysmally silent, devoid of the jubilation of children. It brought a tear to Abram's eye. How he would have relished to play games with the youths who had once filled his settlement in Harran!

Ten years had passed since he had left his flock in Harran and made his way to the land of Canaan. Ten years of the absence of new students and newcomers to the congregation. Ten years of spiritual and physical barrenness, of emptiness and inaction gnawing at the heart of a man whose whole desire was to influence others, to spread his teachings and beliefs among human beings.

A day passed, a new day arrived, Abram and his few people shuffled along slowly, hoping for change and renewal. Throughout most of his life, he had been diligent in understanding what he needed to do in order to fulfill his Creator's will. Turning over in his mind the insights he had gained throughout his life, trying to gain more. Time seemed to stand still, amid the endless repetition of mundane acts. It was as if the dimension of time had no meaning in the stagnant atmosphere of the camp.

A polite cough interrupted Abram's miserable musing, and he looked up. He gazed lovingly at Eliezer, who had returned from his mission in Sodom.

"I hope I'm not interfering. Can I come in, my lord?" He asked humbly.

"Of course, my friend, come sit next to me and have a drink. You look a little tired."

Eliezer sat down in front of his master, his face looking downcast and desperate. Slowly, he drank from the glass of cold water which his master had poured for him.

"What do you have to tell me, my friend?" Abram had eagerly awaited the return of Eliezer from his mission. Many times, Eliezer had been sent by Abram to the great cities near the encampment, to try to find someone who would like to learn and know the Lord. Each time, he returned in miserable failure.

"What can I tell you, my lord, there is no one to talk to. The people there an inexplicably debauched. Once, they revolted against Chedorlaomer and stopped paying taxes to him, they got used to the habit of sitting around all day, just looking for a new way to indulging their hedonistic impulses. Now that the war is over, they have redoubled their focus on profit and pleasure.

"They have fresh fruits and vegetables all the time, endless beef and poultry; very large and handsome houses, expensive and indecent clothes. The truth is that my lord does not really want to hear how they dress, if you can call it dressing. Rich people from all over the country come there to find an outlet for their lusts, and for their money the people of the city provide them with all the abominations of the world. The poorest of the inhabitants of Sodom would be considered rich in another city. They hold nothing sacred but money and property. They despise everything that people worship, they have no idols except silver and gold. Everything is legitimate to achieve more wealth. Any thought beyond the material world is useless and vapid."

Eliezer's look of disgust said it all. "However, worst of all is their behavior toward passersby. Poor people visit the cities of the Jordan Plain knowing that the economic situation there is excellent. The indigent unfortunates who come there and ask for a piece of bread to assuage their hunger are refused; the Sodomites tell them they cannot give them food, but they can give them coins. So the poor roam around the city and collect charity in large quantities, but no one will sell or give them any food; finally, their stomachs burst and they die of hunger. This is a malicious amusement in the eyes of the townspeople, who come afterwards and pick over the corpses, taking the coins that were given to the paupers. Everyone marks his coin before giving it to the poor, knowing that a few days later, when the pauper dies, he will take his money back. These wicked people justify their actions by saying that if the poor are not smart enough to make their own fortunes, it is their problem. Then these monsters excuse their behavior by saying it would be inconceivable to turn the paupers away emptyhanded!"

Abram nodded sadly as he heard about the deeds of the Plainsmen. His pain was twofold: he felt empathy for the suffering of the poor, but he also felt regret over the perversion and perversity of the Plainsmen, who eschewed all knowledge of their Creator.

Eliezer went on, agitated, "these accursed villains have recently invented a new device, and they call it a Sodom bed. If a man comes to town and seeks lodging for the night, they put him in the Sodom bed. If he's too tall, they cut off his legs; if he's shorter than the bed, they stretch his body until it reaches the length of the bed. Many poor people have died on this bed."

Eliezer sighed heartbreakingly, "my lord, I do not know what we are doing here. Nimrod has been defeated by Chedorlaomer, and Harran is free of his rule. Should we not return there?" He begged, despairing and depressed.

Abram looked at his devoted servant; the recognition that he was the son of Nimrod, that he too, was supposed to be as cruel and fierce as his father, made him appreciate Eliezer even more. His heart, inherently hard and determined, had become soft and loving. "What happened to your forehead? Is everything okay?" He asked anxiously, noticing a large cut on Eliezer's forehead.

"Ah, that... It's already healing, but let me explain what happened. I saw a Plainsman beating a pauper. I told him to stop. He picked up a large rock from the ground and threw it at me, causing the cut on my head. So, I sued him. The judge asked me what happened, so I told him that the Plainsman threw a stone at me and cut open my head. You will not believe what he told me: he said I should pay that person who cut open my head ten gold coins for the bloodletting he gave me," Eliezer grinned.

"And what did you do? You paid him?"

Eliezer chuckled, "no, my lord, I just gave the judge a scratch, and I told him that whatever he had to pay me, he could pay to my attacker. I cut out the middleman!"

Abram and Eliezer laughed convivially, which relieved some of the tension from the onerous feeling of depression and helplessness.

"Another funny thing happened to me there," Eliezer said happily. "They have a law that you are not allowed to invite people to feasts and parties; whoever does so will have his cloak seized as a fine. Then, I was a bit hungry, so I went to a feast. As soon as I sat down, the man next to me asked, 'who invited you?' I said to him, 'you invited me!' The man panicked and ran out. That's how I went from diner to diner, until everyone sitting at the table ran away. Then, I sat down and ate. Honestly, I wasn't even hungry enough to finish all the food left on the table."

The two chortled happily, but then their laughter died down. Abram and Eliezer looked at each other, knowing that their amusement did not spring from a positive source, but from pain over the wickedness of the people whom Eliezer had managed to outwit. There were long minutes of internalized silence, expressing their shared disappointment that their neighbors were not interested in change.

"And what about Lot? Did you see him?"

"See him?" Eliezer said in disgust. "It was enough for me to hear about his deeds in Sodom. I have already told my lord that no good will come out of that corrupt man. He spends all day in feasting and revelry, so much so, that even the Sodomites are impressed by it. I did not want to bring up the subject, but now that it has been broached, I will lay it all out. Lot puts on shows in which he dresses up as my lord and mocks him. He presents my lord as the village idiot, saying ridiculous things and behaving crazily. The people of the city love these performances, which are filled with profanity and desecration of all that is holy. He is considered a rising star, and all the townspeople appreciate and admire him. In my opinion, one of the reasons no one visits our camp is the joke and laughingstock your nephew makes of you in Sodom."

Eliezer looked at his master sadly, "I'm sorry, my lord, but I had to tell you that."

CHAPTER SEVENTEEN

Pharaoh

"Excuse me, perhaps you can tell me how to seek an audience with the king?" The ragged nomad asked the clothier in his market stall.

The merchant looked at the traveler in astonishment. The handsomeness of the man and the nobility of his bearing contrasted radically with the worn condition of his garb. It was evident that the man came from a distant land and had not eaten in days. His pale face and shining emerald eyes mesmerized the swarthy clothier.

The traveler smacked his forehead and broke into a captivating smile, "I'm so sorry, forgive me. I forgot that you probably don't speak Sumerian," he said in fluent Egyptian to the staring merchant. "Can you tell me how I can meet the King of Egypt, His Majesty Ostris son of Enem?"

"Ah... you want to see the king?" The man stammered. "I'm sorry, but you probably won't be able to see him for a whole year. He held his annual tour a week ago. He come out of the palace to see us, the common people, only once a year. You'll have to wait for next time, a year from now."

"Isn't there any way to see him before that?"

"No!" The merchant's decisive tone brooked no argument, and the traveler was discouraged.

"Perhaps you can give me something to eat then?" The nomad was begging for his life.

The merchant laughed in a shrill voice. "Here, in town, there is nothing free! If you have money, pay; and if not, stop bothering me!" The laughter intensified, "you know what, there is something free — a grave! When you die, you will be buried for free!"

The foreigner, Rikaion, walked around the colorful town square, the smell of fresh food and roasting meat rising from the vendors' stalls and teasing his stomach. The nagging feeling of hunger soon became inescapable. His hopes of a royal audience had been utterly dashed. He thought, "in vain I pushed myself to travel from Shinar to Egypt, a monthlong journey, just to perish on foreign soil."

He was awash in feelings of loss and despair. He thought, "Ostris is still a new king, and I was sure that if I could just come before him and offer my services, he would be impressed with my wisdom and leadership ability. I was so certain that he would make me an official in his government. Now I have nothing..."

A purposeless stroll through the market district only exacerbated his gnawing hunger. Finally, he found a small, abandoned structure, just as evening began to fall on the city. Rikaion entered the hut, huddled in the corner of the room, and tried to cover his body with his rags of clothing to hide him from the cold that enveloped the ramshackle dwelling.

The next morning, the rays of the sun penetrated into the abandoned shack, awakening Rikaion. A sense of helplessness threatened to smother any glimmer of hope that still remained. Rikaion remained lying in his makeshift bed, refusing to rise to face the next discouraging day.

"You have nothing to get up for! Why bother? Lie here until you starve! You can't survive a full year until the king kindly leaves his palace anyway!" His thoughts gnawed at his flesh, as if trying to devour and bury him in the corner where he lay.

Rikaion angrily got to his feet, repelling the morbidity trying to take over his soul. "No!" He thought to himself. Yesterday, I saw people selling assorted herbs in the city. Surely, I can find something to sell in the nearby forest and revive my soul! I did not leave my father Nimrod's house to die in Egypt! I do not intend to be a humble slave like my brother Eliezer!

Walking to the nearby forest, rummaging through the weeds, a broad smile rose over Rikaion's face as he found, after hours of searching among the wild herbs, what he was looking for-- wild herbs he could sell in the market. Quickly, he gathered the herbs, thinking of the loaf of bread he could purchase for dinner. With eagerness and joy he placed his wares on the ground at the edge of the marketplace, keenly awaiting customers.

A toothless old man walked over to the herbs, looking at Rikaion in amazement mixed with disgust. "They actually look beautiful, the herbs you brought from the forest. But as you know, the forest is free and open to the public, and so I will take some of these herbs for the tasty soup I will make for my supper. Thank you for saving me the effort of walking out to the forest…" The old man grabbed some of the herbs and went on his way without paying. A few minutes passed, and Rikaion found himself standing on a patch of dirt with no wares to sell and without a penny in his pocket, after all the herbs had been taken by the passersby.

Like a condemned man on his way to the gallows, he staggered back toward the abandoned house he'd found. He felt as if a reptile were gnawing at his empty stomach. The gurgling from his belly was the only sound to be heard in the room. He thought, "What to do? How can I survive? I will probably die in a day or two. At least I will be buried for free!"

As Rikaion fell asleep, the voice of the cloth merchant from yesterday came to mind. "Actually, there is something free — a grave! When you die, you will be buried for free!" A slight smile appeared on Rikaion's face as he fell asleep.

"I'm sorry, sir, but the king has promulgated a new decree. There is no more free burial, and it is forbidden to bury anywhere aside from the municipal cemetery, whether inside or outside the city. Burial will cost you two hundred silver pieces! No less and no more!" Said the armed guard stationed at the cemetery gates. The man looked at the guard, puzzled, thinking of how to evade the exorbitant payment demanded for his father's burial. "But... maybe...?"

"No buts, no maybes! There is no free burial! And if you leave this corpse here and try to avoid burying it, it will cost you your head. The law is the law, and no one is allowed to evade paying the new burial tax! We will make sure no one evades it!" The man pointed to the thirty armed fighters flanking him, along the cemetery walls.

"But..."

"Perhaps you want your sons to pay four hundred pieces of silver today?" The boldfaced guard placed his hand on his sword, ready to draw it from its sheath. "I can make sure you and your father are buried on the same day! And by the way, it does not entitle you to a discount!"

The man began to tremble, realizing that he could not evade the king's decree. "Well, I'll go to my house to get the money," he said bitterly.

The guard smiled understandingly, "it's all right. You can leave your father's body here, and we'll keep it for now."

Rikaion stood some distance from what was happening, listening with pleasure to his ploy play out successfully. The thirty warriors he had hired, ostensibly by the king's command, did their job faithfully. At the end of the day, he held two thousand pieces of silver, enough to pay the fighters a month in advance — with a tidy profit for himself!

The days passed, and Rikaion continued to make money, hand over fist. The new burial fee greatly embittered the Egyptians, but they had no opportunity to lodge a complaint with the king, who only left his palace once a year to hear from his citizens. It all redounded to Rikaion's benefit.

Finally, a year had passed, the long-awaited day had come; the king of Egypt arrived to address the needs of his subjects. The palace gates opened, and the royal carriage began to make its way toward the crowd.

"Your Majesty the King!" A forsaken woman cried out, startling the driver of the carriage. He brought the horses to a halt, inches from trampling the woman. She was in rags, with ashes on her head, falling on her face in the road.

King Ostris stuck his face out of the carriage to see what the tumult was about and why his progress had been halted. Anger rose in his heart over the unexpected delay. His only ambition for the day was that he finish as soon as possible and return to his palace and its pleasures.

The ragged woman got up, running towards the king with cries of grief and doom. "Your Majesty the King, why do you do this to your subjects?! Has such a thing ever been done on earth? To levy a tax for the dead?! The way of kings is to demand tribute from the living, not the dead. My husband died, but I didn't have the two hundred pieces of silver required for his burial. For two weeks, his body has been lying in my small home, teeming with maggots and worms, because of the new tax Your Majesty has imposed. Is there no limit to this cruelty?" The woman burst into bitter tears, realizing that her impudence might come at the cost of her life.

The king looked at the widow in amazement, trying to figure out what she was talking about. "Call the minister in charge of the capital!" He commanded one of the cavalrymen escorting his carriage. Minutes later, the minister came to the king, ascending in fear to the carriage, trying to think of an explanation for why he had not seen to the payment of the tax imposed upon the bereaved.

"Can you explain to me what's going on here?" The king barked at the frightened minister.

"Your Majesty the King, to tell the truth, I did not know that this woman's husband had died, and that she had no money to pay the burial tax which the king has imposed. I was also unsure if it was correct to pay for the burial expenses of a private citizen from the city coffers. The city coffers belong to Your Majesty, so I thought it did not make sense for us to pay the king from the royal coffers..." The frightened minister looked at the confused monarch in apprehension.

"Explain everything to me, from the beginning!" The king shouted, feeling that the day was going to prove to be much longer than he had anticipated.

"Your Majesty the King, about a year ago, the new minister Rikaion, whom the king appointed, came and announced the imposition of the burial fee. Minister Rikaion announced that, by royal decree, no one was allowed to evade the tax. Most of the people manage to raise the amount, although some with great difficulty; but as the king knows, sometimes there are poor people who cannot afford the fee, though they are the minority. If Your Majesty agrees, I can pay the tax from the city coffers; alternatively, I can try to set up a fund to help widows and orphans pay the burial fee."

The king sank into thought. "Two hundred silver pieces per burial. There are about ten deaths a day in this city, that is two thousand silver pieces a day. Multiply that by three hundred and sixty-five days, that's seven hundred and thirty thousand silver pieces a year, and all this from only one city, in one year. Ingenious! Simple and ingenious!!!" The shadow of a smile began to appear on Ostris's face. "Set up the fund as you said, and bury the poor woman's husband today! It really does not make sense for the tax to come out of the city coffers!" He rebuked the minister. "And tell Minister Rikaion that I expect to meet him; he must come see me today at the palace." The king ordered the driver to turn the carriage around and return to the palace immediately.

King Ostris was sitting in the throne room, in the great hall of his palace. Hundreds of slaves — young men and women dressed in linen, silk, and embroidery carrying gifts for the king — filled the huge chamber. The slaves had been sent as tribute by Rikaion, who was following them to the palace.

The king looked with pleasure at the gifts. He smiled as the man, who was evidently not Egyptian, prostrated himself before him. "Long live King Ostris, forever!" Declared Rikaion. All the slaves bowed to the king as well, crying: "Long live King Ostris, forever!" After their master.

The king descended from his throne with a smile towards Rikaion, who bowed to the ground again. "Arise, my dear friend," said the king, reaching out to Rikaion as if he were a childhood friend.

"I hope my lord is not angry with his servant," Rikaion said humbly to the king.

The king hugged Rikaion's shoulders, leading him to the chair next to the throne. "Angry? I have long awaited a person like you to come to me. I am proud of you, my dear friend. If there is one thing I love, it is daring and innovation. And it seems to me that you are the right person to be finance minister. I have long been tired of all these puppets serving as my ministers, aimlessly waiting to receive orders."

"I am glad that my deeds have been pleasing to the king. I hope that the rest of the plans I have will also be pleasing to Your Majesty." Rikaion smiled a captivating smile at the king and said in a whisper, "if the king wants it, there are several other taxes that can be levied upon the people..."

The king and Rikaion huddled in intimate conversation, the king's eyes widening in delight. Ostris leaned backed with joyful laugh, "dear Rikaion, you are a naughty one! It seems to me that instead of Rikaion I will change your name to Pharaoh! I have never heard of a man who so relishes collecting a payment (*piraon*) as you!"

For three years, Rikaion- Pharaoh served as viceroy, imposing new taxes every morning, then giving a discount on the tax rate. He collected money at every step in the name of the king. Once people got used to the high rates, he reduced them and filled the masses with the feeling that he was reciprocating with kindness.

After three years, when Rikaion- Pharaoh saw how great his popular support was. With all the ministers following his lead, he organized a military coup and executed King Ostris for the tyranny he had committed against his oppressed people. All the ministers and the people received Rikaion- Pharaoh's coronation, swearing allegiance to the new monarch and his seed after him.

From now on, Pharaoh would be the title of all rulers of Egypt, the whole kingdom agreed, joyfully accepting the good news that the royal tax rate had dropped from fifty-three percent to only forty-four percent.

CHAPTER EIGHTEEN

The War

"Well, I haven't called you all here for nothing. I know that at least some of you were reluctant to make the journey and come to my palace. If any one of you are afraid that I summoned you here with ill intent, set that thought aside." King Chedorlaomer of Elam looked at the other monarchs sitting before him.

"The purpose of this gathering is the renewed threat that is emerging in the land of Canaan — a threat that does not seem so dangerous at the moment, but if we consider the not-so-distant future we can already predict the consequences of inaction. You all probably know that thirteen years ago, the kings of Sodom, Gomorrah, Admah, Zeboiim and Zoar, stopped paying taxes to me. Now, you may ask yourselves why you should care about my not receiving taxes. So, I will tell you. these five kings are beginning to accumulate enormous military power. Their cities are filled with every delight, and that has brought in a tremendous amount of money. My informants tell me that they are planning to fight us, and attempt to conquer all of our lands. They already have mercenaries, war chariots and full armories."

Chedorlaomer looked sternly at the kings, who seemed uninterested in his words. "You think that my words are meaningless to you. Therefore, I will explain to you what these men will do. When they conquer us, they will kill all the men. Your wives, if they are beautiful, will be put in whorehouses for their pleasure. Your sons and daughters will have their ears pierced as slaves, until they're old enough to be sent to the brothels as well. Your idols will be burned and smashed, after they have been desecrated in their circuses and theaters. And finally, you, my friends, will be put on display in their bordellos, so that anyone who wants may do to you what they wish."

Chedorlaomer's bold voice echoed through the chamber. "Do not think that these catastrophes are far off. The war will begin in a matter of months, and if they attack us first, we stand no chance!"

King Arioch of Ellasar, rose to his feet: "I am with you!" He said firmly. "There is nothing more dangerous than a man who fears no god, and that is the Sodomite attitude."

"Me too!" Assented King Tidal of Goiim, with determination.

Chedorlaomer smiled with satisfaction.

"And what about you, Amraphel?" He asked King Amraphel of Shinar.

Amraphel smiled through his disgust: "I am of course with you," he said with no choice. Amraphel was the name given by Chedorlaomer to Nimrod after he conquered his kingdom. Amraphel, who said (*amar*) to Abram, "fall (*pol*) into the fiery furnace!" A cruel joke. This name served to remind Nimrod that he had been incapable of defeating a single man.

"I'm glad you're all with me," Chedorlaomer said boldly. "In two weeks, we wage war against these five pathetic kings. As for the booty, we will divide it equally. Each, will receive a quarter of the fabled wealth of the Plainsmen." Chedorlaomer looked with satisfaction at the smile of the kings, the spoils of war would enrich them to no end.

Chedorlaomer walked among the kings, shaking the hands which would soon be raking in the wealth of Sodom and its neighboring cities. "Amraphel, I have something to talk to you about," he whispered to Nimrod. "Do not go yet, I think it will make you very happy."

A variety of colors and shades adorned the mountains around the Sodom Valley. The warriors of the four armies looked at the flowering valley at the height of its glory. They gazed yearningly at the scene of verdant blooms. Carefully arranged fruit trees decorated with various flowers, made the fertile vale a spectacular sight of natural beauty and splendor. The rippling rivers among the fruit trees seemed to be carved by a wondrous artist. The gentle wildlife meandered peacefully among the people, lounging naked in the face of the caressing sun of early spring. The sound of chirping birdsong melted into the playing of the musicians' instruments, as they ambled through the meadows accompanied by singers, whose melodies entertained the sunbathers. Food and drink in gold and silver vessels were arranged at the foot of the fruit trees for the enjoyment of those lying supine.

"Now!"

Hundreds of thousands of warriors began to flood the valley from three directions. The sound of war cries froze the Plainsmen to the marrow of their bones, echoing from the throats of warriors eager to split the spoils. Screams of terror emerged from the helpless people, who realized that their pastoral indulgence was at an end. The swords sliced their flesh as the horses' hooves trampled their ornamental flowers.

The war whoops continued as the attackers burst through the gates of the five cities of the Jordan Plain. One after another, shattering the serenity of the scene, surprising the defenders who had been indulging themselves moments earlier. The four armies flowed into the cities, killing everything in their path: men, women, and children were trampled underfoot by horses and chariot wheels. The mercenaries, hired by the Plainsmen, fled for their lives, pursued by the bloodthirsty forces of the Chedorlamer and his allies, leaving the once-peaceful cities.

However, the scene in Sodom was different. As Amraphel and his soldiers entered, he ordered, to the surprise of his men, "no one is to be killed without my permission!" Every man captured was taken to Amraphel for confirmation before execution. Thousands of bodies were piled up before the king, as he examined the prisoners before they were slaughtered. Nimrod was excited for the long-awaited captive, envisioning his being transported among his people, haunted by an old memory of insubordination to the king. Nimrod's eyes open with a mischievous smile. "I was told you looked like him, but I did not realize that you looked exactly like him," he said happily to the broken prisoner standing in front of him.

"Save him for me! Woe to you if anything happens to him!" He told his soldiers. "You may now resume combat as usual. We have found the one I was looking for."

The battle continued, Amraphel's soldiers came before their king laden with a wide variety of booty: women and children; gems, silver, and gold galore; clothing and material; sheep and cattle; horses and camels loaded with loot.

"Your Majesty the King, shall we burn the city as we leave?" Asked one of the officers.

Amraphel looked at the officer dismissively. "Why burn it?! I intend to return here after the war to relax in this wonderful place. It would be such a pity to lay waste to all the effort these fools have put in here. This city will be a resort for my people. You do not want to come here for a week or two to enjoy all this luxury?"

The officer smiled ruefully at his master, "Your Majesty, as always, is right. I beg your pardon but I did not think of that." The officer looked at the captive off to the side, "if I may ask, sir, who is this man? He seems awfully familiar to me, but I cannot recall where I know him from."

Nimrod happily clapped his hands, "you are quite young, therefore you do not remember him. You must have seen him when you were still small. The older ones probably know who the prisoner is." Nimrod motioned to the young officer, "go out for a moment and call us one of the veteran warriors, we'll see if he recognizes this captive."

The officer left and returned shortly after with an older fighter. "Tell me, my friend," Nimrod jokingly said to the incoming warrior, "do you know this prisoner?"

The warrior glanced at the prisoner, who shrank in fear of his captors. The warrior's eyes widened in bewilderment, "this is nothing but Abram son of Terah, the insurrectionist!"

A slight tremor passed through the encampment near Hebron. Eliezer looked at his master and came out of the tent to see the cause of all the shaking and rumbling. Eliezer stopped in his place, looked up, and saw in front of him a huge man, before whom he felt like a small ant. "Who are you? And what do you want?" He asked the giant loudly.

"I need to say something to Abram," said the giant. "Tell him that Og wants to see him."

Eliezer hurried to the tent, meeting Abram on his way out. "Og the giant wants to see you," he murmured.

Abram gazed up at his towering visitor. "Og, what are you doing here, my friend?"

Og looked in awe at Abram, aware of the life story of the man standing before of him. "My lord, I am no harbinger of good tidings. A fierce battle is going on, an invasion of our country. Chedorlaomer and Nimrod came with two kings and fought with my people; they destroyed my whole family, and I am left alone." Abram looked at Og in wonder, trying to figure out why the giant had come all this way to tell him the news.

"And...?"

Og looked at Abram with a devilish smile. "We were not their target. After fighting us, they continued to the cities of the Jordan Plain: Sodom and Gomorrah, Admah, Zeboiim, and Zoar. They killed all the men who could not escape. A few managed to escape towards the mountains. King Bera of Sodom and King Birsha of Gomorrah also fled, but they fell into a clay pit in Siddim Valley. You know, the whole valley is full of such pits, from which the Plainsmen produce bricks to build their buildings. The four kings took all the women, children and property." Og widened his smile as he saw on Abram's face the fear for his nephew's life. "Sorry, I said they killed all the men captured, but that's not accurate; they did not kill one man, Lot. They took him captive."

"Well, what do we care?!" Eliezer exclaimed angrily. "All the better! Let the wicked fight the wicked! *When the wicked perish, there are shouts of joy.* What do we care? Did you come to tell us this so that we could hold a celebration?!"

Og's peal of laughter shocked Eliezer. "I heard about you, Eliezer, servant of Abram. Honestly, I thought you were cleverer than that. I was sure you would have more sense and understand why it should be particularly important to you! And that you must go to war against the four kings!"

Eliezer looked at Abram to see if he agreed. Abram's furrowed brow revealed that this was of great concern to his master. "My lord, you know that Lot is a wicked man. Why does this so bother my lord? Is it because he is your nephew?" Eliezer sounded confused. "If you follow that line of reasoning, I ought to have gone to help my father Nimrod when Chedorlaomer fought him and killed my brother Maradon!"

Abram looked at Eliezer seriously. "That Lot is my nephew is neither here nor there. The problem is what you told me when you returned from Sodom-- that Lot resembles me greatly. Don't you wonder why Nimrod took only Lot as a captive? Out of dozens, If not hundreds of thousands, of Plainsmen? Nimrod will now take Lot and carry him along the length and breadth of his kingdom, telling people: 'this is Abram who rebelled against me!' He will make Lot identify himself as me and tell everyone that he was wrong, and is now a chastened and faithful servant of the true deity, God-King Nimrod. Lot will have no problem worshipping Nimrod and deifying him. As you said, he is a wicked man, interested only in the pleasures of the flesh. Nimrod will make sure that Lot impersonates me and pledges undying fealty to the God- King of Shinar!"

Eliezer furrowed his brow, "then what does my lord propose?"

Abram smiled, "there is no choice; we must go to war to save Lot."

"Abram…" Sarai's voice could be heard from the opening of her tent.

Eliezer saw Og looking longingly at Sarai standing in the opening of the tent. "This scoundrel must wish for my lord to die in battle so he can take my lord's wife for himself," he thought grimly.

"Dear, I made matzah for tonight, the fifteenth of Nissan. I think you should take the matzah with you on the road." The woman's voice trembled a little, out of fear of her husband's fate.

"Thank you, darling, do not worry. We will be back by tomorrow night."

"Eliezer, go to Mamre, Eshcol, and Aner, and update them. Tell them I'm going to go to war in about an hour. If they want, they can join us."

Aner, Eshcol, and Mamre were three brothers who had approached Abram during the years he lived in Canaan. The three young men would occasionally visit Abram's tent, coming to hear his wisdom and listen to his wise counsel.

An hour passed, and Eliezer returned with the three brothers. The usually cheerful boys looked surprised. "Abram, do you really think the five of us can defeat the four kings with their hundreds of thousands of soldiers? We are not afraid, we will come with you, but that sounds very farfetched."

"My dear friends, the truth is I did not call you to come and fight with me. Eliezer and I will engage in combat, while you will guard our supplies. The reason I summoned you is so that you may see the greatness of the Lord, may His name be blessed. Until this day, you have only heard stories. Now, you may personally witness who is worthy of your worship." The boys looked at Abram in admiration, appreciating the integrity of their master's faith.

"Come on, friends, we're going to war," Abram said with a smile.

"Just a moment, my lord, I will bring our swords," said Eliezer, and he turned toward the tent to retrieve their weapons.

Abram laughed with pleasure, "Eliezer, my dear, what will two swords help against hundreds of thousands of soldiers? Do you think that Gd needs our help in this war? Come, my friend, *it is not by sword or spear that the Lord saves; for the battle is the Lord's!*"

The five men advanced toward the coordinates Og had given them. The men felt that their accelerated pace was unnatural. They felt as if the ground was contracting beneath their feet.

In the Valley of Siddim, Abram paused for a moment, looking up, "Master of the Universe, please bring the kings of Sodom and Gomorrah out of the mud so that all the unbelievers will believe; for You may take them out of the mud just as You brought me out of the fiery furnace!"

A jubilant smile broke out on Abram's face, then spread to his comrades, as they saw two men, white as ghosts, emerging from the bowels of the earth, landing at Abram's feet.

"Thank you, God," Abram said delightedly. The two men began to bow to Abram, realizing that his prayer had saved them.

"Come on, we need to keep going!" The five continued in the direction of Damascus.

Midnight came, with Abram and his men watching the vast camp spread out before them. "What now?" Eliezer whispered.

"I will attack from the right, and you from the left," Abram laughed. "The young men will stay here and watch the show."

"What?!"

"Listen, my friend. All you have to do now is just believe, with complete faith, that nothing is beyond the powers of the Creator, may His name be blessed. Take a handful of dirt and straw, and throw it towards the camp. The dirt will turn into swords, the straw into spears which God will bear, to strike only the Elamites and their allies. Do not think too much, just do as I have told you and witness the Lord's salvation!" Abram picked up a handful of dirt and straw. "Watch..." The bits of dirt and straw that rushed toward the camp became swords and spears that hit the enemy soldiers. Screams and shouts of agony arose from the camp as it was attacked by unknown hands, striking the fighters with great precision. They tried in vain to avoid the swords and spears piercing their bodies. The mysterious battle lasted a few minutes. Abram and Eliezer stood on two hills, throwing dirt and straw at the enemy until it was routed.

The five men descended toward the devastated enemy camp, taking Lot, all the captives, and loot back towards the Jordan Plain.

The convoy made its way back from the battlefield. The shadows of night faded before the bright glare of the sun, warming the hearts broken by the loss of their people. Abram and his friends marched toward Sodom and its neighboring cities. A multitude of women and children mourned their loved ones who perished in the war, but rejoiced being saved from their cruel foes.

King Bera of Sodom, miraculously ejected from the bowels of the earth, waited anxiously, doubting whether Abram would succeed in defeating the immense enemy who had conquered his kingdom, destroyed his army, and taken his people captive. Then he heard the sound of sheep bleating and cattle lowing, accompanied by the noise of a great camp. It sent chills through the body of the humiliated man.

In the vast valley that stretched far and wide, the king stood and looked forward to welcoming the returnees. He hesitated fearing that Abram would want to take the captives and property for himself, as he had saved them.

Suddenly, he noticed another convoy of people, coming from the city of Salem. The king of Sodom looked at the two caravans, coming from opposite directions: Abram's convoy with the captives on one side, and the king of Salem, wearing his crown and accompanied by many nobles and ministers, on the other side.

"My lord, it seems to me that they have prepared a reception for us," Eliezer happily said to his master. He was filled with the joy of victory, the exaltation of the supreme power given to those who do the word of God in faith and perfection. He smiled boldly at the sight of those who had come to welcome them back. The knowledge that his father Nimrod had fled the battlefield left a strange feeling in his heart: on the one hand, a sigh of relief that he had not been forced to kill his own father; on the other hand, a groan of disappointment at the escape of his master's nemesis.

Abram agreed, "yes, I recognize him. That is Shem, son of Noah, who is known by the locals as King Melchizedek of Salem. He is my longtime friend, who now rules the city which contains the altar built and used by Adam himself. Noah did the same when he returned from the Ararat Mountains after the flood." Abram hurried to meet the man who had been his friend throughout his youth.

The tables were set with bread, wine, and other delicacies for those returning from the battle, spread out in the valley for the weary people. There was a loving embrace between the two longtime friends, an embrace that dispelled any concern of unease or resentment on the part of Shem for killing his descendants, who had started a war with the people of Sodom and Gomorrah in order to deny the Creator's providence over His creatures. *"Blessed be Abram by the Supreme God, Maker of heaven and earth,"* he greeted Abram happily, knowing that victory in this war had been delivered by God Himself. Shem thought to himself, "apparently, this is the man the world has been waiting for, to bring about the ultimate rectification of the universe!"

He concluded with an admiring smile, *"and blessed be the Supreme God, who has delivered your enemies into your hand."*

Abram lovingly embraced Shem, although he was a bit uneasy at what he had heard. God should always be the first to be blessed, before any human being! Aloud, he said to Shem, "I was very saddened to hear that your righteous father passed away fifteen years ago. I miss him very much. But I am sure that from his place in heaven, he is happy that he left behind a son like you. My friend, as you are a priest of God, I take a tithe from all that is here as a gift to you, as a priest deserves," ordering Eliezer to set aside tithes from their booty for Shem son of Noah.

King Bera of Sodom advanced towards the two friends, but aside from his proud gait, it was not apparent that he was a monarch. His tattered and lime-soaked clothes made him look like a commoner, but his bearing proved that he was a king. "My lord Abram, I do not know how I can thank you for saving my people and my property. I know that now, by right, everything is yours, both my people and my property," the king said apprehensively to Abram. "But I ask you to give me the people; I am their king. You may take all your property because it is yours by right. You may also take the remaining property in Sodom because you won it, as you have acquired my people by saving them. I ask for nothing but my people."

Abram smiled at Bera, who was sure that Abram would take the property and the slaves. The thought of returning the captives to the king of Sodom distressed Abram, who knew the evil of his deeds. He thought to himself, "if I take them and convert them, two evils may come out of it: first, they may not follow the ways of the Lord; second, even if they do, the nations of the world will say that I coerced them, that they only serve the Lord because they fear me."

He mused further, "If I take the property, the world will say that for the sake of wealth, I went to war; and because the Lord could not enrich me, I became affluent from the looting of Sodom. However, I was not alone in the war; Aner, Eschol, and Mamre earned their share, and I cannot withhold it from them."

Abram looked at Bera, who eagerly awaited what his response. Abram declared, "*I have lifted up my hand unto the Lord, the Supreme God, Maker of heaven and earth, that I will not take a thread nor a shoe-latchet nor aught that is yours, lest you should say: I have made Abram rich; save only that which the young men have eaten, and the portion of the men which went with me, Aner, Eshcol, and Mamre, let them take their portion.*"

Bera prostrated himself before Abram, rejoicing in his heart over the good that had been given to him; both the property and the people that belonged to Abram were being returned to him. The rest of the kings and ministers, who had gone with Melchizedek to greet Abram, also bowed down, accepting Abram as their supreme king.

CHAPTER NINETEEN

The Covenant Between the Parts

The heat of the spring sun caressed the silent land with its rays. The war had ravaged the country, leaving the roads desolate. People huddled in their homes, trying to heal their traumatized souls. Abram's encampment was free of visitors, its handful of residents conducting themselves lazily and with disinterest.

Abram took the flock and went out into the wilderness to graze, seeking refuge from the disturbing silence that dominated the tents, to flee to a place where the calm expanded and nothing disturbed it.

The little flock devoured the fresh grass of early spring and quenched its thirst from the waters of the gurgling stream. Abram lay on the grass, judging and criticizing his actions, words, and thoughts. His eyes stared into the distance, his mind penetrating his innermost core, exploring his intricacies. "Perhaps among the warriors of the four kings I killed were some honest people. Is it possible that the sons of those kings may gather and fight me, to repay me for defeating their fathers? Maybe I should have kept the Sodomites I saved in my possession!" His heart observing, his mind exploring, his whole being straining to encompass the deliberations that filled his soul. Time was gone, space was gone, reality was fading.

He saw a fire blazing without any fuel, kindled by its innermost quintessence, rising and falling. The flames were in a variety of shades and colors, and they seemed to encompass all facets of Abram's existence. Abram stared into the conflagration, merging with it... disappearing...

"*Fear not, Abram, I am your shield, your reward shall be exceedingly great.*" Abram listened, mesmerized, to a perception that nullified everything, refuting all his thoughts. "The warriors you killed were thorns and briers in the vineyard. If their sons dare to fight you, I will protect you. The Plainsmen you saved will never seek shelter beneath the wings of the Divine Presence. The miracles I wrought on your behalf are insignificant compared to the vast merits of your righteousness. There is a great reward which I maintain for you, both in this world and the world to come."

Like a drop bursting through a seemingly impermeable dam, a cold tear streamed down Abram's cheek. He felt a twinge in his heart, as the globule of resentment swelled and grew, clawing, gnawing, trying to break through the battlement of rock-solid faith. The first drop was followed by another drop, diligently widening the crack in the fortification; still more came, rivulets now, soaking and seeping the packed mud of the wall, until the dam burst with a torrent of bitterness. "*Lord God, what will You give me?*" With a cry of utter heartbreak, of a man who had lost everything, he went on, "This world? For what? What good will silver and gold do for me here? Who will inherit my wealth when I pass from this world?

"Is it honor? For what purpose? To distance me from You?" The hidden sorrow erupted, poured forth, enveloped Abram.

"Is it the world to come? What will my experience be in the next world? An eternity remaining on the first level? What is there to be enjoyed in perpetual fixity? How can I ever advance in the world to come, *seeing I go hence childless?* After all, you have not given me a son. A person can only be complete when he has children or students to continue his path. All the students I taught, can they spread Your will in Your world? Will they continue to teach their sons what they have absorbed from me? I have one faithful student, Eliezer of Damascus, can he continue your way in the world? As great and righteous as Eliezer is, he is a descendant of Ham, whom You cursed. Can a cursed man be the one to carry Your message on to the world? Can he be my successor, studying Your law and fulfilling Your commandments, so that I will continue to advance in the world to come thanks to his actions?"

His heart, sliced to ribbons by grief, seized up as he cried, *"behold, to me You have given no seed, and, lo, a member of my household is to be my heir.* Am I less worthy than the idol-worshippers, who have children to love and to leave everything to? As for me, *he that shall be possessor of my house is Eliezer of Damascus!"*

A conciliatory Voice spoke, like a father embracing his broken, shattered son, holding him to his bosom with deep and abiding affection, caressing his head with compassion. *"This man will not be your heir, but a son who comes from your own innards will be your heir."*

Still Abram was inconsolable; he thought his Heavenly Father's comfort to be untrue, a temporary measure to keep his wounded heart from collapsing in grief. "I know that I will not have children. I have seen it in the stars: Abram will never be a father and Sarai will never be a mother. That is just the way it is; it all depends on astrology, and I understand the two of us were born under the influence of Jupiter, when it was in the west. Therefore, we can never be parents," Abram said, like a child lovingly accepting words of comfort from a parent while realizing they are nothing more than words.

However, the voice roared back at him, "Abram! Defy your horoscope! Who do you think created the planet Jupiter? Who determined its orbit, when it would be in the west and when it would be in the east? I can toss it back into the east if I so desire! Astrology has no power over you, nor will it have power over your descendants. You are above the stars! Set aside these thought and ideas; it is time that you base all of your identity on faith alone."

Abram felt himself flying into the air, drawn into the high heavens, so that he could look down on the earth as it rushed away from him, just a small marble in the infinite expanse. His eyes opened wide, perceiving endless constellations and heavenly bodies. He felt how indignant man was, in the face of the infinite.

"*Look now toward heaven, and count the stars, if you be able to count them,*" Abram tried to do as he had been told, but he knew it was impossible. "*So shall your seed be.*"

Abram began tearing up, not tears of grief and heartbreak, but warm tears of gratitude and thanksgiving.

"*I am the Lord brought you out of Ur Kasdim, to give you this land to inherit it.*"

Abram feverishly considered this promise, trying to discard his preconceived notions and to fully accept this guarantee. "*O Lord God, whereby shall I know that I shall inherit it?* If I inherit the land, how can I know that I will pass it on? How can I know that this inheritance will be a legacy in perpetuity? By what merit will my seed retain it?" Abram asked, painfully, knowing that his questions were superfluous.

God explained what would happen to his children. "*Know of a surety that your seed shall be a stranger in a land that is not theirs, and shall serve them; and they shall afflict them four hundred years;*

and also, that nation, whom they shall serve, will I judge; and afterward shall they come out with great substance."

"Will I accompany them to this strange land of servitude?"

"But you shall go to your fathers in peace; you shall be buried in a good old age."

"Then what am I to do?"

"Take Me a heifer threefold, and a she-goat threefold, and a ram threefold, and a turtledove, and a young pigeon."

Abram got up, enthralled, as if his body were acting of its own accord, his hands moving as if they were being adjusted by a supreme will, without any intentional action on his own part.

He slaughtered three heifers, three she-goats, three rams — each three years old — slicing each in half and placing one half opposite the other. The turtledove and pigeon were seized by Abram, placed living and tranquil on the halves. Abram suddenly recoiled, looking at the abattoir, wondering why he had been commanded to sacrifice so many animals on this occasion. "Forget logic!" He ordered himself. "It is time to discard human intellect and embrace what the divine will tells you to do!"

God explained, "it is by virtue of sacrifices such as these that your descendants will last forever. They may sin, but by way of the offerings, they will always have a path to return to Me and win My forgiveness.

"Later on, there will be four empires who will subjugate your children: the heifer-like Empire of Edom, the goat-like Empire of Greece, the ram-like Empire of Persia and Media, and the dove-like Empire of Ishmael. The first three empires will fall, but from the fourth, the Empire of Ishmael, will arise the man who will bring redemption to your children — and to the world as a whole. Your descendants are the pigeon, which will survive the subjugation of all these empires."

Abram experienced a vision of the upcoming millennia and what his descendants would experience. "When the Temple lies in ruins, how can my children maintain the sacrificial service?"

"They will study its laws and aspire to rebuild it; then I will credit it to them as if they had brought those very sacrifices in the flesh."

Abram raises his eyes to the sound of wings flapping over his head. Huge birds of prey, hovering over the carcasses, tried to devour them. Abram's feet carried him reluctantly to beat back the attack of the birds of prey. "What are the birds of prey? Whom do they represent?" The question arose.

"From among your descendants, a man will arise who will be capable of bringing redemption to the whole world, even before its proper time; as the birds of prey want to destroy the carcasses, he will also want to eradicate these empires prematurely. He will be the king of Israel, complete in every way, fit to be the final redeemer: David son of Jesse, king of Israel. However, I will not let him do so, for My children must go through one purification after another, until they are worthy of perfection. For many years, My children will endure upheavals until one will arise who will lead them to the ultimate goal for which I created this world. A person who will discover faith in the heart of each and every one of My children as a tangible thing. A person who will bring all My people to a degree of faith that is above the degree of faith of the prophets."

Abram felt that his body was incapable of containing what was revealed to him. Slowly, he sat down on the ground, his eyes closing of their own accord.

And it came to pass, that, when the sun was going down, a deep sleep fell upon Abram; and, lo, a dread, even a great darkness, fell upon him.

Abram could hear the screams and shouts of his descendants, throughout the generations. Innocent children were slaughtered, pregnant women were dashed to pieces, men were tortured beyond the limits of human suffering. For the amusement of their oppressors, people were left to be devoured by wild predators and children were buried alive inside buildings. In the background, the delighted laughter of their killers rang out. Tens of millions were slaughtered with a cruelty that the human mind quailed to consider.

"Isn't there another way???" Abram burst out, perplexed.

The Voice in his mind declared: "either foreign subjugation or Hell..."

Abram came to the realization that his descendants would undergo refinement and purification solely for their eternal good. "If that is how It must be, foreign subjugation is preferable, as it will benefit my children in the end."

On that day, the Lord made a covenant with Abram, saying: "Unto your seed have I given this land, from the river of Egypt unto the great river, the river Euphrates; the Kenite, and the Kenizzite, and the Kadmonite, and the Hittite, and the Perizzite, and the Rephaim, and the Amorite, and the Canaanite, and the Girgashite, and the Jebusite."

The vision dissipated, Abram felt himself sinking into a long slumber, merging into the abyss, drawn into peace of mind.

"I am afraid of what will happen now with the people we have left in Harran," Abram mused, the worry clear on his face. "The fierce battle here, along with the escape of your father Nimrod from the battlefield, tell me that I must find see to our people in Harran. After the humiliating defeat of the four kings at our hands, they may want to harm our allies. We must return to Harran," Abram told Eliezer. "Tell Lot and the slaves to start packing. Tomorrow, we set out. I will talk to Sarai..."

Abram, Sarai, Eliezer, Lot, and the people with them made their way back to Harran. The few provisions they took with them were no burden for the people happily returning to the place they had left ten years earlier. The sounds of laughter and joy rising in the distance put a spring in their step, despite their tired legs. Old and young, men and women, boys and girls welcomed those who came with happiness and admiration, as children meeting their parents who had been reluctantly separated from them. Even Terah and Amathlai came out to greet their son returning from afar.

CHAPTER TWENTY

"Go for Yourself!"

The stream flowed slowly, the banks covered with playful fruit trees, the sound of the wind spreading the leaves of the trees and rattling among the fully-grown stalks of wheat. The laughter of the children frolicking in the sprawling woods and the sound of the men filling the benches of the study hall soothed Abram's soul. Along with that, the sound of the women giggling in the kitchen and the racket of the rattling pots indicated how large the camp was.

At an hour past midday, Abram sat under an ancient walnut tree, his eyes closed, meditating on incorporation with his Creator, a pleasant feeling of warmth filling his being, floating in unknown realms. A slight tremor gripped his body, as he felt that the spirit of God was landing on him. The separation of the spirit from the body that bound it to the physical being, which enslaved the spiritual soul to the world of material substance began to occur.

A voice spoke in Abram's mind, filling his self and erasing it, leaving only the Communicator: "*Go for yourself from your country, and from your kindred, and from your father's house, unto the land that I will show you. And I will make of you a great nation, and I will bless you, and make your name great; and be you a blessing. And I will*

bless them that bless you, and him that curses you will I curse; and in
you shall all the families of the earth be blessed."

Conflicting feelings ran through Abram's heart, each one displacing its predecessor. On the one hand, there was the recognition that he would have to leave the flock again and go to an unknown place, leaving the converts who congregated and multiplied every day, setting out once again when his last journey abroad had ended in such great disappointment; on the other hand, his prophecy had explicitly stated, *"and I will make of you a great nation,"* implying that he and his wife might finally merit to have a child of their own. On the one hand, he had a path lying before him in Harran, together with his many disciples; on the other hand, he saw the enticing potential of finding new students in the forgotten lands, of disseminating the light of the true faith.

Abram opened his eyes and put a smile on his face, knowing that what God had told him, he must do; the divine decree could only be for his good and for the good of all mankind. Quickly he got up, directing his steps towards the great encampment, happily prepared for the adventure that awaited him and his people.

"Cutie," he turned to one of the mischievous children, caressing his head. "Can you please run to Eliezer and tell him to come to my tent?"

The boy looked admiringly at his father's master, "yes, milord, I will find him straightaway." The boy happily ran to carry out his mission.

"Eliezer, we must go on a journey again. I do not know where we are going; the Lord will reveal this to us further down the road.

Gather all the men, women, and children, and inform them that I want to tell them something," Abram directed his devoted servant.

A short time passed and Eliezer came before his master to let him know that the congregation had gathered to hear what he had to say.

"My dear friends," Abram addressed the many gathered at his feet, as he surveyed the faces looking up at him. "The word of God was revealed to me today, telling me that I must leave this place. I do not know where I will go, or how long the journey will take. I cannot promise any of you anything. One thing I do know is that I must go. Anyone who wants may come and accompany me. However, you must know that the road is unclear and the goal is unknown. This path is the Lord's path, and only He knows where and why I should go. I do not ask or require you to come with me on a journey into the unknown. Whoever decides to stay here, know that I bear no ill will about that choice; whoever decides to join me must be prepared for the many trials that are inherent in exile. As we wander from here to our ambiguous destination, we may expect many difficult tribulations."

Sounds of astonishment and groans of sorrow arose from the crowd, which, until that moment, had been silently listening to their master. Abram quieted them again to give his valediction.

"It has been my pleasure and honor to spend time with you and to teach you what I know. Tomorrow morning, I will begin the journey; whoever wishes to join me is welcome. And to all who remain here, I will always love you, and you will always have a place in my heart."

A large crowd gathered to set out on the journey with Abram and Sarai.

Terah and Amathlai came before their son, their eyes full of tears and their faces downcast. "We cannot go with you, my son," Terah said to Abram. "Your mother and I are old, and we cannot withstand the travails of travel. Here we were born, and here we want to die. May the Lord be with you, my son, wherever you go." Terah lovingly embraced the son who had become his mentor. Amathlai burst into bitter tears over her separation from her beloved youngest son, yet again.

Abram dried his tears with his hands, saddened by yet another separation from his parents — it seemed to him, the last. He knew that he had no choice but to take the first step on his journey of a thousand miles or more.

The caravan began to move into the unknown. It followed the feelings of Abram's heart, leading them in the direction outlined for him. They would pitch their tents each night and continue traveling each morning, going south and west. Passing established cities, camping outside them. Some of the people quit tearfully, going back to their birthplaces, but many of the people clung to Abram and his household.

Beside Abram, Lot walked, to Eliezer's displeasure. "I'm not sure where we're going," Lot grumbled as the caravan passed near the city of Tyre. "We left a flourishing and fertile city to head to this place! Look at the people of this land: working in the fields all day, toiling and toiling to feed their household. In Harran, we did not have to work, whereas here, it seems as if the people work all day, every day. In Harran, we could sit all day without doing a thing, while in this country they seem to be slaves to their livelihood."

Abram glared at his nephew, ruing his irresponsibility. "I would rather be among people who work for their sustenance, than those who pass their days pursuing pleasure and amusement," Abram said, as if to himself.

Abram's heart trembled with joy, as they entered the lands of the Canaanites, where he had spent, studying in the academy of the righteous Noah. Still, his happiness was accompanied by a feeling of regret that he had not taken advantage of the opportunity to address the sinful cities of Sodom and Gomorrah years earlier.

The metropolis of Shechem arose before the eyes of Abram. The Canaanites of the city had a particular reputation for being fierce and cruel, becoming notorious. Abram and his entourage encamped outside the city, hoping they were far enough away not to draw the residents' attention.

A strong tremor gripped Abram as he sat in his tent at midday. He sensed that a prophecy like no other was being revealed to him, the reality of divinity revealed to him in all its power, as if he could see God. *"To your seed I will give this land!"* The prophecy was just a few words, but Abram envisioned his descendants fighting fiercely and capturing the city of Shechem, their first conquest in the land of Canaan. Battles, victories, and slaughter; joy and sadness; destruction and construction — everything passed before him in the blink of an eye.

Abram went out of his tent, built an altar to the astonishment of all those who were with him, and made a sacrifice of thanksgiving to the Lord for this revelation. His mouth was filled with prayer, an entreaty that no descendant of his might be harmed in the conquest of the city.

The journey continued, and Abram felt that he needed to head in the direction of Mount Moriah, the place on which Adam built his altar and sacrificed on it, the altar on which Noah offered his sacrifice.

After two days of walking from Shechem, Abram and his people passed between two cities, Bethel to the west and the Ai to the east. These were peaceful towns, one day's journey from Mount Moriah.

Abram pitched his wife's tent and his own special tent for study and the worship of God. An altar was erected, and on it Abram again offered a sacrifice of thanksgiving, seeing in his mind's eye his sons conquering the Ai.

Many months had passed since Abram left Harran, months of upheavals on the roads and arduous travelling, months that depleted the great camp that came out of Harran. Nearly everyone who had left Harran had found a place to settle along the way. The small encampment was, essentially, Abram, Sarai, Lot, and Eliezer.

Thus, it was a pleasant surprise when, one day, Eliezer cheerfully said to Abram as he sat in his tent, "my lord, people have come to learn your way."

A spark of joy twinkled in Abram's eyes. "Call them in, my friend, and bring them food and drink." Abram rose from his seat to welcome the new students who had come to his door. A group of five teenagers shyly entered Abram's tent, and he greeted them glowingly.

The days went by as Abram explained and clarified, answered questions, and countered challenges, instilled faith and resolved doubts. The number of students increased day by day. Happiness flooded Abram when he saw his multiplying disciples; but this soon turned to displeasure when he saw that his students were unfocused and uninterested in their duty to the world.

"Eliezer, please bring these fine young men some more food. They look a little hungry to me," Abram whispered to his servant.

"My lord, I'm very sorry, but there's almost nothing left to offer them," Eliezer replied weakly. "We have no flour, and we have already slaughtered all the sheep and cattle. There is almost nothing to eat in the kitchen, not even for you and your wife."

Abram looked at Eliezer in amazement. Day and night, he had been preoccupied with his studies and his students; he had never stopped to think about what was going on in the kitchen. "What happened? Why did the food run out?"

"I do not know, my lord; I have never encountered such a thing. There is nothing in this land to eat, the land does not produce grain, and there is also nowhere to buy food from." Eliezer looked at his master sadly. "Has my lord not noticed that most of the boys come here only to eat? I am not angry with them, but that is why they do not understand my lord's words. They don't come here for spiritual enlightenment. I do not believe it, but traders passing by our camp say that the famine has come to the land because of us. I have heard some say that if we do not leave the country, they will come to attack us. Honestly, I find it hard to believe that they will do so, as they still remember our war with the four kings; but hungry men dare to act wildly and nonsensically."

"What? There's nothing to eat?!" One of the students, who was listening intently to the conversation between Abram and Eliezer with a disappointed look on his face, exclaimed, "I'm starving!"

Abram looked at the young man sadly, "I'm sorry, my son, our food is gone."

"So why did I come here?" He cried, broken.

Abram looked at the student innocently, "why, to learn the will of God..."

"Look, old man, if all you have to feed me is nonsense, I'm leaving. Maybe you can find someone else to swallow your tripe!" The young man got up, flipping the empty table over. "Are you staying?"

He asked his fellow students. The other young men arose, their faces distorted with rage and disgust.

"So it seems," one of them bitterly observed, "that my father was right! Our gods must be mad at us for letting you live here! Thanks to you infidels, we are going hungry!" He approached Abram, screaming, and raising his arm to hit him. Eliezer stood as a buffer between his master and the young man, his fiercely determined face convincing the would-be assailant to turn on his heels and abandon his attempt to attack. On his way out, he stopped to scream, "This isn't over!" With a bloodthirsty look in his eyes.

Abram looked at the tent emptied of students, feeling a familiar burning sensation. "It seems that we must embark on yet another journey," he whispered to Eliezer.

The journey began with four people: Abram, Sarai, Eliezer, Lot. They began to make their way towards the land of Egypt, a place that was rumored to have no famine or scarcity. The four nomads made their way through the desert, where they were greeted with sour faces by those who dwelled among the dunes. Their hosts were kind enough to open their tents and give their guests a bit of dry bread and a swallow of water to revive their souls — as long as they kept moving far away.

Still, they had nothing but ridicule and mockery when Abram revealed that unlike his pagan hosts, he and his people worshipped a single God, ruling over all creation.

"And He has no ability to support you in your home?!"

"If you really believe that, why are you in exile?"

"The whole world is His, but you're poor and delusional?"

These were the questions which tried to poke at and crack the wall of Abram's faith, explaining to his hosts that God was testing him.

The response was inevitably a burst of laughter and contempt.

The four nomads were then left with no choice but to leave the encampment and continue on their way to the land of Egypt.

CHAPTER TWENTY-ONE

Egypt

Finally, the four wanderers reached the Nile. They began looking for a secure way to cross. Sarai, accompanied by the love of her life, felt safe with him by her side. They looked into the clear waters of the great river, as smooth as a mirror. Abram could see Sarai's face, as young and comely as any maiden's, though she was far past seventy. Her face was as tranquil and noble as if she had just emerged from her dressing room, despite the travails of many weeks of travelling.

She had a heavenly beauty that overshadowed the attractiveness of all the other women in the world, a sublime exquisiteness which by comparison made anyone else appear barely human. Abram felt that trembling and fear gripped him, as the people of the land of Egypt were known to be lewd and hedonistic; this thought made him shudder in horror, realizing that he and his wife were in danger from the inhabitants of the land. Distressing ideas began to spring up in his mind.

He thought, "If we enter Egypt, and the Egyptians know that she is my wife, there is a likelihood that they will kill me and marry Sarai off to one of them. If we were to turn around, it would be a terrible desecration of the name of the Lord. Our only option, to emerge from this unscathed, is to present Sarai not as my wife but as my sister. Then the people of the country will try to please me in order to marry her, and I can always postpone the match by demanding an outrageous bride-gift. Or perhaps, I should hide her in this crate? Yes, I will try that; and if they discover her, I will say that she is my sister, and I am only trying to protect her virtue…"

Sarai looked at her champion; she could see the emotions seething within him, and she tried to figure out why his body was shaking so. "Dear Sarai," he finally said. "I have known, since my youth, that you are a beautiful woman. Since, I first met you your image has been engraved upon my heart. I have not dwelled on it since then, but now that I have seen your face, anxiety has gripped me, knowing we are coming to a land inhabited by homely, swarthy people. They have never seen a woman with features such as yours; all the more so, they have never seen a woman as beautiful. You still look young and comely, like the day we first met. Now, unfortunately, your attractiveness is a cause for concern." Abram looked at her, having poured out his heart. "I will try to keep you concealed in this crate, but they may open it. *Please say you are my sister; that it may be well with me for your sake, and that my soul may live because of you.*"

The three men approached the river crossing, with Abram and Eliezer carrying the crate; next to them walked Lot, laughing inwardly at his sister Sarai's boxed state.

"Halt!" A swarthy guard, stationed on the riverbank challenged them. "Where are you going? What's in the box?"

"Some clothing and some barley," Abram replied, trying to keep his voice flat and causal.

"You say barley, but maybe it's wheat. Open the crate!"

Abram smiled at the guard. "Okay, let's say there is some wheat in here, do I have to pay customs for it?"

The guard froze, looking at Abram penetratingly, "maybe there are pearls and diamonds in there?"

Abram met the guard's gaze, trying to distract him from the box. "Do you think that a poor man like me has pearls and diamonds? And even if there are pearls and diamonds here, what of it?"

The guard gestured to his comrades, who were watching their commander, "open the box!" he ordered.

Eliezer stood between the crate and the guards, ready to defend his mistress with his body. Abram's gaze instructed him to fade into the background and let the guards open the box.

"Ahhh..." The guards retreated in amazement, seeing a beautiful woman standing nobly in front of them.

The commander's staring eyes were enthralled, unable to break away from the aura which seemed to emanate from the woman. He was literally salivating and slack-jawed in amazement. "Yes, this is far more valuable than diamonds and pearls... Who is she???" He asked, captivated by Sarai's magic, trying to take his eyes off her and look at Abram, who stood there quietly.

"She is my sister," he said softly, praying in his heart that they would be able to get out of the situation safely.

"This is a woman worthy of King Pharaoh!" said the commander to his soldiers, ordering them to take the woman and escort her to the palace, Abram and Lot following.

Rikaion stood in his palace, straining his eyes at the amazing woman standing with her head bowed before him. His cheerfulness increased with pleasure at the thought that a woman worthy of being his wife has finally been found. Though he had been king of Egypt for many years and had dalliances with many local women, he had not found an aesthetically pleasing spouse among the native population. Because he could not conceive of marrying a woman whom he was not conventionally attracted to, he had thought quite often about importing a bride; but he had been discouraged by the thought that his subjects might see this as an unbearable affront. He even thought, at times, about abdicating and leaving Egypt, but he could not bear the idea of becoming nothing more than a regular person in another land.

Rikaion made a circle around the woman, like a merchant considering the goods brought before him. "So, she is your sister?" He asked Abram, who was standing at the side of the magnificent hall. At no point did Rikaion take his eyes off the goods.

"Yes," Abram replied, feeling the desire to pluck out the eyes staring at his wife so lasciviously.

"Indeed, the guards were right, she deserves to be the king's wife!" He said with a smile, as a shrewd merchant discovering that an invaluable commodity has fallen into his hands. "How much do you want for her?" He asked, knowing that he would be willing to pay any price that would be imposed on him.

"My sister is not for sale!" Abram answered stiffly.

A slight laugh came from Rikaion, "my friend, do not be a fool, tell me how much you want, and I will give it to you. You know that I can take her for free and kill all who escort her in the blink of an eye. However, I do not want the next queen of Egypt to be sad and mourn for her brother." Rikaion looked at Abram, pointing at the armed guards standing in the throne room, eager to carry out his orders. "I understand you. It's very difficult to name her price. She's really something extraordinary." Rikaion noticed Sarai's tears. "Look, now she's sad," he told Abram sourly.

"You know what?" Rikaion suddenly said. "I understand you do not have the capacity to estimate the price. I'll tell you what! I'll give you this in return: the heads of three thousand sheep, the heads of one thousand cattle, five hundred donkeys, two hundred male and two hundred female slaves, five hundred camels, and five hundred donkeys. I will also give you the land of Goshen, so that you will have a place to live with all the things that I have given you."

Rikaion looked into Abram's opaque face with displeasure. "I understand that it is not enough, so I will also give you two hundred talents of gold and two hundred talents of silver, and I will fill the crate in which you brought her in with diamonds and pearls."

"I'm her brother too!" The cry erupted from Lot's mouth in frustration.

Rikaion looked at the other man standing at the side of the room, and for the first time saw the resemblance between him and Abram. "I understand now! It's okay! You will not have to share all this," he said, consoling Abram. "I will give him the same as I gave you, except the land of Goshen. But you will surely get along there together. You are probably an even more shrewd trader than me. It does not seem to me that anyone has ever sold his sister for as high a price as you have. But I forgive you, because I do not think there has ever been a such beautiful woman like your sister!" Rikaion looked at the overjoyed Lot, "well, at least you're happy. It's a good trait to settle for what is given to you, and I'm sure your brother Abram will be just as happy with what I gave him, once he comes to terms with the fact that your sister is going to be my wife."

Pharaoh called one of the guards, "go to the minister of finance and tell him to get everything I mentioned for these two people. Take them from here and give them all I promised."

The guard nodded momentously and turned to carry out his order. "Please, my lords, accompany me," he told the newly-rich men.

Abram followed the guard with displeasure, while Lot walked in front with a smug look.

"Please, my wife, do me the honor of accompanying me to my room," Abram heard the jarring request. All he could do was raise a prayer in his heart for his wife's welfare.

"Please God, I followed Abram, my husband, out of my faith in You. I trusted in You, and out of my belief in You, I surrendered my life, I left my home and family to cleave to You. Abram left Aram under Your promise to guard him, and he was delivered from every trouble; but what I did was out of faith, without revelation and without prophecy. Now this evil one will come and abuse me?!" It was heartfelt prayer, tears flooding the usually bright and joyful face. The prayer of a woman who was in fear of an enemy who desired to defile her pure body and soul.

"Beautiful, you know that it is good for you to be my wife," Rikaion tried to appease Sarai. "Once you accept it, there will be no happier woman in the world. I am not like my Egyptian subjects, who are cruel to their wives. In my house, you will be a true queen."

"Do not come near me, I am a married woman!" Murmured Sarai.

A slight laugh came from Rikaion, "and where is your husband?"

"Ahhh… he's not here now; he should be here soon."

Rikaion chuckled, "lying does not become you, darling."

"I'm not lying! I'm a married woman!" Sarai stood up straight, feeling within her the belief in the Creator, who would not abandon her in the hands of this unclean man.

Rikaion began to approach Sarai, eager to enjoy his purchase, feeling his lust increase in the face of the woman who had rejected him.

"I'm warning you, don't come near me."

Rikaion, ensorcelled, approached Sarai, who stood defiantly against him. He stretched out his covetous hand to touch the woman whom he had bought for himself. A scream erupted from his mouth as he felt a tremendous blow hitting his chest, tossing him towards the other side of the great bedchamber. Rikaion was lying on the ground, trying to figure out what had hit him. Seconds passed, and the humiliated man got to his feet, trying to claim his purchase once more.

"I will tell you again, you should not try to touch me. I am a married woman!" Said Sarai, knowing that heavenly angels were guarding her from the despicable man.

Rikaion moved towards Sarai, captive to the passing thoughts of his lust, dismissing in his heart, what had happened a few seconds earlier as a figment of his imagination. Suddenly, he screamed and grabbed his lacerated shoulder, from which blood flowed as if he had been whipped by an unknown assailant. He could hear distant shouts, coming from other members of the royal household elsewhere in the palace.

"You still do not believe me?" She said, as if taunting him. "I told you I was a married woman!"

Pharaoh fumed at the humiliation he had suffered. He could think of only one thing, accomplishing his goal, which was being withheld from him by something beyond understanding. Rikaion tried to pounce on his prey, to dash over and grab the woman.

Then he heard, "Strike!" The peaceful commandment was issued by the protected woman, directed to an unknown servant who was obeying her will. His body was flung to the back of the room, and he writhed, bruised and injured. The shouts, rising in his ears from a distance, grew and grew. All night long, Rikaion tried to reach the woman, who warned him with a smile that he dare not approach her. Rikaion tried to throw objects at the woman; if he could not have her, then he would kill her! However, whatever he threw at her bounced back at him, without her even pointing a finger.

The door of the room was finally broken open, and the injured guards rushed in to find their wounded king, realizing that it was all due to the woman standing like a towering palm tree in the heart of the bedchamber. Due to her, Pharaoh and his entire household had been beaten soundly all through the night.

"Bring Abram here now!" Pharaoh, commanded in an attempt to maintain his air of power and authority.

The door to the room opened. Abram, fearing for his wife's safety, was ushered into Rikaion's bedchamber. A slight glance proved to him that his wife had been protected by heaven. The destruction that prevailed in the room and the sight of Rikaion, broken and shattered, made it clear to Abram what had happened to Pharaoh during the night. The sight of the noble figure of his wife, smiling at him, let Abram sigh in relief, with thanksgiving to God for saving Sarai.

The contemptible Pharaoh screamed at Abram, "*what is this that you have done unto me? Why did you not tell me that she was your wife? Why did you say: she is my sister?*"

Abram offered a Pharaoh conciliatory smile, trying to come up with an answer the monarch would accept. "My dear friend, I tried to make it clear to you that you could not take this woman for yourself. If I had told you that she was my wife, you would have killed me and taken my widow as your wife. Since I did not want innocent blood to be shed, I identified her as my sister. Now you know that you cannot marry her, so you have no reason to shed my blood."

"But how did she do that?" Pharaoh's voice sounded like the voice of a student realizing he has not yet learned anything.

Abram approached Rikaion in the spirit of fraternity, placing his hand on the king's lacerated shoulder, "understand, my friend, the Creator of the world created man with wondrous psychic powers. When the Creator formed the universe, He created spiritual and physical worlds. Our world is a physical world, but spiritual worlds and spiritual entities overlap infinitely. Usually, the connection between the physical world and the spiritual worlds is not felt by most human beings, although there are a few human beings who know of it. Sometimes, they can use inferior spiritual powers as demons and spirits, but these are not real and primary forces. When a person nullifies himself utterly before his Creator, he has neither place nor limit, because he is like nothing. When a person has reached a level that is outside the physical world, both the physical and spiritual worlds are open before him. When you tried to touch my wife, she turned to the Creator, asking Him to send one of His spiritual emissaries to protect her from you; and this was the result."

Abram looked at the bruised Rikaion with compassion, "do not worry, my friend, I will take care of your wounds." Abram ran his hand over the laceration in Rikaion's shoulder. Rikaion looked in astonishment as the cut sealed and healed itself before his eyes.

"Listen to me, Lord Abram," said the shocked Rikaion, "I do not know what you are and how you do what you do. Therefore, all that I have given you is yours, but I have a small request to make of you: I have a young daughter, and her name is Hagar. I want you to take her with you, and she will be a slave to your wife. It would be better for her to be a slave in your house than to be a princess in mine."

Abram nodded in understanding.

"And there is one more thing you must agree to: you must leave this land. You must know that the Egyptian people are lewd; I do not want anyone to attempt to do what I tried to do. Therefore, it is better for all of us if you to return to the land from which you came," Pharaoh begged.

"Certainly, my friend..."

Abram's convoy began its journey back toward the land of Canaan. Abram, now stupendously wealthy, returned to the same places where he had camped on his way to Egypt, paying back those who had provided for him in his time of need. He was living proof that within the blink of an eye, God can make the poor man rich. The encampment stretched between Bethel and the Ai, the place from which Abram was ejected the first time; now, he re-established his study hall.

"Why do you graze your animals in the fields of strangers who live in the land?"

Lot's slaves looked with ridicule at Abram's slaves reproving them. The herds of sheep, goats, and cattle grazed in fields sown with grain and vegetables by the people of the city near Abram's encampment.

"What?! You don't know why?" Lot's servants laughed. "It is clear! All the land of Canaan belongs to Lot!"

Abram's shepherds were confused. "And how did you come to this conclusion?"

"It's simple! Lot told us that God promised Abram the whole land of Canaan. And Abram is as barren as a mule; he has no children. His closest kinsman is his nephew Lot, our master. Since Lot is Abram's heir apparent, the land of Canaan belongs to Lot!" The shepherds laughed as they laid out their master's stratagem. "If you want, take Abram's gagged beasts to another pasture!" Lot's shepherds mocked them by pointing to Abram's muzzled animals, which were prevented from grazing in the fields of strangers. "The truth is that these beasts are also Lot's, and you are Lot's slaves too, but as long as Abram is alive, you and they are still in his possession. When the sanctimonious fool breathes his last, then you'll see..."

Infuriated, Abram's shepherds viciously attacked Lot's shepherds, who had ridiculed their master. When the melee was over, the shepherds returned to their respective masters to tell them what had happened.

"Lot, my friend," Abram turned to his nephew, fearing that it would not be long before blood was shed, *"let there be no strife, I pray thee, between me and you, and between my herdsmen and your herdsmen; for we are brethren. Is not the whole land before you? Please separate yourself from me; if you will take the left hand, then I will go to the right; or if you take the right hand, then I will go to the left."*

Abram and Lot stood on a clifftop, looking out at the Jordan Plain. Lot gazed at the region of Sodom and Gomorrah, enjoying the pleasant sight of the land carved by valleys wending their way through the colorful fields full of stalks of grain and fruit trees. On the other side, was a land of mountains, rocks, and hills, an arid and desolate land. His heart despised his uncle, who behaved submissively in his dealing with the people of the land which God had promised him.

"I do not want our people to quarrel, God forbid; any of them could be mortally wounded. It seems to me that it would be best for us to part ways for the time being. After all, the whole country is in front of you."

Abram looked at Lot, understanding his hesitation; even though his nephew disrespected him, Lot knew that his uncle had protected him in his most desperate hour, and it was hard to leave. "Do not worry! If you need my help, I will be there for you."

"I will go to the Jordan Plain then," Lot said, happy in his heart that he could finally part with the man who was trying to convince him at all times that the world had a Master and Ruler, that he must ignore his desires and impulses.

Their roads diverged; Lot turned toward Sodom and Gomorrah, the cities of sin.

Abram turned towards Hebron. He built an altar and received another prophecy, assuring him that the land would be given to his seed.

CHAPTER TWENTY-TWO

Hagar

T he camp which bustled by day, fell silent at night — except for the infants. The murmuring wind bore on its wings the cry of a newborn seeking nourishment; then the bawling stopped. A few more minutes of the air rustling, and then another baby woke up crying, only for loving hands to cuddle and swaddle it, in the lap of a loving mother who sustained the most precious thing in her life with the nectar she produced.

However, in the very center of the camp stood a tent that had never known the cry of a suckling; instead, its pillows were wet from the tears of the mistress of the encampment, who longed to be a mother. The desperate sense of being incomplete seeped through her eyelids, shut tightly in pain, trying in vain to dam the river of grief flowing from within. Her heart ached with the realization that she would never experience the most profound intimate connection between two human beings: a mother nursing her child.

The tears flowed, in a bitter torrent, with self-flagellation from the depths of the heart, which refused to believe that she could be good and honest. If she were blameless, surely she would not suffer from the abysmal status imposed on her. Pain pierced her body like a sword hacking at the limbs. Her lips squeaked, stifling the cry which yearned to break out and tear asunder the very heavens; instead, she drowned her agony in the silent depths of a pillow.

"I know that it is because of me and my evil deeds that I am childless. You are a righteous, O Lord, but I have sinned. I do not deserve the fruit of my womb, and I have no right to embrace a child," Sarai sobbed in her bed, trying to drive out of her heart any heretical notion which might be produced by her anguish and sorrow. The pillows were accustomed to absorbing her tears, the outburst released almost every night. Her heart twisted in pain, trying to forget the sadness and instead, acknowledge the good in her life; nevertheless, she continued to hurt, to ache, to bleed…

Abram walked among his students, watching with pleasure the eager repetition of the lesson he has just finished passing on to them. He noticed one father sitting next to his son, his arm encompassing the youngster, the son's head resting lovingly on his father. There was a slight twinge in his heart as he realized that he would never be allowed to express such affection to his own offspring. An audacious tear tried to make its way from his eye, encountering a finger that wiped it away quickly and a mind that commanded the heart to stop. It was like a rat trying to gnaw at the bonds of love and faith that linked Abram to his Creator with the teeth of jealousy, but it was captured and destroyed by the heart that knew that no injustice had been committed.

Still, the thought enthusiastically gnawed at him. "You are eighty-five years old, and your wife is seventy-five! Forget your desire to hug a son!"

The heart tried to brace itself, but the thought, along with a mocking and dismissive laugh that echoed in the depths of his mind, dismissed the attempt. No fortification can last forever!

Abram forced himself to disengage from the thought that was eating away at him, quickly striding towards a student who was sitting alone on the far side of the tent, his face downcast. The student raised his head, trying to muster a smile to match Abram's beaming face as his teacher sat down next to him, and lovingly put his arm on his shoulder.

"My dear, what is troubling you?" Abram asked the young man. Abram could feel the war taking place in the young man's heart, seeing the rebellious tear seeping past the eyelid trying to hold it back.

"I do not know how to tell you this, sir. It feels impolite and foolish to tell you what I am going through. I know it is due to my own lack of faith, so I prefer to stay silent." The young man wiped away the now-flowing tears.

Abram embraced him enthusiastically, knowing the pain the youth was experiencing. "Do not feel this way, my friend; if you feel bitterness, you must talk about it. The worry and acrimony that reside within the heart are poisonous, toxic to the soul. Whatever doubts and concerns you have, you must talk about it; if you do not remove it and root it out, it will be noxious to your whole body and soul."

The young man started crying like a little boy, "it's been three years since I got married. About a year ago, my wife and I came to your camp, and we still haven't had a baby. I know that it is rude of me to even think about ever having a child after all the sins I have committed in my life, and how can I complain to God after all I have done?"

The sound of his sobbing penetrated to the depths of Abram's heart, and he felt the sorrow that pierced the young man's heart. His hand gently caressed the head of the broken young man.

"I… I know that I am the vilest villain, insolent and cruel! How dare I even resent my condition, when you, my lord, have not been blessed with children!" The surging sorrow enveloped the young man's being. "How, my lord? How can you continue to live like this? I have been childless for just three years and I already begin to have suicidal thoughts. There is no purpose to my life! Why should I be alive? How do you go on living, even smiling? What is your secret?"

Abram beamed lovingly at the young man who looked so shattered, "my secret, my love, is that I know that the very purpose of life is that life has no purpose."

The young man looked confused, "I don't understand."

"I will explain. There is nothing in the world but the Creator. He has done, is doing, and will do all deeds. There is nothing He is unable to do. By His will, one is rich or poor; by His will, one is wise or foolish; by His will, one is strong or weak. When you serve the Creator, the most basic and important knowledge to have is that the Creator directs you by His will. He puts you through varied and strange trials to see if you worship Him, or if you are only fulfilling His laws for your personal good. In fact, you are not master of the experiences you go through — it is neither your power, nor your intellect, nor the strength of your will which directs what occurs in your life; it is all from Him, may He be blessed."

"If so, it doesn't matter what I do in life. It does not matter if I am righteous or wicked," the young man challenged him.

"It certainly does matter! If you are righteous, you can sometimes act to change what is decreed upon you. By praying and asking the

Creator you can sometimes change the laws and decrees that were supposed to come upon you."

"Sometimes!?""

Abram smiled understandingly, "yes, sometimes, not always."

"But why?!"

Abram pointed to a small ant walking on the ground, "do you think this ant can understand our conversation? Do you think it is capable of understanding why we do what we do?" The young man shook his head. "All the more so, my child, we cannot understand the actions of the Lord. We only know that He directs the universe and watches over us at any given moment."

"But why? If He can do anything, why does He not grant me children? And why not you?!"

"I do not know..."

"But you deserve children!" The guy looked like he was going crazy.

"Apparently not. If I deserved children, I would have them already."

"If you do not deserve them, who does deserve them?!"

Abram laughed affectionately, "everyone who has them."

"Pharaoh, Nimrod, Lot — they deserve children, and you do not?!"

"Yes, indeed!"

"Where is the justice? Where is the truth?"

"My dear, it seems that you still do not understand. Children are not the purpose of life! There is no purpose in life but one thing: to fulfill His blessed will with joy! There are people who have children who are rotten apples. Are such children the purpose of life for their parents?! There are powerful people, with stunning physiques, who pursue nothing but lawlessness and debauchery. Does their life have what you would call a purpose?! There are even unfortunates who keep the commandments of the Creator and feel that their lives are an unbearable burden; they too do not appreciate the purpose of life. There is one single, solitary purpose: to follow His ways and to fulfil His will happily, without considering the hurdles and obstacles in your path. You should be happy about every difficulty in life, knowing that He is the one who gives you the difficulty, having faith in you to get through it. Even if you go through the greatest trials in life and your spirit is grieved, that is not the purpose of the work. The purpose is to be happy with everything you experience, even if it appears to be bad, by being confident that it serves the most perfect good for you."

"My lord, are you always happy?"

Abram smiled understandingly, "I try very hard, and if I feel joy has escaped me, I know that I have lost my composure; so, I settle my mind to see what the source of dissatisfaction is and revive myself in the good that exists in me and for me."

"And if you do not succeed? If the sadness does not give way to peace?"

Abram chuckled aloud, "I do everything to rid myself of it. Even this…" Abram reached out and started tickling his student. Abram's laughter proved contagious, eventually overpowering his young student until they were both chortling. More peals of laughter were heard throughout the crowded tent. The young man looked up and saw that many of his colleagues in the tent had joined in his and Abram's mirth…

"Hagar, dear, could you please wash the dishes?" Sarai said to her young maidservant.

Hagar rushed to do her mistress's will. A few months had passed since Hagar had joined the household of Sarai and Abram on the orders of her father, Pharaoh. Months in which she served her righteous mistress with infinite loyalty.

Hagar thought to herself, "this woman is such a paragon of ethics. Even though I am a slave in her house, she never commands me anything, she just calmly asks me for what she needs. In my father's house, the reality was completely different. The slaves were oppressed and humiliated by us. The way I behaved with my slaves, it was as if they had no existence in their own right, as if their whole purpose was solely to serve me and my whims. Sarai, on the other hand, treats me like I'm her young daughter, always speaking kindly and lovingly. My father was right when he told me to go with them and become Sarai's slave. If I had stayed in my father's house, I would have become a cruel predator. I have much more to learn from this poor righteous lady. She is such a good person, but has never borne children!"

Hagar hurried to keep her lady's commandment happily. "Ma'am, is there anything else you want me to do?" She asked happily after completing the task.

"No, darling, we'll have to get dinner ready later, until then you can rest," Sarai said, caressing her devoted maidservant's head.

She thought, "this girl has come a long way in a little while. In the few months she has been with us, she has undergone such a change, night and day! She has become a very modest and righteous woman. She tries with all her heart to learn what we have to teach her, and to be punctilious about all the rules we have told her. It seems to me that she is ready for marriage. I will have to talk to Abram to find a decent man to marry her. It seems that she would be a good wife: modest, respectful, and hardworking. She has to find a boy who is as good and attractive as her. She is a very beautiful woman, although she does not seem to internalize it."

Sarai looked lovingly at Hagar, who refused to go to rest and diligently arranged her mistress's room. She thought, "I wonder which of the boys Abram would want to marry her? I must tell him that the boy must be righteous and God-fearing like him. I hope he will soon find her a decent husband. The girl is already mature enough to bear children. I am sure she will be a very good mother."

Sarai felt the thoughts running through her, wrestling with each other, her face downcast, hiding the tears which threatened to break through.

Maybe I'll tell Abram...

No I cannot...

She will be a good wife...

I couldn't stand it...

You think only about yourself! What about Abram...

It would be too great a trial...

You will be able to with stand the test...

And if not?

You owe it to your husband...

I'm going to collapse.

You will not collapse; you will be built up! Bring her into your house; then perhaps the Lord will have mercy on you and give you children too...

And if He does not give me children? I will not have the strength to withstand it...

Do not underestimate the powers you have! In any case, her son will grow up and be like your son for all intents and purposes...

But she will be his mother...

She is your slave, and therefore, her children belong to you...

There is no other way?

This is the only way!

Will Abram agree?

Only if you show him that you really want it...

Sarai looked up resolutely, wiping her tears with the scarf covering her head. "Hagar, sweetheart, can you please call Abram my husband and ask him to come to my tent?"

As she waited for a few minutes, Sarai felt a storm of emotions trying to shatter her resolve. She felt like a small boat in the middle of a tempest, refusing to succumb to the waves breaking on it, getting stronger against the waves trying to drown its resoluteness in the depths of the sea. The tent was opened, and Abram stood in the doorway, marveling at his wife's unconventional call in the middle of the day. "Everything okay, darling?"

Sarai, who was standing out of respect for the champion of her youth, gestured for him to sit down. "I have to talk to you about something. Can you sit for a few minutes?"

Abram sat down calmly, trying to decipher the strange summons.

"Abram, my dear husband, you know that I am no longer young. I am already seventy-five years old..." Said Sarai, as she tried to find a way to convey to her husband what she was thinking.

"The Creator, blessed be He, has not given us fruit of the womb until now; it appears that He will not ever let me bear children to you." Sarai hurried to silence Abram as she wiped away a rebellious tear. "Please, my husband, do not try to console me. I know for myself that I am no longer capable of bearing a child, that I no longer have my monthlies. Apparently, I will never have children. However, even if I cannot have children, that does not mean you cannot one day hold your son; on the contrary, I will benefit as well, as I will be like a mother to the newborn."

Abram looked at his wife as she laid out her plan, and he felt the great strength of her character, the massive reserve of self-control required for her to express her idea. "It is my maidservant, Hagar. She is a fine young woman, gentle and intelligent, understanding and diligent. In her brief time with us, she has learned well what I have taught her, and I see how she is punctilious about the commandments and about modesty. So, this is what I thought: *go in, please, unto my handmaid; it may be that I shall be built up through her.*"

Abram looked at the ground. It seemed to him that she wasn't simply voicing her own views, but that the spirit of God within her was expressing itself through her. He knew full well that no excuse or effort could allow him to defy his wife's will.

"As you wish, my beloved wife..." He whispered after a few moments.

Hagar stood staring wide-eyed at her mistress. "My lady, I cannot... I, with Lord Abram?!... I don't deserve... I cannot do this to you. He is your husband!"

Sarai hugged Hagar's shoulders, trying to overcome any resistance. "Who is more worthy than you, my dear? You are fortunate to be associated with such a pure and holy man..."

"My lady, are you sure...?!"

"Absolutely! Prepare yourself and let me know when you are ready..."

Hagar wiped her face, brushing away the sweet tears of joy. She would soon be the wife of a righteous man.

"Hagar, darling, could you wash the dishes please?" Sarai asked.

Hagar, lazily lying on the large pillows in the tent, happily stroked her small belly, which had begun to protrude. "I have no strength! You wash the dishes; I am resting. Can't you see that I'm pregnant?!"

Sarai looked at the pampered handmaid, seeing the contempt that filled the slave's heart for her mistress. "So what if you're pregnant?! You're neither the first nor the last pregnant woman, you can still move around and do something!"

"'So what if you're pregnant?!'" Hagar mimicked Sarai with contempt. "Of course you say so! You've never been pregnant, have you? You play it as if you're righteous, but you harass a pregnant woman! It's not for no reason that God made you barren! You're not really righteous, you're just a good actress. I'm Abram's real wife, not you; if you ask him, he will admit that! I spent one night with Abram, and I became pregnant right away — while you, how many years did you spend with him? Thirty? Forty? Fifty? Still you have no child from him! Do not tell me what to do! If you want the dishes washed, wash them yourself! I am now resting! Do not disturb me!"

Sarai glared angrily at Hagar, her eyes flashing fire. "You may be pregnant, but you'll never give birth!" She promised furiously.

Hagar grabbed her belly, feeling an ominous twinge.

Sarai left the tent feeling that she could no longer bear the repeated abuses of the past few months. With teary eyes she ran to Abram's tent. Abram jumped up when he saw his wife crying and bursting into his tent. He knew that something terrible was about to happen.

Though she knew it was not his fault, she cried aloud, "*my wrong be upon you: I gave my handmaid into your bosom; and when she saw that she had conceived, I was despised in her eyes.* Since she's become pregnant, she's acted like she is the mistress and I am the slave! And it's all because of you. You prayed for God to give you a son, but you did not pray for God to give you a son from me. *May the Lord judge between me and you!*"

Abram looked at his unhappy wife with love, knowing that her words were right, that Hagar had done an about-face and started acting like Sarai served her. "My dear, I tell you this once and for all, you are the mistress and she is the slave. *Behold, your maid is in your hand; do to her that which is good in your eyes.*"

Sarai straightened up and declared, "yes, I will!"

She hurried back to her tent, hearing a moan as she entered. Hagar, stretched out on her pillow, looked anxiously at the blood dripping between her legs, raising her face to her mistress, who was watching from above.

"You...?" Hagar whispered in fear.

Sarai smiled triumphantly: "Yes, me! Now get up and clean the mess you made, and after that I will let you rest until morning. Early in the morning, you will go into the kitchen and do everything that an ordinary slave girl must!"

The days went by, as the loving relationship between Sarai and Hagar was replaced by cold and contentious alienation, a mistress and her rebellious slave. "Wash the dishes! Wash the clothes! Clean the tent! Prepare food! Clean! Wash! Wash!" What had once been gentle requests became harsh and humiliating orders. The chores did not change, the burden did not increase, but the cordial attitude was replaced with something cold and stiff.

"Wash!"

"Clean!"

"Sweep!"

"Cook!"

Every task seemed like abuse stemming from abysmal hatred. "There is no end to the work... I can't stand it anymore... I'm so tired..."

Finally, Hagar reached a fateful decision. She had to escape from Sarai, who endlessly told her what to do.

Before dawn, Hagar left the encampment, fleeing from her mistress towards her homeland. The walk became difficult as the sun began to rise over the land, beating upon her head. The little water that was in her canteen ran out, and the food ran out soon after.

Hagar longed to find water to quench her thirsty soul. Her feet were heavy and weary. Her lips, swollen with thirst, trembled in prayer for salvation, for deliverance. Her head swam, thoughts pecking at her head. Had she behaved properly towards her mistress Sarai? The thought that she was about to return to her father's house, to idolatry and lewdness, made a shudder pass through her body. The truth planted in her in the house of Abram would not let her go back to the vanity and folly of her birthplace in Egypt.

In the distance, she saw a well. With the last reserves of strength, Hagar forced her legs to carry her to the source of life. Her heart was pounding with prayer to God, as she had learned at her mistress's house. The clear water revived her tormented soul; her heart was filled with gratitude for the salvation and providence that had not been withheld from her. Hagar quenched her thirst eagerly, feeling the rejuvenating freshness pulsing through her veins.

"Hagar, handmaid of Sarai, from where have you come and where do you go?"

The voice emerging behind her shoulder produced fear and trembling in the runaway slave. She was filled with trepidation; the realization that she could be apprehended in her depravity, even in this remote place, increased the understanding that she was being watched at all times. Hagar turned on her heel in fear of seeing the source of the voice. The majestic and glorious figure, somehow both visible and invisible, was revealed to her wide-open eyes in terror. She thought, "this is no human being, but an angel of the Lord, as I was wont to see in the home of my lord Abram."

"*I flee from the face of my mistress Sarai,*" she whispered in awe.

"*Return to your mistress and submit yourself under her hands!*" Said another figure, revealed to her gaping eyes as she turned around again.

The thought arose in Hagar's heart, "yes, she is my mistress, but I am her pathetic handmaid."

"You are indeed a handmaid, and you must act accordingly!" The figure said.

She thought, "but she will never take me back. By now, she must know that I've run away, that I rebelled against her. I will not be able to return there, even as a slave.

"She will take you back, rest assured. *I will greatly multiply your seed, that it shall not be numbered for multitude,*" a new voice announced. Hagar turned back, as another figure, glorious as the first two, appeared.

A fourth voice declared. "*Behold, you are with child, and shall bear a son; and you shall call his name Ishmael, because the Lord has heard* (shama) *your affliction. And he shall be a wild ass of a man: his hand shall be against every man, and every man's hand against him; and he shall dwell in the face of all his brethren.* Sarai your mistress will give you back to Abram, but you must know your place!"

Hagar fell to her knees in tears, as the vision shimmered and vanished. Her bones rattled intensely; she had witnessed personally, the ubiquity of Divine Providence, and realized that a significant role had been given to her. Hagar got up from her place, gathered herself with the last of her strength, retracing her steps towards her mistress's house, accepting upon herself her original path: to be a lowly slave as she had been when she first came to Sarai.

The sound of rejoicing and celebration rose from the large encampment. A son had been born to Abram from Hagar, Sarai's handmaid. There were dancing and revelry all through the night until dawn, prayers of thanksgiving and exaltation of the Lord, who had taken account of Abram and granted him a son at the age of eighty-six years. Abram named his son Ishmael because God had heard his prayer.

CHAPTER TWENTY-THREE

The Covenant

"Let me! I want to slaughter it!" Ishmael grabbed the calf's halter from Eliezer.

"But Master Ishmael, why get blood all over yourself? I will do this work, you do not have to! Better that you go to the study hall, no?" Eliezer tried to dissuade his young master from doing the dirty work.

Ishmael looked at the slave impatiently. "I said I would slaughter the beast, so I will slaughter it! Stop annoying me! You are starting to upset me. Don't make me angry!" Ishmael swung his long knife at the slave with menace. Eliezer backed away, disgusted by the young man.

Ishmael slit the calf's throat, washed his hands with pleasure in the warm blood. Then, skinned and cut the calf into pieces with a look of satisfaction and joy on his face. "'Go to the study hall,' this idiot says. It's boring there! Here, it's fun," he pronounced with a smile.

Abram sat in his tent, peering out at his son who relished slaughter, basking in the blood of the calf. He thought, "what will happen to him. All day long he spends with the manservants and the maidservants, going out to hunt with his bow and helping in the kitchen. He never visits the study hall, just the dining room. There he finds his place, as if this is his purpose in life. He is very good at welcoming guests and seeing to their every need, but all his actions seem to be artificial. He speaks beautifully, but it is mere lip service." Abram felt a twinge in his heart. "He is already thirteen years old, and still plays all day, like one of the wild children." The depressed Abram tried to distract himself from his reckless son, trying to cling to the thought of offering a prayer to his Creator, that his son might change for the better.

The sound of Ishmael berating the slaves could be heard from far away, as Abram closed his eyes and connected with his Creator. A tremor passed through his elderly body, auguring prophecy.

"*I am God Almighty, walk before me and be perfect,*" said the voice that filled Abram's being.

Abram felt a strong twinge inside him, "am I not complete already? Am I not perfect? Is there something indecent in me that I have not corrected?"

"You are as complete as you could have been, but that is not the apex of perfection according to My will, for *I will make My covenant between Me and you, and will multiply you exceedingly.* You have done everything that you could have, whatever was within your capacity; but now it is My will to make a covenant between Me and you, a covenant never to be abrogated."

Abram fell upon his face, overwhelmed by the experience, his body shaking and his soul rattling inside him, like a clapper in a bell. "*As for Me, behold, My covenant is with you.* I have wanted to make a covenant with human beings since I created My world, but you are the only one I have found to be worthy. Therefore, *you shall be the father of a multitude of nations. Neither shall your name any more be called Abram, but your name shall be Abraham; for the father of a multitude (av hamon) of nations have I made you. And I will make you exceeding fruitful, and I will make nations of you, and kings shall come out of you. And I will establish My covenant between Me and you and your seed after you throughout their generations for an everlasting covenant, to be a God unto you and to your seed after you. And I will give unto you, and to your seed after you, the land of your sojourning, all the land of Canaan, for an everlasting possession; and I will be their God."*

Abraham rejoiced to hear this, ecstatic at God's promise to give him and children the land of Canaan.

And as for you, you shall keep My covenant, you, and your seed after you throughout their generations. This is My covenant, which you shall keep, between Me and you and your seed after you: every male among you shall be circumcised. And you shall be circumcised in the flesh of your encumbrance; and it shall be a token of a covenant betwixt Me and you. And he that is eight days old shall be circumcised among you, every male throughout your generations, he that is born in the house, or bought with money of any foreigner, that is not of your seed. He that is born in your house, and he that is bought with your money, must needs be circumcised; and My covenant shall be in your flesh for an everlasting covenant. And the uncircumcised male who is not circumcised in the flesh of his encumbrance, that soul shall be cut off from his people; he has broken My covenant.

Abraham's heart twinged. He thought, "will I have more children from Hagar? More bad apples like Ishmael? Is this a desirable goal? Could Sarai ever withstand it?"

The prophecy continued, reading Abram's thoughts. "*As for Sarai your wife, you shall not call her name Sarai, but Sarah shall her name be. And I will bless her, and moreover I will give you a son of her; yes,*

I will bless her, and she shall be a mother of nations; kings of peoples shall be of her."

Abraham was overjoyed at this news. His beloved wife would finally bear his child. He laughed (*vayitzhak*) as an expression of his joy at the shocking idea. "*Shall a child be born unto him that is a hundred years old? and shall Sarah, that is ninety years old, bear?*"

Abraham was concerned about his wayward son Ishmael. He knew that Sarah's having a child was a supernatural occurrence, a miracle; but Ishmael's repentance was a more easily accomplished natural feat. "I am not worthy for you to work miracles and acts of loving-kindness for me; *oh, that Ishmael might live before you!* All I seek from You is that my son Ishmael will follow Your path and revere You, nothing more," he begged out of concern for his rebellious son.

The voice responded in a mild reprimand, "*'nay, but Sarah your wife shall bear you a son; and you shall call his name Isaac; and I will establish My covenant with him for an everlasting covenant for his seed after him.*" Then the prophecy became calmer, responding to the somewhat inappropriate request of the beloved student. "*And as for Ishmael, I have heard you; behold, I have blessed him, and will make him fruitful, and will multiply him exceedingly; twelve princes shall he beget, and I will make him a great nation.* Still, he is not capable of passing on your way to the rest of humanity. You bore him before undergoing the covenant of circumcision, with Hagar the handmaid. There was imperfection within you, by virtue of your being the son of Terah, brought into the world in great impurity; this flaw you passed on to Ishmael. However, now this imperfection no longer exists within you, so you may beget a child who will follow your path. I will forge the covenant with you, as you enter the covenant now with the wife of your youth, the love of your life, Sarah.

A woman who so dedicated herself to My glory, every day of her life — should I not bestow My blessing upon her?! *But My covenant will I establish with Isaac, whom Sarah shall bear unto you at this set time in the next year."*

Abraham rose to his feet, feeling the vision of the prophecy still shaking his body. His heart threatened to explode from sheer happiness and great enthusiasm to fulfill the terms of the covenant.

"Aner, my friend," Abraham addressed his longtime ally, "I have received a prophetic message from God, who told me to circumcise myself and all the men of my household." Abraham decided to consult his friends about the command he had received. In his heart, he had arrived at the decision to check whether his comrades were indeed sticking to the path he had sought to instill in them.

Aner looked at his friend in bewilderment, "does he want to make you deformed?! In my opinion, either you did not understand what He was saying, or He is testing you, to see if you would do something so illogical and nonsensical." Aner laughed, then turned serious. "You know, if you perform this nonsense, the kings around you will jump on you like flies on an open wound and try to hurt you, after you have destroyed so many of their people."

Abraham looked at Aner, feeling in him an aversion to the man whom he had thought to be his companion, walking the path of truth. "Thank you, Aner, I have to go now," Abraham said and left Aner's tent.

"Eshcol, my friend," he addressed his second ally, "God told me to circumcise myself and my household. What do you think I should do?"

Eshcol burst out laughing, "Abraham, do you not know how to relax?! You are close to a hundred years old! Do you want to die ?! If you circumcise yourself, you will not survive it! You will surely die from blood loss!"

"Thank you," Abraham said and went out of the tent.

Disappointed by two of his friends, Abraham turned to the last one, hoping to find in Mamre a deeper attachment to the Creator.

"Mamre, my dear friend," Abraham said, fearing that Mamre would respond just as his brothers had. "The Creator of the world appeared to me and told me to circumcise myself and all the males in my household. I came to ask you for advice. What should I do?"

The look of astonishment that came over Mamre increased Abraham's apprehension.

"Abraham! Are you asking me for advice on this?!" He replied reproachfully. "We have all seen how God saved you in your war with the four kings! We heard how He saved you from Nimrod and the fiery furnace! And you ask for advice? You ask whether to do the will of your Creator?!"

A slight smile of satisfaction rose over Abraham, happy to receive the rebuke from his friend.

Mamre continued without noticing Abraham's response, "He has saved you, body and soul, countless times, and now that He is asking you to circumcise one body part, you are asking for advice?! Get up and circumcise yourself!"

Abraham happily arose and embraced his friend, who walked the walk of the faithful. "Mamre, my boon companion, I now know that you are a friend of mine and a friend of the Lord. The truth is that I asked in order to test your sincerity in your faith. However, I now have a true question, the Lord spoke of 'the flesh of your encumbrance.' What do you think He means by that? It cannot be the encumbrance of the heart, because what man can cut into his own heart? But perhaps it is the encumbrance of the ear? Or the encumbrance of the tongue? Alternatively, does it mean the encumbrance of the organ of procreation?"

Mamre thought for a moment, "according to what you said, the Lord gave this command to you and all the men of your house. So, it must be an encumbrance that is exclusive to males. The Lord must mean for you to circumcise your foreskin."

Abraham was happy for his friend's counsel and honesty. "And when do you think I should do it? Day or night? In private or in public?"

Mamre laughed happily, "Abraham, I know you know my answer, and it is what you think as well. Of course, you must do it during the day, not early in the morning but at midday, in front of the whole world. As far as I know you, my friend, you are not afraid of the mockers and scorners who will try to make you a laughingstock. All your days, you have not let fear of them keep you from fulfilling the will of God, even before He revealed Himself to you and told you, His word; now that He has given you an explicit command, you must stand as a solid cliff before them."

"Come with me, my dear friend, and we will go and fulfill the will of God," Abraham said to Mamre.

The sun blazed over the heads of the many people who had come to watch the old man who had said he was about to circumcise his foreskin, as part of the covenant between him and the Creator. Thousands of curious people filled the blooming valley. Hundreds of slaves from the household of Abraham stood in fear before their master, afraid of the cut he would make in the most sensitive and private part of the body

Abraham stood proudly on a small wooden stage in front of the large crowd. "My disciples, my friends, and my loved ones! The time has come to make a covenant between us humans and the Blessed Creator. The Lord has ordered me to circumcise all the males in my household. I know the fears and anxieties that reside in your hearts, but do not worry. We are fulfilling the will of the one who spoke and brought the universe into being. He binds every wound and heals every injury. To remove the fear from your hearts, I will circumcise myself first; and then Ishmael, my son." Abraham took out a small, sharp knife from his pocket, as if guided by the passing thoughts of the supreme being. He put his hand beneath his robe, feeling an unknown hand directing his own, keeping him from shaking. His face twisted slightly, but he continued to smile, happy to fulfill the commandment of his covenant. A few seconds passed, which seemed like an eternity to those observing the scene; then Abraham stuck out his hands, one holding a knife and the other his foreskin.

"Do you see?" He said with a smile covering the pain. "It's not that bad." Abraham looked for his son. "Ishmael, come to me," he said to his son, who was trying to hide behind the line of slaves. "Do not worry, my dear, it is not as terrible as you think."

Ishmael was pushed toward Abraham by Eliezer. "My lord, I want to be next, after him," the servant requested.

Abraham gestured to Eliezer to grab his son, who wanted to escape. Eliezer gladly did the will of his master. A few seconds later, the sound of Ishmael's screams filled the valley.

"Run to your mother," Eliezer laughed as he let out the howling Ishmael.

"Now it's my turn," he said, wanting to fulfill God's word *like someone who finds a priceless treasure.* Eliezer was circumcised next, followed by all the men of Abraham's household.

CHAPTER TWENTY-FOUR

The Guests

A scorching, unseasonal spring heat wave drove people into hiding in their tents. In the abysmal silence that prevailed, Abraham heard the moans of his heart. Now, on his third day of being circumcised, the pain was worse than on the first day; he felt waves of agony pounding hard on his arteries. The air was humid and unmoving in the Mamre Plains, the place where Abraham had settled down after his friend Mamre had given him such sound spiritual counsel.

Eliezer, who was also in pain, stood before his master, "can I do anything for you, my lord?" Abraham looked at his devoted servant with affection. "Yes. If it is not too difficult for you, check outside if there are any passersby we can bring into our house. Obviously, if there are people outside, they must be very thirsty."

Eliezer left the tent to look for passersby. Abraham sank into the depths of his mind happily, meditating on incorporation with his Creator. Pleasantly inspired by the Divine, he felt God sheltering him, as if he were a child in pain held in his father's bosom, indulging in the warmth of His love without saying a word. He took delight in just being present, relishing the closeness of lovers who do not have to use words to communicate — words which, in any case, would fail to express the essence of their emotions.

Eliezer returned from his mission, looking at his master communing with the Divine. "I have not seen anyone outside, my lord," he said quietly. Abraham nodded in disappointment to Eliezer, and he dismissed him with a gesture.

The pleasure continued, convergence under the wings of the lover. Abraham raised his eyes to the horizon, where three figures suddenly appeared, standing in the distance. "O Lord," he said to the master of the world who had come to visit him in his time of pain, "I will go and receive the guests who have come to take refuge in the shade of my roof."

Abraham felt within himself a divine consent, and with the agility of a young boy he got up and ran toward the three nomads walking in the light of the blazing sun. The three impressive men looked like desert-dwelling Arabs. They tried to elude the old man running towards them, but Abraham rushed over and caught up with them, *"my lords, if now I have found favor in your sight, pass not away, please, from you servant."* The nomads stopped at the sound of the voice begging to receive them in his home.

"Let now a little water be fetched, and wash your feet, and recline yourselves under the tree. And I will fetch a morsel of bread and stay you your heart; after that you shall pass on; forasmuch as you are come to your servant," he begged the travelers, who appeared to be idol-worshippers, who would bow to the very dust on their feet.

The nomads looked at each other reluctantly, but they were too embarrassed to refuse the old man's request. *"So do, as you have said,"* the one in the middle said, indicating that he did not want Abraham to trouble himself any more than what he had initially offered.

Abraham rejoiced at the opportunity to host people in his home, and he enthusiastically escorted those who had come to his tent. He showed his guests where they could rest under the tree, while he hurried into one of the tents to take care of his duties as host. A servant brought water for the guests to wash their feet, while Abraham ran to his wife's tent, ordering her to bake bread for the guests.

The guests reclined comfortably under the tree, watching the old man who was so eager to bring them into his home.

Abraham ran towards his flock, selecting three young calves to prepare delicacies for the guests. His son Ishmael, stood in displeasure at his side, angry and grumbling that his father had commanded him to slaughter calves for the guests, while he was still in pain because of the wound his father had given him three days earlier. One of the calves bolted, escaping imminent death.

Abraham ran after the calf, feeling his legs carry him lightly away from his place. The calf entered a cave, and Abraham followed it. The intoxicating scent hits Abraham's nose, distracting him from his purpose. Abraham went deeper into the cavern in awe, a glowing light filling the place, candles still flickering, lights which seemed to have been kindled long ago. He saw two beds, and on them were two figures in repose, each splendid, glorious and beautiful in a manner surpassing all human beauty. The figures seemed to be peacefully sleeping. Abraham retreated in awe, realizing that these were Adam and Eve. The idea came to him naturally, "I too, wish I could spend my eternal slumber in this place." Abraham felt the inner struggle between staying in place and returning to his guests waiting for his return. "Come," he said to the calf, "we must do what we have to do."

Meanwhile, Sarah happily toiled away in the tent, joyously knead-
ing the dough to bake bread and cakes for the guests. A tremor
passed through the old woman's body, a strange feeling that she
had not felt in many years, a long and lasting twinge in her belly.
Sarah stared at her slightly cracked hands as the wrinkles seemed
to spread and disappear. The hands that had worked so hard for so
many years became like the hands of a nubile young woman. The
shock was exacerbated by the recognition that her monthlies had
returned — years after they had ceased, ostensibly for good. She
felt confused and puzzled by the wonder taking place inside her.
"Then the dough is defiled, and I cannot serve it before the guests,"
she thought sadly, but the realization was mingled with joy at her
rejuvenation.

Abraham returned to his son Ishmael, who finished slaughtering
the calves. Abraham's eyes were shining with joy at what had been
revealed to him.

He hurried to serve the guests milk and butter, while the meat
was being cooked. Abraham stood by the guests, ready and willing
to serve them while they ate the viands that had been prepared for
them. A calf tongue cooked in mustard was placed before each of
the important guests, and the rest of the meat was cooked for Abraham's many household members. The impressive travelers seemed
to happily eat the food that was served to them. When they had
finished, they relaxed and reclined with gratification, like people
who were fully satisfied with their meal.

A noise could be heard in the tent, *"where is Sarah your wife?"*
one of the guests asked Abraham with a smile, aware of what was
happening to Sarah and knowing that she was eavesdropping.

Abraham smiled at the guests, knowing that they too, had heard his wife listening to them. "*Behold, in the tent,*" he smiled, pleased by Sarah's great modesty.

The traveler closed his eyes, as if communing with his Creator, "*I will certainly return unto you when the season comes round; and behold, Sarah your wife shall have a son.* The Lord will reveal Himself to you a year from now, and the two of you will have a newborn."

A noise was heard from inside the tent. Sarah, hearing these things, had sunk to the ground, laughing. "*After I am waxed old shall I have pleasure, my lord being old also?* Even if this withered womb could hold a fetus, even if these shriveled breasts could suckle a newborn, my husband is elderly and has already separated from Hagar!"

Abraham looked at his guests, realizing that these were not people born of a woman, rather angels from heaven, who had come to confirm the prophetic message which he had received a few days earlier about the birth of a son to him and Sarah. He realized that he had never told his wife about the prophecy he had received. A shiver went through his body at the sound of the reproving angel. "*Wherefore did Sarah laugh, saying: 'shall I, who am old, truly bear a child?' Is anything too hard for the Lord? At the set time I will return unto you, when the season comes round, and Sarah shall have a son.*"

The angels rose from their seats, affectionately parting from their host who had accompanied them for a long time.

Abraham happily returned to his wife's tent, but had to ask the awkward question. "Why did you laugh at the words of prophecy?" Abraham asked in bewilderment

Sarah, embarrassed and ashamed, was afraid to admit to her husband that the miracle the angels had promised had made her chuckle, "I did not laugh…"

"No, Sarah! Tell me the truth, because you did laugh!"

Sarah nodded her head, acknowledging that Abraham was correct.

CHAPTER TWENTY-FIVE

Sodom and Gomorrah

"Shhh, don't ask questions. Take the bread, and tomorrow I will return and give you more food," the girl said with trepidation, worried someone might see her.

"But who are you? What is your name?" The emaciated man pressed.

"My name is Pelotith daughter of Lot, but now you must stay quiet," the girl pleaded with the pauper. "If anyone else were to see me, my life would be forfeit,"

"But please, tell me, why are you so afraid?"

The girl wiped a tear from her eyes, "have you not witnessed the conduct of the people of this city! There is a law here that forbids supporting the poor; whoever comes here and has no money in his pocket gets the death penalty. And so does whoever helps him."

The man looked at the noble-hearted girl who supported him with devotion, realizing that the stories he had heard about the conduct of the citizens was true. "But why are you not like them? How do you have the courage and fortitude to risk doing a kindness for a stranger?"

The girl straightened her back proudly, "I was privileged as a child to live close to Abram and Sarai. In their house, I saw their acts of kindness, and to my delight I learned something. But now I must leave, lest someone see me, for then they will put us both to death." The girl hastened her steps, moving away from the cistern in which the man was hiding.

King Bera of Sodom angrily banged on the table, his crystal goblet of wine falling over and rolling off the surface smashing on the ground. The ministers and judges standing in the room looked at each other in horror. "It cannot be! For three weeks he has been walking around the city, and he is still alive!" There was a tense silence in the glorious hall that formed the king's throne room.

"If I may say something else..." Said one of those present.

The king looked at the man, nodding his head affirmatively, trying to remember who he was.

The man stepped forward, and a smile appeared on his face, "Your Majesty the King, this is a very simple and clear thing! There exists, in our city, a man who breaks the laws of the kingdom! Someone must be feeding this traveler."

The king looked at the man, and his gaze indicated contempt. "Do you think that is news to me?" He asked cynically.

The man laughed with pleasure, "Your Majesty, I know that this is nothing new, but the king's anger and bitterness have so saddened me that I feel compelled to point out that there is a way of finding out who the criminal is that dares to feed this traveler."

"So?"

"Your Majesty, this is a simple matter. Let this man be followed constantly for a day or two, night and day. You have to watch him from a distance and see who brings him the food." The man smiled, knowing that it would be difficult to find volunteers for the mission. "I know it will be difficult to impose the task on any person. It is not easy to work continually, for hours on end, without enjoying some of the magnificent parties and feasts which fill our days and nights. However, due to the seriousness of the matter and the displeasure it causes the king, I am willing to volunteer to do my patriotic duty, to find the miscreant who rebels against the king. I would do it alone, but I'd be happy if another person or two were to join me so we might catch the offender red-handed. Your Majesty may observe that I am not the strongest man."

The king looked at those gathered to see if there were any other volunteers for the mission. The people's eyes eluded the king's piercing gaze. "I see..." He said angrily, "I will give you two of my strongest servants. You will track down the criminal, and they will apprehend him."

Late at night, the sounds of singing and revelry rose from the many homes and taverns. The people of Sodom, who spent their nights in lewdness until dawn, were unlikely to frequent the desolate, darkened streets. The young spy's eyes were wide open as he looked towards the cistern, which he had seen the traveler enter as evening fell.

His stomach, accustomed to being full of delicacies at this time, began to bother him. A thought popped into his head, "whatever honor he might receive from the king, if he succeeded in catching the offender, could not be worth the price of his suffering right now, hidden in this dark corner." His pampered body trembled in the drafty night. The two burly guards, who were concealed alongside him, made him quiver with disgust.

Suddenly, the man opened his eyes wide and smiled. At the edge of the street, he could see a furtive figure, advancing toward the cistern surreptitiously.

"Get ready to grab him!" The man whispered happily, thinking of the huge feast he was about to hold, to celebrate catching the offender. "Wait, not him… Her!" He murmured. The approaching figure was unmistakably female. The furtive figure stopped near the cistern, the traveler emerged and she gave him something.

"Now!" The watcher ordered. The two burly guards ran towards the pit, seizing the traitor in a viselike grip, the spy following right behind them, eager to confront the perpetrator, now caught red-handed. The silent woman, with her head bowed and a thick veil covering her face, knew her fate. The man happily pulled the veil off the woman's face, wanting to see with his own eyes who had dared to rebel against King Bera.

In shock, he stumbled back: "Pelotith… My wife!"

Bera's rolling laugh filled the room. The two burly servants carried the delinquent woman in their hands, and behind them the adviser was trailing. "So I understand that it did not go the way you planned, my friend! To catch your wife red-handed defying the king's law?!" The king's laughter became cold and sarcastic, "what you deserve, my friend, you will receive. Due to your loyalty, you shall become a minister in my kingdom."

Then Bera turned to Pelotith with a sneer. "And you, lawbreaker, will also receive what you deserve! You love to feed the poor, do you? You do not care that the wretches come and suck our blood! These leeches swarm here to get food which we labored for! These people stroll in our gates without shame and seek to eat! Well, I will let you feed many paupers. Every last bit of you will feed the poor!" The king screamed angrily at the frightened young woman.

To the guards, he said, "tomorrow morning strip this woman who likes to feed others, smear her with honey, and put her near the beehives. The unfortunate bees will show her what it is to give food to the poor, when they sting her to death." He looked at the condemned young woman. "You wanted the poor to sting us financially, but the bees will sting you, when you feed them with your body!"

The king leaned back on his throne, surveying the feckless husband angrily. "Who is the father of this girl? Who cultivated this rotten apple?"

The husband lowered his eyes in disgrace, "Lot son of Haran."

The king looked at one of his servants, "hurry and fetch this man for me, at once."

Within the hour, the servant returned to the king. Lot followed him confidently, resplendently dressed in his elegant clothes. The news of Pelotith's deeds had reached him before the guard arrived. At first, thinking that he might have to justify his daughter's actions to the king made his heart tremble, but immediately afterward he settled his mind and decided to make the most of it.

Lot prostrated before the king.

"Are you the girl's father?!" The king's thunderous voice and sharp glare startled his servants.

Unruffled, Lot sighed ruefully, "yes indeed. Unfortunately, I am the father of this wayward girl, Your Majesty the King." He then turned on his daughter with fury, "stupid wench! How many times do you have to be told that your way is the wrong one? You, an unintelligent and impudent girl, have walked the evil path you have chosen for yourself! Now you will suffer the punishment you deserve!"

The king looked at the scene playing out with a smile and asked Lot, "is that how you educated this girl?! To be rebellious and recalcitrant?"

"As Your Majesty the King must see, I am not a native of the region," Lot began to sweet-talk the monarch. "I came to live in the city quite a long time ago with my family, my slaves, and my many flocks of sheep. I bought several houses and businesses in the city, so I could take part in paying taxes to maintain the city and its taverns. I have five daughters, most of whom have found their proper place in the city's entertainment district and society. However, this daughter of mine decided to get married right after we got here, and she regards herself as if she is different from and unlike all the girls in the city." Lot sighed, as if from the bottom of his heart. "What can I say, Your Majesty? I am ashamed of her and of her deeds! She is aping the sanctimony of my uncle Abram, who lived near me for many years."

The king looked at Lot in amazement, seeing that his appearance was remarkably similar to that of Abram, who had saved him many years earlier, "Abram is your uncle...?!"

"Yes, Your Majesty. As the king knows, Abram's way is completely different from ours. He is obsessed with welcoming guest and all such nonsense. I presume that because he is childless, he wants to waste all his money while he is alive, so that whatever property he leaves behind upon his death will not go to his servants and slaves."

"But I have heard that he already has one son; Ishmael is his name, if I am not mistaken," Bera exclaimed.

"Yes, I heard about him..." Lot laughed out loud. "That's exactly what Abram got! His son, if you can even call him that," he whispered, as if imparting a delicious secret. "Do you know that Ishmael is not even the son of his wife Sarai? They say that Sarai gave her Egyptian slave girl Hagar to old Abram, and the handmaid bore him that child." A peal of laughter erupted from Lot's mouth. "An Egyptian slave girl... Has Your Majesty ever visited the land of Egypt?"

The king shook his head.

"Oh, oh my lord, what shall I say? What can I tell you? The truth is that we Sodomites have much to learn from the Egyptian connoisseurs. They really know how to have a good time...!"

The king looked embarrassed and ashamed, hearing that there was a place which surpassed Sodom in licentiousness.

"There, in Egypt..." Lot reflected nostalgically, "they do everything. And when I say everything, I mean it." Lot winked at the king, as if he could read his thoughts. "Does the king know whose daughter Abram's slave girl is?" he asked with a smile.

"No..."

"Hagar is a princess, Pharaoh's daughter! One can only imagine what entertainments the princess used to enjoy there. And I'm sure she still continues to pursue these pastimes, right under Abram's nose..."

The king scratched his head, "I do not understand..."

"Your Majesty, it is simple. Of course, Abram knows that this son is not really his. Do you know how many slaves are roaming around that encampment? The young Hagar simply must have saved herself for old Abram, if the king catches my drift..." He said with a wink and a leer.

The king laughed with pleasure at Lot's juicy gossip.

"As for the matter at hand," Lot said with a wicked smile, pointing to Pelotith, "this daughter of mine spent a great deal of time around

Abram and Sarai. Unfortunately, even though I remonstrated with her many times to stay away from their evil company, she would not listen to me. Now the king will do what he has to do, so that the people may hear and see it."

Lot whispered to the king, "if His Majesty wants, I can come to the king later to tell him and teach him about the things I learned in Egypt."

Dawn broke, and the terrified girl was stripped and smeared with honey. She was then bound tightly to a tree, to prevent her from fleeing. A swarm of bees emerged from the hive, landing on the body of the girl like a writhing carpet, sucking and stinging, as the young woman twisted in agony.

The suffering of the girl was a sight to see, as the large crowd in attendance reacted wildly, laughing and pointing enthusiastically at the young woman's misery.

"Ahhhh!" She screamed, in her death throes; her shout rent the heavens, all the way to God's throne of glory.

Abraham returned to his spot, overjoyed at his opportunity to welcome guests and the wonderful news he had received. He was meditating on incorporation in his Creator, as he had been before the guests' arrival. The prophetic voice rushed into him, penetrating and encompassing his existence. It warned him, "*verily, the cry of Sodom and Gomorrah is great, and, verily, their sin is exceeding grievous. I will go down now, and see whether they have done according to the cry of it, which is come unto Me.* If they do not change their behavior, I will end them. *And if not, I will know.*"

Many reports of what had been happening in the five cities of the Jordan Plain had reached Abraham. The cruelty and debauchery that dominated these cities had become more sophisticated over the years. Pain pierced his heart with the realization that not only had the Plainsmen not changed their actions after he had rescued them from the four kings, but their behavior had become more depraved. He thought, "it cannot be that there are no righteous left in that place; even for the sake of a few honest people, it is worth saving these cities."

"*Will You indeed sweep away the righteous with the wicked?*" He asked, shocked. "*Peradventure there are fifty righteous within the city.* There must be at least ten decent people in each city; are they not enough for You to show pity on the region? *Will You indeed sweep away and not forgive the place for the fifty righteous that are therein? That be far from you to do after this manner, to slay the righteous with the wicked, that so the righteous should be as the wicked; that be far from You; shall not the Judge of all the earth do justly?*"

The reply was clear, "*if you find in Sodom fifty righteous within the city, then I will forgive all the place for their sake.*"

Abraham pondered the issue fervently. "*Behold now, I who am but dust and ashes have taken upon me to speak unto the Lord. Peradventure there shall lack five of the fifty righteous; will you destroy all the city for lack of five?* If there are nine in each town, You can join each and to form a quorum for salvation."

"*I will not destroy it, if I find there forty and five.*"

"*Peradventure there shall be forty found there.*"

"*I will not do it for the forty's sake.*"

Abraham felt awkward negotiating with his Creator, but he would not relent. "*Oh, let not the Lord be angry, and I will speak. Peradventure there shall thirty be found there.*"

"*I will not do it, if I find thirty there.*"

"Behold now, I have taken upon me to speak unto the Lord," Abraham begged, knowing in his heart that God wanted to show mercy to His creations. *"Peradventure there shall be twenty found there."*

"I will not destroy it for the twenty's sake."

Abraham mused to himself, looking for some argument to save the Plainsmen. Noah, his sons, and their wives had been eight souls, yet they could not save their world; perhaps if they had been ten... *"Oh, let not the Lord be angry, and I will speak yet but this once. Peradventure ten shall be found there."*

"I will not destroy it for the ten's sake."

CHAPTER TWENTY-SIX

Rescue

The streets began to empty of people, the last hawkers collecting their wares in a hurry to get to the bordellos before they filled up. The sound of dogs barking at each other disturbed the silence that descended on the city preparing for another wild night.

A man dressed in elegant clothes sat at the city gate, savoring the honor which had been granted to him that day to be a municipal magistrate. Joy filled his heart at the prestige he had received from King Bera. The monarch had been so happy that such a worldly man had taken up residence in his city that Bera had appointed Lot a judge in Sodom.

Lot relished hearing the requests of his inferiors, who begged that His Honor adjudicate their suits. The old man sat alone, wishing for a little more respect, pursuing the slim chance that he would find someone else to honor him before he was forced to go home.

Suddenly, the sound of footsteps could be heard at the city gates. The man looked up quickly, readying himself to once again sit in judgment over his fellow citizens. Two men appeared, their faces beaming with a splendor and grace that struck Lot. Lot felt that these could not be normal human beings.

The newly minted judge rose from his bench, bowing deeply to them. His heart was brimming with anticipation. He thought, "if these two magnificent individuals want me to hear their case, it will redound to my greater glory and prestige!"

The two newcomers seemed intent on continuing on their way, without paying attention to the distinguished figure bowing to them in humility. Disappointment clouded Lot's mind; the people were not seeking his services as a judge. He thought to himself, "maybe I'll invite them to stay at my house! It's not forbidden to bring strangers into one's home, just to give them food. If I invite them to my house, my wife Irith will see these esteemed people, and think that they are my friends, and she will show me honor for their sake."

Lot said, drawing the attention of the newcomers, *"behold now, my lords, turn aside, please, into your servant's house, and tarry all night, and wash your feet, and you shall rise up early, and go on your way."*

The newcomers looked at Lot dismissively. *"Nay; but we will abide in the street all night."*

Lot, who saw his shot at prestige slipping away, began to beg the newcomers to come to his house. After long minutes of pleading, the two men agreed to accompany him. Lot wended his way to his house, taking a circuitous route out of fear that some of the townspeople would see him bringing guests into his house.

"Irith!" Lot exclaimed to his wife as he entered the house, "We have important guests, hurry up and make matzah, and bring water for our guests."

"Guests?!" Irith said in shock. "You're bringing guests home?! Are you crazy?! Wasn't it enough what we went through with Pelotith⬛? Now you are trying to bring this bad habit into our own house?! I won't make matzah — or anything else! If you want, you can make it! Either they leave, or I will!"

"But Irith..."

The door slammed shut behind Irith's back. Now, there were nine left in the house. Lot and his two guests were downstairs. Upstairs were his four remaining daughters: two engaged to be married and two single. From the room shared by the former, he could hear rolling peals of licentious laughter. That meant their fiancés had come to spend the night.

Lot hurried to make matzah for the strangers to eat, before anyone could see what he was doing.

"Sorry, I wanted to ask if I could borrow a cup of salt until tomorrow," Irith said aloud to her neighbor down the street. The confused housewife looked at Irith in amazement. Never had any of her neighbors asked for anything, and now Irith was at her door to ask for salt — in the middle of the night!

"I understand your confusion, but I'll explain," Irith responded, practically shouting. "My husband Lot has brought home two strangers he found on the street! He wants me to make some food for them; I told him that I didn't have any salt and left."

This piqued the curiosity of the neighbor's husband and two children. "What did you say?" The former demanded.

"Yes, it's true, my husband Lot must have caught the hospitality bug from his uncle. He brought some riffraff from the road, and he wants me to feed them. Can you believe it?"

The husband ordered his children, "come with me! We'll teach this schemer some manners! Just this morning, he got his judge's robes, and tonight he's already committing felonies?!"

The father and his two sons left their home and headed toward Lot's. On the way, they pounded on the doors of the bordellos and taverns, alerting the men inside about the deviant behavior of the new magistrate.

Furious pounding on the door startled Lot. He could hear the shouts from outside. "Traitor! Conspirator! Open the door immediately!"

Lot ran to the window to see who was at the door. He saw a motley assortment of men, women, children, and elderly. The entire citizenry of Sodom seemed to be there, filling the streets which were usually desolate at this hour.

"Where are the men that came into you this night? Bring them out unto us, that we may know them," they screamed.

Lot looked fearfully at his guests, "don't worry! I'll speak to them! The townspeople have the greatest respect for me," he said with a panicked smile. The men grinned tranquilly at Lot.

Lot opened the door a crack, then squeezed through the narrow opening. The massive crowd was like a river, foaming with rage. Lot slammed the door behind him, looking at the furious townspeople, who were eager to toy with a new plaything.

He pleaded with the agitated throng, offering his two nubile daughters to the crowd to appease them. *"Please, my brethren, do not so wickedly Behold now, I have two daughters that have not known man; let me, Please, bring them out unto you, and do you to them as is good in your eyes; only unto these men do nothing; forasmuch as they are come under the shadow of my roof."*

The crowd looked at him with astonishment and anger. Lot's impudence and audacity in protecting his guests drove the mob mad.

"Get out of the way!!!" Said one of the men angrily. Suddenly, Lot felt a hand gripping the collar of his shirt, "you think that because you were appointed a judge today, you can do whatever you want?! So what if you're a magistrate? Do you think you can break the rules and no one will touch you?! Or perhaps you have promulgated a new statute, that judges are above the law and can do whatever they want without facing any consequences?! *This one came here as a foreigner, but he's acting like a judge! Now will we deal worse with you, than with them!"* Their faces twisted in cruelty, the townspeople pulled Lot out of the doorway, looking at him with abysmal hatred. A few burly men approached the door to break it down.

However, the giant door suddenly slammed outward, hitting with tremendous force those who had come to break it down, knocking them over. The two guests stood in the doorway calmly; they grabbed Lot and pulled him into the house. One of the guests raised his hand and it began glowing like a blazing fire. The townspeople were suddenly struck blind, from the smallest to the greatest. Screams of pain and terror rose from the agitated crowd which could not see a thing. The door closed on the mob angrily groping, trying to find it and enter the house.

Lot was trembling with fear, knowing that his judicial career in Sodom would end the day it had begun; he looked at his guests and realized that these were not human beings at all.

One of the angels urged him on, prompting the terrified and frozen Lot to get moving. "Do you have anyone else here — sons or daughters, sons-in-law, anyone else in the city who belongs to you? Get them out of here, for we are destroying this place, because the cry of them is waxed great before the Lord; and the Lord has sent us to destroy it."

Lot charged up the stairs to the bedroom of his betrothed daughters, throwing the door wide open. He had found them in the midst of pleasuring their fiancés. "*Up, get you out of this place; for the Lord is destroying the city,*" Lot shouted at the two young men, who could not help but stare at the old man barging into the bedroom disgracefully.

"Why don't you go drink another glass, old man?" One of them chortled, dismissing the dire warning.

Lot desperately screamed, "no, it's true! The Lord is going to destroy this city for our sinful actions."

"What a nuisance! Leave us alone!" The young man angrily got up from his bed, slamming the door in front of his prospective father-in-law. The derisive laughter of the girls and their fiancés echoed through the house.

Lot hurried to the other bedroom, panicking his single daughters. "Come with me now! We need to pack!" Lot and his two single daughters rushed through the house, trying to grab any jewelry, gold, and silver in the house.

At that moment, Irith, Lot's wife, entered the house from the backdoor, seeing the ominous scene. She heard the cries of horror rising from the front of the house, looked in terror at the two people sitting calmly at the table and observing with a slight smile her husband and two single daughters trying to pack up all the belongings in the house.

"You have no time to linger, dawn is breaking!" One of the angels said to Lot. "*Arise, take your wife and your two daughters who have been found, lest you be swept away in the sins of the city.*"

Grief filled Lot's heart. "How much silver and gold, precious stones and pearls will be lost if the city is overturned!" He lamented. "At least I will be able to save something."

"Aren't your lives enough? Forget the money!" Said the angel to Lot. The angels seized the four survivors, one holding the hands of Lot and his wife, and one holding the hands of his two daughters. In the blink of an eye, without feeling any movement, they found themselves standing far from the city walls, watching the sun about to rise over them.

The angel Raphael said, *"escape for your life; look not behind you, neither stay you in all the Plain; escape to the mountain, lest you be swept away.* Flee to your uncle Abraham; it is only on his account that God has spared you from destruction."

Lot looked at the angels with trepidation; he could not bear returning to Abraham and taking shelter beneath his roof. The thought of going back to Abraham's camp — especially penniless — sent a shudder through his body.

"Oh, not so, my lord; behold now, your servant has found grace in your sight, and you have magnified your mercy, which you have shown unto me in saving my life; and I cannot escape to the mountain, lest the evil overtake me, and I die. Behold now, this city is near to flee unto, and it is a little one (mizar) oh, let me escape there — is it not a little one? — and my soul shall live. The town of Zoar is smaller, and therefore its sins are fewer. Let me flee there!"

The angel responded, *"see, I have accepted you concerning this thing also, that I will not overthrow the city of which you have spoken. Hasten you, escape there; for I cannot do anything until you have come there."*

Lot, Irith and their two daughters grabbed each other's hands as they ran towards Zoar.

Rumbling and trembling shook the ground, as Lot began to run towards Zoar, pulling his wife and daughters. A rolling boom of thunder struck fear in their hearts, as Irith felt the hot tears running down her face in an unstoppable torrent, thinking about her two betrothed daughters left behind. The thought of losing two more of her daughters along with the townspeople forced her to turn her head back to see what was happening in the city. At the sight of the horrors unfolding behind them, her body was petrified. All the moisture within her dried up, and in an instant there was a pillar of salt standing in her place. Her daughters looked in horror at their petrified mother, trying hard to pull her after them.

"Do not look back, if you do not want to die!!!" Lot screamed at his daughters for fear that they too would become pillars of salt. "We must keep running away!!!" His hands gripped his daughters' hands tightly, pulling them toward the surviving city.

The sound of screams and cries of terror rising from the ruined cities could be heard the entire time Lot and his daughters ran towards Zoar.

The city gates were wide open, as Lot and his daughters ran through them in a panic. Death and doom filled the lifeless town. Carnage lined the streets, the stench of charred corpses, sulfur and fire strewn everywhere. The silence of death and the stifling stench were unbearable. "We cannot stay here," Lot whispered to his daughters, holding a handkerchief to his face to protect himself from the foul odors. "We must go spend the night in one of the caves up in the hills, until we figure out what to do next."

In short order, Lot found a cave in which they could breathe in. They were overjoyed to escape the stench of death which had permeated Zoar. As night began to fall on the world, Lot and his two daughters entered the cave, hiding from the horror of the destruction of the world. Cool air, bearing a pleasant smell, filled the interior of the cavern; they soon discovered that it was a wine cave, where the people of Zoar had stored their oenological reserves.

The two young women curled up in a corner of the cave, looking at their disconsolate father mourning his money, his wife, and his daughters. He looked from the entrance of the cave towards the ruins of the cities of the Jordan Plain.

"I think the entire world has been destroyed, and we are left with only us and our old man," the older daughter whispered to the younger.

Her sister sighed tearfully, weeping over the death that pervaded their world. "That's it! It's all over! The entire world has been destroyed! Wouldn't it have been better for us to die together with the rest of the world?! In the end, we will die childless, with no man in the world to marry us! Why did God have to save us? So we could die slowly and in agony?!"

The older sister put an encouraging hand on the shoulder of the weeping sister, "I do not think so. Obviously, He had a good reason to rescue us and our father. Surely, he wants the world to survive through us!"

"But how?! Only we remain, the two of us and Father. How can we bring life into the world?!" The younger sister continued to cry.

"Just like that!" The older sister said decisively. "Us and our father!"

The younger sister looked in astonishment at her older sister, "but that is forbidden!"

"Brother and sister are also forbidden, yet Cain and Abel fathered offspring with their sisters," she explained calmly. "There are times when there is no choice. We must commit this sin in order to save the world! I feel in all my limbs that we must do so. The existence of the whole world depends on us. Do you think that God put us here together with Father for no reason at all?!"

The younger sister looked at the older sister in astonishment, "do you think he would agree?"

"I don't know how he would respond, but I do not intend to ask him. It is not by chance that the Lord brought us to a cave full of wine. Ply him with alcohol until he doesn't know what he's doing! I do not intend to wait for tomorrow; he may be dead by then. Don't you realize? Father is old, and it is impossible to know when he will pass away."

The older sister got up decisively and opened one of the wine barrels; just the smell of the vintage was overwhelmingly intoxicating. She filled a large jug and sweetly said, "father, drink some wine. You must be very thirsty."

Lot looked at his daughter holding the wine jug. "Yes, I am quite thirsty," he said wistfully, sipping the wine served to him.

"Drink some more, dear father," she whispered in a soft and loving voice. "The wine will drown the sorrows of your heart."

Lot eagerly gulped the wine and relished the feeling of warmth that enveloped him, suddenly feeling his clothes being peeled off of him...

"I did it," the older sister whispered to the younger sister the next morning. "Tonight is your turn..."

"Do you think he will drink tonight too...?"

"As far as I understand, he will do it happily," the older sister laughed, knowing her father's heart.

Night came, and Lot saw his younger daughter pouring him wine. A slight smile played across his lips, as he realized that the previous night's events were being replayed.

Nine months passed quickly. The older daughter gave birth to a son and called him Moab, "from the father."

The younger daughter also gave birth to a son, but was a bit more bashful in the name she gave: Ben-Ami, "son of my people."

CHAPTER TWENTY-SEVEN

Abimelech

"I told you, my lord, this man is utterly despicable!" Eliezer entered Abraham's tent with shock on his face.

Abraham looked at his servant, trying to figure out what had so disturbed him. "Your nephew Lot!" He cried, nauseated. "This contemptible man escaped from Sodom, thanks to you. Then, he fled with two of his daughters to a cave, where he impregnated them!"

Abraham looked at his servant in astonishment, "are you certain?!"

"My lord, there is no doubt about it!" Eliezer said, embarrassed. "If he had not shared this with everyone he met I would not have conceived of it. Even I did not think the man was so depraved! He plundered the city of Zoar, and now he is extremely wealthy. He says he needs all that loot because these newborn children are both his sons and his grandsons!"

Abraham sighed, dismayed at his nephew's lowly behavior. He felt he needed to get away before Lot came calling. He knew that after the destruction of the cities of the Jordan Plain, there would be no more guests passing by his tent. "Eliezer, tell our men to pack up the camp. We are leaving forthwith! We will head south, towards the land of the Philistines, to Gerar."

Eliezer bowed happily to his master, willingly rushing to break camp so as to avoid any further encounter with the despicable Lot and his daughters.

"Oh my! I did not believe their description, but I tell you they really did not exaggerate..." King Abimelech of Gerar said as he completed his circuit around Sarah, who had been brought to his palace by his servants.

"Where have you been hiding all this time?" Abimelech continued to circle, as if a dealer had brought merchandise to him, a connoisseur, to happily examine the rare wares.

Sarah, confident and forceful, replied, "I tell you, it is not worth your while to try touching me!"

Abimelech laughed, enjoying the verbal sparring. "You are both attractive and self-assured! How fortunate, I need such a woman as my queen."

"I told you, send me back to my brother's house! I'm a married woman!" She uttered in a commanding voice.

"And where is your husband...?"

"It's none of your business! Send me back to my brother, otherwise..."

Abimelech's laughter intensified, "I hope you will not hit me..."

Sarah scoffed, "I would never lay my hands on a filthy man such as yourself, I assure you!"

"Fine, then I'll lay my hand on you, my d—" suddenly, Abimelech faltered, groaning, falling to his knees. It felt like an invisible leg had kicked him hard in the stomach.

"I don't think you should keep trying..." Sarah grinned at Abimelech, who was trying to catch his breath.

Abimelech staggered to his feet, while his mind struggled to make sense of what had just happened, trying to distract himself from the strange sounds rising from across his palace. His feet led him, enthralled, towards the beauty he coveted; but then his body was suddenly lifted up and dumped upon the table set with viands and delicacies. The table collapsed under his clumsy body, and his clothes were immediately befouled with a mélange of sauces, juices, and relishes.

Sarah laughed aloud, "and here in my naïveté, I thought the King of the Philistines would know a little history. At least keep abreast of current events! It was not so long ago — just a few years — that Pharaoh had to learn this lesson personally. Really, Abimelech," she chuckled reproachfully, "do you think that this is a regal presentation? Look at yourself!"

The despised Abimelech glanced at his filthy clothes, trying to understand what was happening.

"Listen to me carefully, boy! I'm going to the next room to sleep. I will not go out at such an hour. Now, if you want to go on living, I advise you not to approach the door. You must understand that until now you have been treated gently. I suggest you go to sleep, and first thing in the morning, call my brother to come and pick me up from this repulsive place! If you have enjoyed your experience thus far, you can try your luck with my door!" Sarah turned her back on Abimelech, left the king's bedchamber with her head held high, and slammed the door behind her.

Another thump could be heard in the king's bedchamber, followed by a shriek of pain; this brought a smile to Sarah's face.

Soon afterward, the door of the king's bedchamber was forcibly opened by two slaves who had heard the shriek of their master. Abimelech was lying on the ground, wounded and in pain, trying to hide his disgrace.

"Your Majesty the King!" One of the slaves screamed as if ignoring the destruction and devastation in the room. "Something terrible is happening all over the city: pregnant women are unable to give birth, no person can use the chamber pot or privy, even the chickens are not laying their eggs. All orifices are clogged, and we do not understand why."

Abimelech looked at his brazen slaves who ignored his suffering. "Help me get into bed!" He shrieked at his servants. "Do you not see what has happened to your king?! Do you want me to decapitate you?!"

The two slaves looked at their king, realizing the situation he was in; they rushed to help him move to his bed.

"Get out of here right away!" He commanded in pain. "And do not disturb me until morning. I cannot think right now."

Abimelech lay back in his bed, groaning until he fell asleep.

He began to dream. An angel appeared, brandishing a sword at his head. He shook in terror. "But what have I done...?"

"Behold, you shall die, because of the woman whom you have taken; for she is a man's wife."

Abimelech objected, *"Lord, will you slay even a righteous nation? Said he not himself unto me: 'She is my sister'? and she, even she herself said: 'He is my brother.' In the simplicity of my heart and the innocence of my hands have I done this."*

"There is no innocence of hands here, because you should not have enquired after the woman at all, whether she was Abraham's wife or sister. *Still, I know that in the simplicity of your heart you have done this, and I also withheld you from sinning against Me. Therefore suffered I you not to touch her. Now therefore restore the man's wife; for he is a prophet.* You need not worry that he will think you have defiled her, because as a prophet, he will know that you did not touch her. *And he shall pray for you, and you shall live."*

"But how will the world know?"

"Every orifice in the capital will remain clogged until you appease Abraham. At the moment he consents to pray for you and your people, they will be opened." The prophetic voice admonished him, *"and if you restore her not, know you that you shall surely die, you, and all that are yours."*

Abimelech opened his eyes, terrified by his nightmare, waiting coolly for dawn. He could not help but hear the cries and moans of anguish from the stopped-up men and women of his kingdom.

Abimelech complained, *"what have you done unto us? and wherein have I sinned against you, that you have brought on me and on my kingdom a great sin? you have done deeds unto me that ought not to be done."*

Abraham looked at Abimelech trying to exonerate himself of his corrupt deeds by shifting the blame to another.

"What did you see that you did this thing?!" Abimelech attacked him. "Have you seen some sins, some untoward behavior among us?!"

Abraham looked at Abimelech as he twisted, "what did I see? I saw all manner of things, even good things, but not the most important thing, the fear of God. And when there is no fear of God, everything that people can do to satisfy their lusts, they will — even kill a man to take his wife. We told you that Sarah was my sister and this was no lie. She is the daughter of my brother Haran, and so we are both the offspring of Terah. Therefore, she is like a sister on my father's side, but not on my mother's side. Because we have traveled far and wide, encountering many disreputable people, we have an agreement between us, that if we arrive at a place and are interrogated about our relationship, we say that we are siblings. So, way they will not kill me to seize her."

Abraham rebuked Abimelech, "tell me, what is the first question a wayfarer should be asked when he arrives in a strange place? Whether the woman with him is married or unmarried, or whether he needs food, drink, and lodging? It is abundantly clear that the people of this country are neither ethical nor moral, but rather lewd and lascivious!"

Abimelech looked down, knowing that the man in front of him was correct in his reproach, and in full control of the situation. "*Behold, my land is before you: dwell where it pleases you,*" he declared.

Abimelech turned to his servants, commanding them to bring a gift to Abraham: sheep and cattle, male and female to appease the Prophet.

Sarah was brought to the room, walking with her back straight, knowing her husband's heart.

"My lady," Abimelech turned to Sarah in humility, "*behold, I have given your brother a thousand pieces of silver* as a bride-gift — to your husband the Prophet that is. I thought, at the time, that he was your brother and would give me your hand in marriage; *behold, it is for you a covering of the eyes to all that are with you; and before all men you are righted.* As you are in fact his wife, I am entitled to demand my money back, but now I give it freely, as a gift, so that everyone will know that I reluctantly returned you to your husband, not because I was tired of you; and anyone who tries to despise you, you can prove to him by my gift that you are pure."

"My Lord Prophet Abraham," Abimelech pleaded painfully. "Will you pray for us...?"

Abraham closed his eyes in prayer, meditating on incorporation in his Creator, until...

Abimelech's eyes lit up, "excuse me, I must run to the privy!"

CHAPTER TWENTY-EIGHT

Isaac

The leaves murmured their thanks for the precipitation, even as the howls of the jackals joined them. This night on the edge of winter. The raindrops dripping on the roof of the tent sounded like the peals of bells; it was an evening that delighted the heart. Warm tears of happiness and gratitude flowed from the eyes of the old woman who had returned to her youth.

Sarah was lying on her bed with her hands touching her bulging belly, which indicated that her pregnancy was reaching its fruition, heralding a new period in her life. She felt, at her fingertips, the movements of the newborn in her womb, relishing the feelings she had been sure she would never experience. Her lips expressed praise and glory unto her Creator for the miracle He had wrought for her late in life.

Abraham was sitting in his tent listening intently to the sounds rising from his wife's tent, which was next to his tent. He thought, "spring is arriving; tomorrow marks the anniversary of the visit of the three guests who told me that my wife Sarah was going to give birth to a son. According to the angels who visited me, tomorrow at noon Sarah will give birth."

Dawn broke, a vernal sun caressing the plant-life, drying out the small puddles of water that had accumulated from the night's drizzle. In response to the sounds rising from Sarah's tent, Abraham rushed to its entrance.

"Is everything all right?" He whispered to Sarah anxiously.

Sarah smiled at her tense husband. "Yes, darling. Everything is wonderful. It seems to me that he is getting ready to come soon. If you can, please call two maids to come attend me. I am sure it will not be too long; I have had birth pangs since midnight."

"Does it hurt?" He asked, feeling her discomfort in his own body.

"It is the sweetest pain in the world," she smiled lovingly. "Come, my dear, call them and pray for our safety. They will let you know when it is over."

Abraham ran to the slaves' tent, urging them to attend to Sarah, who was about to give birth.

"I'm telling you, my dear lady, your husband Abraham ran like he was twenty. He was so excited that he didn't even notice he was running like a youth," the midwife giggled as she walked towards her lady.

"You can understand him," said the other midwife, "the whole camp seems to be hovering a few feet off the ground in anticipation of this birth. And if we are so excited, then our Lord Abraham all the more so."

Sarah chuckled happily with her maids, but a pain passed through her lower abdomen, bringing the merry laughter to a halt. "It's very close..." She smiled, her lips clenched in pain.

The midwives quickly approached their work, moans of pain rose from the tent, and after them there was the sound of a baby bawling.

A few minutes passed, and one of the maids went out of the tent to tell Abraham about the birth of his son.

The sounds of dancing and merriment filled the crowded encampment, an uproar of happiness and rejoicing. They all loved Abraham and Sarah, and reveled in the salvation of the beloved couple — and the birth of their heir apparent!

On the eighth day, the tent of Abraham's study hall was filled, cheek by jowl. All the people in the encampment gathered early in the morning to be present at the circumcision of the newborn.

Abraham sat on a magnificent chair, thanking his Creator profusely for the profound privilege of being able to circumcise his son. Jubilantly, Abraham declared, "and his name shall be… Isaac — 'He shall laugh.'"

The large crowd burst into dancing and singing that continued until the end of the day, and the celebrants enjoyed a royal feast, sharing in the joy of Abraham and Sarah.

"Believe me, I would never have believed how much money a man is willing to spend to back up his lie," Og laughed at the Canaanite kings sitting with him in the great tent. "I thought he would eventually admit that this boy… What is his name? Isaac… Yes, Isaac… He's certainly having a laugh! I thought Abraham would admit that this is just some foundling he and his wife picked up in the market and adopted. But Abraham is not willing to admit it, so he holds such an extravagant feast, as if to prove to us that it's his son. Two years have passed since he found the boy, and now he's saying the boy's about to be weaned, so he's having a party for him. He's ridiculous, this Abraham! Who could believe that he has fathered a son at one hundred? And his wife at ninety!"

One of the kings laughed with pleasure, "do not worry! I have something they'll never see coming, a trap my wife and I laid for Sarah. I also have a baby, about a year old. When he starts crying, my wife, who is at the women's feast with Sarah, will lament that she has forgotten to bring the nursemaid. Then she will ask Sarah to nurse our son just like she has nursed who she says is her son. I tell you, it will be very funny..."

Another king began with a rolling laugh, "believe me, great minds think alike. My wife and I did exactly the same thing!"

"Me too," another king grinned.

"And I..."

"And I..."

Abraham was enjoying the feast with his father Terah and brother Nahor, who had come from Harran for the occasion; also present were Shem, Eber, and King Abimelech of Gerar. All the great men of the generation had come to celebrate this milestone in the life of Isaac with Abraham. Eliezer approached his master, whispering in his ear, "Lady Sarah asks you to come for a moment, my Lord; she wants to ask you something..." Abraham apologized to his guests and walked over to his wife with a smile.

A baby's cry could be heard from the tent where Sarah was holding the banquet for the wives of the important guests.

"Abraham, I do not know what to do. The wives of the kings brought their babies with them and did not bring their nursemaids, and now they are asking me to nurse their sons. I know they did it on purpose to see if I really nursed Isaac with my own milk or if we bought a foundling from the market, as the gossip scandalmongers and mockers claim. I know they want me to nurse their babies in front of them." Sarah looked confused, helpless, looking at her little son snuggled in her arms. "How can I do such a thing? It is not modest to uncover my body, even though there are only women present."

Abraham looked at his wife with understanding, also knowing about the vicious gossipmongers. "This is not the time for piety and extreme modesty, my dear. Go and suckle their sons before their eyes, and in doing so, sanctify the name of the Master of the Universe, and let them all know that Isaac is our son."

A tear rolled down Sarah's cheek over the immodest act she was supposed to perform. "And what about the clowns who say that even if he is my son, he is my son from Abimelech…?"

Abraham smiled lovingly at his wife, "God has already put this matter to rest. Just look at Isaac's face! Everyone says that he is remarkably similar to me, that we look like identical twin brothers — born a century apart! Bring me Isaac for a few minutes, and I will show him to all the men, so they know he is my son."

Abraham entered the tent of the men, carrying his son in his arms. All the attendants murmured in astonishment, seeing with their own eyes the marvelous resemblance between the aged father and his little son.

"A foundling? Brought from the market, you said?!" One of the kings whispered to Og disbelievingly. "They look exactly the same! *Abraham begot Isaac!*"

Sarah entered the women's tent, sat comfortably on her upholstered chair, and smiled at two of the women trying to reassure their screaming babies. "Kindly bring them to me; I will let these poor ones eat…" Sarah opened her robe to feed both the babies simultaneously. A line of women holding their babies in their arms formed before Sarah, who happily nursed all the little princes.

"Isn't she getting tired...?!" One of the women whispered to her friend in astonishment. "She's already shown us she can nurse; she could have stopped after the first two kids, and that would have been enough to put an end to these rumors. But she keeps going, as long as there are crying kids." The queens looked at each other in disgrace, realizing that Sarah was showing compassion to them and their children, even though their plan had been to embarrass her.

CHAPTER TWENTY-NINE

Banishment

"Tell me, what do you think you're doing?!" Eliezer screamed at the young man, bowing to a statue on the outskirts of Abraham's camp.

The young man got to his feet, his face expressing contempt for the person shouting at him. "Old slave! You think I do not hear you scream like crazy?! What do you care what I do?"

"What do I care? Because you are the son of Abraham, and here you are bowing to idols!" Eliezer screamed in shock.

"If you do not stop cawing at me like a black raven, I will shoot an arrow at you and kill you, slave!" Ishmael pointed at the bow and quiver at his feet. "If you do not fly away from here immediately, you will no longer be able to fly anywhere, slave!"

Eliezer realized that Ishmael was capable of doing so and tried to recover, to appeal to his young master's heart. "Ishmael, you know that it is forbidden to bow down to these statues. Why would you engage in this nonsense?"

A peal of laughter burst from Ishmael's throat, "I'm just studying! This is how the idol-worshippers serve their god, so I am imitating their actions. What does Father always say? The best way of learning is by doing." He continued with a grin, "so I'm studying now, and you're bothering me! And you know what? This ritual is far less taxing than what Father says should be done. Now leave me alone, slave!"

Eliezer looked at Ishmael with disgust; his young master was falling into the pagan ways of their neighbors.

Eliezer hurried to Sarah's tent, and once she granted him permission to enter, he began speaking.

"My lady, please, I must talk to you. I saw Ishmael on the outskirts of the camp near the great forest, and he..." Sarah sat in her chair, watching her son play happily.

Eliezer's expression was serious and hard. His gaze turned to Isaac, who had stopped playing after noticing Sarah's gesture telling Eliezer not to continue speaking in front of the boy.

"Eliezer!" Isaac exclaimed happily and ran towards his favorite servant, jumping into his sturdy arms. "Did you come to play with me?"

Eliezer hugged the boy lovingly, stroking his head affectionately. "A few more minutes, good boy; I need to talk to your mother, and then I'll come play with you, all right?"

"All right," Isaac said with an understanding face. "I'll wait for you outside until you finish talking to Mother." Eliezer set Isaac down, and the boy left the tent.

"Yes, Eliezer, did something happen? You look very upset," said Sarah. She was used to seeing the servant's smile all the time; now she was amazed at his sad look.

Eliezer pondered how to convey the situation as it truly was, without putting into words his displeasure and disgust with Ishmael. "Yes, my lady, a terrible thing is happening in the camp. Ishmael brought a statue from somewhere and began to bow down to it. I told him to stop, but he mocked me and said he was learning how idol-worshippers practice their religion. However, I know that he is being swept away after idol worship. I do not know how to inform my lord about this; I do not want to aggrieve him, and I know that this will cause him very great sorrow." Eliezer sounded as if he was about to burst into tears and tried to conclude his words. "My lady, I do not know what to do. Does he not see what Ishmael does? Perhaps he prefers not to see?"

Sarah closed her eyes in silence; she knew that Ishmael's actions were corrupting, and she knew how much anguish this would cause Abraham. "I'll consider what to do about it," she whispered gravely.

"The truth is, ma'am, I'm most afraid for Isaac. He's still a little boy, barely three years old, and I'm afraid Ishmael will ruin him."

"I'm afraid of that, too." Sarah put her hand on her face. She thought, "Eliezer told me some of the terrible things that Ishmael does. The poor slave girls come to tell me their grief after he forcibly defiles them. He constantly brings stolen goods back to the encampment from his 'hunting trips,' claiming he found them in the fields or the forests. I have even heard that he killed a man who tried to resist when he accosted him. But how do I tell this to my dear husband? How do I tell him that this bad apple has fallen far from his tree?"

"My lady," Eliezer said as he stopped her train of thought. "First of all, I think you should command little Isaac not to speak to or walk near Ishmael. The sooner the better!"

"You are right," she said, realizing that Eliezer made a good point, and that she should have done so long ago. "Please call him, and tell him I want to talk to him," Sarah asked.

Eliezer quickly stepped outside to carry out his mistress's request. "Isaac! Isaac!" Sarah heard him calling.

"My lady, I do not understand where he is. He always waits for me when I tell him to." Eliezer looked confused as he entered Sarah's tent, fearing for Isaac's fate.

Like a hind let loose, Sarah shot to her feet and ran out of the tent. Eliezer looked at his lady and immediately understood her apprehension. "Perhaps Isaac went to see what Ishmael was doing..." He also ran out, following Sarah into the thick forest at the end of the camp.

Isaac left the tent at the request of Eliezer, his good friend. "I do not understand Ishmael. He constantly does things that upset Eliezer and insults him all the time. I need to talk to him. He will surely listen to me; we are brothers. I need to make peace between him and Eliezer! Ishmael must not understand what a good and nice man Eliezer is. So what if Eliezer is our slave? Hagar, Ishmael's mother, is also my mother's slave, that does not mean I am allowed to insult her!" Isaac began to run in the direction where Eliezer had left Ishmael, feeling that he had to carry out an important mission.

The little legs ran fast, devouring the distance easily. "Here he is!" Joy filled Isaac when he saw Ishmael; he hoped that his brother would hear his words. "Ishmael!" He exclaimed happily, waving his hand towards his brother, hunched on the ground.

Ishmael raised his head from the ground, seeing Isaac running towards him. "Ugh... That annoying kid!"

Isaac stopped near Ishmael, trying to catch his breath. "Yuck, what is that?" He said, pointing to the statue with a fish's head, a lion's body and an eagle's feet, which lay next to his brother.

"Just a statue I found in the woods," Ishmael muttered casually, trying to avoid explaining anything to the little boy. "I wanted to ask Father what this statue is."

"It looks like... an idol!" Isaac whispered in disgust. "I do not think my father would approve if you brought it into the camp."

Ishmael hid his hostile gaze from Isaac: "Perhaps you are right," he said, as if agreeing with his little brother. "Perhaps you will help me, and we will throw this statue back into the forest."

"Happily!"

Ishmael and Isaac lifted up the statue together. Ishmael then slung his bow and quiver over his shoulder, and the two entered the forest. "Ishmael, I saw something that made me sad, you know," Isaac said lightly, in the earnestly carefree manner of young children, as they stepped beneath the shade of the great trees. "Eliezer seems to be in a bad mood today, and it's a shame. He is so good to my father and to me."

Ishmael thought angrily, looking away so Isaac couldn't see his furious gaze. "'My father' again! This twerp think he's the old man's only son. 'My father?' He's our father! In the end, he will try to steal my inheritance. After all, I am not only Abraham's son, but his firstborn; I should get twice as much as Isaac."

Ishmael tried to hide the rising anger within him, "what happened to the slave —Eliezer?" He asked.

"I don't know," Isaac said, straining to see Ishmael's face. "It seemed like the two of you were fighting."

"Well — here we are!" Ishmael abruptly said, moving on to another subject as they arrived at a clearing. "See, you can throw anything into this." Ishmael pulled on a rope, uncovering a large pit with a net over it, full of leaves.

"What is it?" Isaac looked in amazement at the huge hole, "who dug it?"

Ishmael laughed with pleasure at the boy's astonishment, "this is an animal trap! The forest is full of traps I dug, and I hunt all kinds of animals."

"What do you do with them?" Isaac asked his hunter brother.

"Sometimes I eat, sometimes I take their hide, and sometimes I just leave them for the other wild animals. But now I have a much better way to hunt..." Ishmael laughed and patted his bow affectionately. "Want to try to shoot an arrow?"

Isaac looked at the great bow, and his heart was filled with a desire to try it. He thought, "wow, like a big boy."

"Yes, yes, will you let me?"

"Certainly, my dear brother..." Ishmael unslung the bow over his back, putting it into Isaac's small hands, then handing the boy an arrow to teach him how to shoot.

Isaac tried to stretch the string and shoot the arrow. The arrow fell not far from his feet.

Ishmael laughed out loud, "come, I'll show you," he said and picked up the arrow. "Do you see that branch dangling from the tall tree?" He pointed to a thick branch. "Look how I knock it down." Ishmael stretched the string with skill, firing the arrow directly at the target. The branch shook with force and fell loudly onto the ground.

Isaac clapped happily, "wow, you really are a sharpshooter!"

"Oh, that's no problem!" He said, slapping his kid brother's shoulder. "I can show you something better... unless you're afraid...?"

"Yes, yes, please!"

"All right then, take this leaf, and stand next to that tree," Ishmael said, pointing off into the distance. "Hold that leaf against the tree, and I will shoot an arrow right through it, into the tree. But you must not move!"

"Are you sure about that?!"

Ishmael laughed mockingly, "if you're still a scared little boy, we don't have to…"

Isaac overcame his fears, declaring defiantly, "no, I'm not." He grabbed the leaf from Ishmael, marching toward the tree his big brother had indicated.

Ishmael looked at Isaac with contempt, the whippersnapper who dared to call Abraham "my father." The scheme came together quickly in his mind, as he thought, "the brat will be eliminated soon! One arrow, and then I will throw his body into the pit and cover it. No one will ever be able to find him. Abraham will grieve, but in the end I will be the sole heir. And even if they find him one day and see that an arrow fired at him, I can always say it's like what happened to Lamech, who accidentally killed Cain in the woods.

"I'm ready!" Cried Isaac, standing heroically by the tree, his hand holding the leaf tightly. Ishmael notched his arrow and drew his bow taut, aiming for the heart of the hated child. He thought, "two more seconds and he's done."

His fingers readied to let the arrow fly. He thought, "your story is over, boy!"

Just as he loosened the arrow, a shriek of terror shook the forest, "Isaac!" The little boy jumped, turning towards the sound of his mother's scream. The arrow flew past his arm, tearing the fabric of his sleeve — exactly where he had been standing a split second earlier.

"Mother…" He whispered in amazement, realizing that only Sarah's cry had kept him from certain death. He looked toward where Ishmael stood, but his older brother was already gathering his quiver and bow, hurrying away from the clearing in displeasure.

"Stay in the tent with Eliezer, and do not come out!" Sarah commanded Isaac and hurried to her husband's tent.

"You must drive them out of here! Get them the hell out of our camp, so they never come back here!" Sarah felt her body vibrate with fear and rage, her tear-filled eyes obscuring the world around her.

Abraham, who was bent over a scroll in his tent, jumped up when he heard his trembling wife. "What happened?" He demanded apprehensively.

"What happened?! You don't know what's happening here?" Sarah cried out, uncharacteristically hysterical. "Your son Ishmael attempted to murder Isaac, that's what happened! He tried to kill our little boy, who survived by a miracle!" Sarah collapsed, feeling her body sapped of all its strength after the storm of emotions which had ravaged her, to the depths of her soul.

Abraham ran to the corner of the tent, poured his broken wife some water from the jug sitting on the small table, and served it to restore her soul. It took several minutes for Sarah to calm her crying. Sarah stabilized her breathing as much as she could and began to tell her beloved husband about his firstborn's deeds: the attempted murder of Isaac, along with all the past incidents of murder and idolatry, the impurity sexual immorality, robbery, and looting.

Abraham looked at his wife, finding it hard to accept what he was hearing. The truth was undeniable, but he still tried to defend his firstborn. "How can I do such a thing? Kick my son out of my house? I try to bring all the people of the world closer to the Creator, but I am to banish my own offspring?! Is there no remedy for the boy?" Struggling in his mind, he tried to find a way to keep his eye on the young man. "And if he behaves like this while he is still close to me, how will he behave if I send him away? It would be blasphemous if I threw him out!"

Sarah watched her husband, feeling his distress; still, she was resolute that there was no alternative. "There is no choice, my husband! You must send them away from us, the sooner the better," she said gently, gazing into the face of her tormented husband. Abraham heard his wife, feeling the spirit of prophecy descended upon him. *"Let it not be grievous in your sight because of the lad, and because of your bondwoman; in all that Sarah says unto you, hearken unto her voice; for in Isaac shall seed be called to you. And also of the son of the bondwoman will I make a nation, because he is your seed."*

The prophecy passed, and Abraham felt the tears flowing from his eyes in sorrow. "I will do as you say," he whispered to his wife.

The rays of the rising sun filled the land of Gerar, the crimson-painted horizon looking more beautiful to Eliezer than ever. He was eager to keep the command of his master, and he ran to wake Hagar and Ishmael.

Abraham stood in the doorway of his tent, waiting for Eliezer to return with his firstborn and the boy's mother. His heart brimmed with sorrow as he faced the mission which had been placed upon him; he felt the need to fortify himself against the current of emotion rushing through him.

Eliezer returned smiling, ignoring the imprecations hurled at him by Ishmael, followed along by Hagar.

Hagar looked at Abraham in amazement at the early-morning summons. "Have you called us, my lord?" She asked apprehensively, seeing a bundle and a waterskin. Abraham extended his hand to Hagar, holding out a piece of parchment.

"What is this?" The handmaid asked.

"This is a bill for divorce," Abraham said as he tried not to show the turbulent feelings inside him. "You and Ishmael need to leave this place immediately. There is bread and water here. It will be enough for you, until you reach Beersheba."

Hagar opened her eyes in panic, "but my lord..."

"No buts!" Abraham said firmly, fortified by the command he had received. "You are to leave the camp immediately." Abraham took the waterskin, tying it around her waist so all would know that she was a slave, and handed her the bundle, which contained bread for the journey. "Take your son now and go!" Abraham declared, turning his back on his firstborn and the boy's mother. Tears ran from his eyes as he strode back to his tent.

The blazing sun beat down on their heads, confounding all thought. "What did you do that made him angry enough to kick us out of the camp?" Hagar shouted at her son, trailing behind her.

"Nothing! He just did it for no good reason." Ishmael felt his feet ache from the long journey, knowing that his actions had landed himself and his mother in this awful predicament. "I was playing with Isaac, and his mother saw it and thought I was trying to kill him."

"Stupid!" Said Hagar, angrily smacking Ishmael on the back of his neck. "You should have done it cleverly, so that they wouldn't see you!" Her uncertainty about their future was driving her mad. "What shall we do now? Where shall we go? If we had some statue or idol here, like I had in my father Pharaoh's house, it might help us; but there is nothing here!" She cried in despair.

"I want water! Bring me water!" Demanded Ishmael, who felt that his throat was dry. Hagar pulled the waterskin tied to her waist, offering it to her son.

"It's empty! You drank all my water!" He shouted angrily.

"I drank it?! You finished the water!" Hagar felt her dry lips cracking. "We will find some water soon enough," she whispered in an attempt to calm herself.

"I have no strength to keep going! Either pick me up or leave me to die here!" Ishmael sat down on the yellow sand, watching his mother bend over.

"Ishmael, get up and walk," she pleaded. "Surely we will find water soon."

Ishmael challenged his mother. "Either lift me up or your son will die because of you!"

"Ishmael, you're too big. I cannot pick you up!"

"So go on alone, and I'll die here!"

Hagar surrendered to her son. She knew that she would not be able to carry him for a long time, but she could not conceive leaving her son alone. Ishmael hung on his mother's neck, with his bow and quiver on his back. Hagar staggered, feeling her heavy legs sink into the desert sand. "A few more steps..." She whispered to herself, "a little more…"

She fell to her knees next to a bush, which offered the tiniest bit of shade from the desert sun. She knew she could not go on walking. She placed her son, who was burning up, under the bush. Slowly, she crawled towards another bush, a few paces away. She was aware that she and her son might soon die of thirst. She moved away, enough to prevent her son from firing his arrows at her out of grief. All she wanted was to avoid witnessing the death of her poor son. The mother's heart was torn in two at the impending death of her son, feeling as if her flesh was being torn off her body.

A cry burst forth from Hagar's throat. "What did You say? *I will greatly multiply your seed*? Now the boy is dying of thirst!" Tears ran down her face as she challenged heaven.

Meanwhile, Ishmael offered his own complaint to the Creator. "If You are the king, as Abraham my father says, and You kill me by thirst, then You are a cruel king! Remember how I entered into Your covenant, when my father commanded me, when I was thirteen years old, and I did not stop him." His body was wrung-out and seething, dampness covering the eyes, wide open with the impending terror of death. "I know that I have committed unspeakable acts. And I know that by Your will, You give life or death. My father told me that You do not judge a man until he is twenty years old, for then his soul is developed enough to know between good and evil; but I am only seventeen years old! Are You condemning me to death in defiance of Your own rules?! I am sorry for my corrupt deeds, and I repent before you at this time. Am I not the son of Abraham? Do You not want to prevent him from experiencing the grief of being bereaved of his firstborn?" Ishmael stretched out on the hot sand, his lips trembling, begging for his life from the Creator of all things.

He could hear the voices of the accusers, "he does not deserve a miracle! After all, he and his seed will murder Your children in the future! They will cruelly slaughter children, women, and the elderly, utterly innocent people. They will try to exterminate Your children in any way possible!"

"I know all this, but I do not condemn any man for what he will do in the future, but only for his past deeds. In the present, the boy has repented before me," God replied to his angels.

"But all the troubles?! All the atrocities?! The murders?! Terrorists?! And Hamas...?"

The voice was soothing, "I know, but this is what is necessary..."

"What ails you, Hagar?"

She tried to locate the source of the voice, fearing that her mind was producing hallucinations and delusions as she breathed her last. *"Fear not; for God has heard the voice of the lad where he is. Arise, lift up the lad, and hold him fast by your hand; for I will make him a great nation."*

Hagar rubbed her eyes forcefully, hoping she wasn't dreaming. A well of water burst from the ground. Hagar crawled towards the well, seeing that it was no mirage, that there was water to quench her and her son's thirst. The water revived the unfortunate soul. Hagar filled the waterskin and ran towards her son, praying that she was not too late.

CHAPTER THIRTY

Repentance

The encampment was bustling with life, as people came in all day to get food, a drink, and a place to stay. The hosts made only one request of the many guests: to give thanks to He who spoke and brought the universe into being.

With the sound of children's laughter in Abraham's ears, thoughts ran rampant through his mind. The news brought by travelers from the south was about his son, Ishmael, who married and had sons. The rumor was that his son had become a bandit, waylaying wayfarers; this clouded Abraham's mood. The knowledge that Hagar had found an Egyptian wife for Ishmael disturbed his peace.

He thought, "perhaps there is hope that he will change his ways. Three years have passed since I sent him and his mother way from me. He is a clever young man, and he has probably thought a lot about why I had to send them away from my son Isaac. Three years is quite a long time to take spiritual inventory and arrive at a personal reckoning. He was a teenager at the time, but perhaps the years have done their work, allowing the wound of his banishment to heal."

Abraham dove into his thoughts; he longed to see his son, along with the grandchildren he had never laid eyes on.

He thought, "I must talk to him! Surely he will not hurt me. I must go to him!"

Sarah's mouth gaped in astonishment at her husband's words, "but why? What do you see in him? Have you not heard about his bad behavior? About the Egyptian woman he married? You know that nothing good will come of him! He is a blasphemous seed! Are you not the one who always speaks of how important it is to stay away from bad influences and people who pursue devious ends? Why would you want to have anything to do with this bad apple?"

A tear flowed from Abraham's eye, knowing that his wife was right, but feeling that he had to go. "This bad apple is my son," he whispered with sorrow, words piercing the heart of the loving mother.

Sarah looked at her husband, trying to plumb the depths of her soul, considering how she would have felt in her husband's situation . She realized that she, too, would at least try to see if anything had changed with her wayward son, to investigate the possibility of bringing him back to the path of truth. "I see," her voice, full of sympathy for her husband, made it clear to him what his wife was about to say. "I, too, would go on such a journey if the situation was reversed. Goodbye, my dear husband, but promise me something: when you arrive at Ishmael's place of residence, do not dismount from the camel, not even to eat or drink. You know better than me that staying in such a place may cause enormous spiritual damage. Go, get the lay of the land, but then come back here as soon as possible."

Abraham was happy in his heart that his wife agreed with his plan. The worry of doing something his wife might disagree with would have kept him from sleeping a wink. "Thank you, Sarah, I will do as you say."

In the Paran Wilderness, the golden horizon seemed infinite and desolate; still, he felt joy that every step was bringing father and son closer to their reunion. The camel's legs devoured the road briskly, a few hours separating the father from the encampment of his eldest son. Abraham sank into thoughts about his son's condition, remembering the day when he had been forced by the situation to send his son away from him. He wondered if there was a possibility that his son would one day admit that his father had done the right thing.

He thought "after all, even Abimelech of Gerar changed his mind! King Abimelech and Lord Commander Phicol came shortly after I sent Ishmael from me and asked for my forgiveness for what they'd thought about me."

Abraham smiled to himself in satisfaction, recalling that event. He reflected: Abimelech and Phicol saw that my place was blessed after I had sent Ishmael away, and that God was granting me success in every endeavor. Then they asked to make a covenant with them, that I would not seek to conquer the land — all because they had seen how much our camp had grown.

"Abimelech…" Abraham laughed to himself aloud at how crooked the man was. He thought, "even his name shamelessly demonstrates his desperation: would that (*abi*) I were king (*melech*)! All he seeks is greater authority and power… So pathetic, he even dared to ask me if I would spare his son and his grandson too. After all, a king who cannot pass on his crown to his heir is no king at all. I had to rebuke him because it was his servants who stole the well my servants dug. A man must be honest about the issues he has with his fellow; otherwise, resentment festers in one's heart. This is even more true when the other comes to appease and make peace! From the expression on the faces of Abimelech and Phicol, it was clear that they didn't know about the stolen well..."

The camel seemed to be hovering over the desert, bringing the father closer to his longed-for reunion with his firstborn. Over the hill, a spacious encampment came into view. It was an oasis, with palm trees reaching toward the heavens, swaying in the light wind. A spring of water sustained the few fruit trees, a dot of life in the heart of the desolate desert. Two small children could be seen in the distance, one toddling and one crawling by the door of the tent. "Surely these are my grandchildren..." A wide smile spread across his face as he thought, "what a wonderful surprise it would be for the residents of the camp."

However, as he grew closer, he heard: "beasts! Stop driving me crazy! You're garbage! I wish you and your father would die!"

Screams, imprecations, and profanity echoed through the desert, dismaying Abraham; then there were shouts of pain and weeping.

"You'll die, bitch! Stop beating me, you shrew!"

There was the jarring sound of the smashing of earthenware, then a haunting shriek of pain. Abraham edged his camel closer to the tent, seeing a two-year-old boy, whose head was dripping blood, come screaming out of the tent.

Abraham, who felt the urge to get off the camel to help the bruised child, remembered the promise he had made to his wife. "Boy, what happened to you?" He asked sadly, feeling the injury in his body.

The boy looked up, startled, at the strangle old man riding the camel who had suddenly appeared. "Aisha, the shrew, threw a clay jug at me and hurt me."

The boy looked at the old man, wondering what this interloper was doing in his father's camp.

"Who's that? Who's Aisha?" Abraham interrogated him.

"My mother! The shrew who sliced my head open is my own mother!"

"And who is your father?"

"Ishmael," the boy replied without thinking why the man was asking questions.

"And what's your name?"

"Nebaioth," the boy said proudly.

"And where is your father?"

"Went with his mother to hunt. Who are you anyway? What are you doing here?"

"Just a wandering old man," Abraham replied. "Would you call your mother?" He asked.

The boy hesitated for a moment, thinking how best to satisfy the old wanderer's request. "Aisha!" He shouted into the tent. "There's an old man here who wants you!" The boy picked up his feet and ran away before his mother could lay into him again.

"Call me a bitch, will you? I'll show you, you stinking bastard!" The woman shouted as she exited the tent.

Abraham looked away from the sight before his eyes. A bareheaded woman, dressed in horrifically immodest clothing, came out of the tent in a rage.

"Who are you?! What do you want?!" She spat at Abraham, sitting on his camel.

"I'm just an old wanderer, thirsty for water," he replied in a low voice.

"Come on, get the hell out of here! Go find another sucker who will give you water!" She shouted, waving her hands in all directions.

Abraham breathed deeply, filling his lungs with air, trying to overcome his feelings of disgust towards his son's wife. "I'm going on my way, but please, when your husband gets back, tell him: an old man came from the land of the Philistines looking for him, and he wanted to let him know that the door to his tent is in disrepair and he must replace it! " Abraham turned his mount around and galloped back to his house.

Three more years passed before Abraham went out again to Ishmael's camp. The subsequent journey was also predicated on his promise that he would not dismount when he reached the tent of Ishmael; he was unsettled by the concern that the scenes of his first visit might repeat themselves. Abraham advanced toward the tents with apprehension, silence prevailing in the camp.

"I remember you!" A five-year-old boy said to Abraham, "You are the old wanderer who came here that one time."

Abraham looked at the child, knowing that the boy was his grandson, "I remember you too," Abraham smiled, "your name is Nebaioth, right?"

The boy laughed kindly at Abraham, "you may be old, but you have a good memory."

"And your father is called Ishmael, and your mother Aisha, am I right?"

The boy nodded affirmatively, marveling at the old man's memory of the short meeting that had been so long ago. "How do you remember after so long?"

Abraham laughed out loud. "The mind, like a field, must be constantly tilled," he said, tapping his head. "Is Ishmael, your father, at home?"

The boy shook his head, "father went out with Grandmother to graze the sheep."

Abraham pondered whether to ask anything else; a few seconds passed before he ventured apprehensively, "and Aisha? Is your mother at home?"

The boy's face looked pensive as if he did not know what to feel. "No, she's not home. The truth is that she doesn't live here anymore."

Nebaioth looked at Abraham as he tried to connect the events that had happened in the past. "Actually, now that I think about it… Father came back after you were here the last time, and Mother told him something about replacing the tent door. Father smiled understandingly, and that day he banished Mother." The boy gazed into the old man's eyes looking at him tenderly, feeling that he could lay his conscience bare to this old man whom he'd only met twice. "I don't know how to tell you this, but I was not at all sad when she left. Do you remember how my head was bleeding when you came here? That used to happen every day. Then, when Father brought another woman, I was even more happy that she left. Now she's my mother; her name is Fatima."

Abraham felt relieved that he would not meet Aisha again. "Would you call her? Tell her that there is a very thirsty old man here."

The boy did not hesitate and entered the tent, shouting, "mother, there is a very nice old traveler here who wants to drink."

Fatima came out of the tent carrying a jug of cold water in her hand. "Why do you not come down from the camel, sir?" She said, her eyes lowered. "Please sir, come down! Drink, eat, and wash your feet after your long journey."

"Thank you, Lady Fatima, but I am unable to come down," Abraham said to the kind woman. "But if you could give me just a little bit of water to drink, I'd be very grateful."

Fatima poured a glass of water for the old wanderer and whispered in Nebaioth's ear to run to the kitchen and bring the wanderer some fine food. The boy ran happily to fulfill his mother's wish.

Abraham sat, drank, and ate on the camel, as he had promised his wife. "Please, tell Ishmael, when he comes, that the old man has come again from the land of the Philistines looking for him; this time I must say that his tent door is splendid, and he must keep it well."

Fatima engraved on her heart the words of the traveler without understanding their meaning, then asked him to rest a little inside. Abraham declined the invitation, wished farewell to the woman and her son, and returned to his place in Gerar.

"Father, the old wanderer came here again from the land of the Philistines!" Nebaioth ran to greet his father and grandmother, who had returned from grazing. Ishmael raised his son in his arms, feeling disappointed that he had again missed his father's visit. He felt a desire to return to the bosom of his father and his lifestyle. Hagar looked at her son angrily, clearly perceiving her son's desire to return to his father. "Do you want to go back to him?" She asked her son in a whisper.

"With all my might," he replied, aware that his mother would not return to his father's encampment as long as Sarah was there. The mother and son had had many conversations while grazing the flocks in the desert, long discussions about the vanity of their current life as opposed to the ethical life which Abraham had tried to instill in them and all his household.

"You have to go back," said Hagar to her son as they approached the tent. "You have nothing to look for elsewhere..."

"What about you?" He whispered.

Hagar felt her son's heart torn between dueling loyalties, "I'll manage!"

Fatima, hearing their voices as they approached the tent, happily went out to greet them, filling bowls of water and washing the feet of her husband and mother-in-law. "My lord," she said to her husband humbly, "a very kind and generous old man was here today, from the land of the Philistines, and he was looking for you. When I gave him food and drink, he refused to come down from the camel and told me to tell you that the door of your tent is excellent and you must maintain it. Do you understand what he meant? " She asked confusedly.

Ishmael looked at his wife, realizing that the reception Abraham had received this time had pleased him. "I know him well," he said with a pleasant smile to his ingenuous wife. "It was my father, and soon we will move and go to live near him." Ishmael looked at his mother and saw a tear make its way down her cheek.

CHAPTER THIRTY-ONE

The Trial

Twenty-six years had passed since Abraham's arrival in Gerar, years of prosperity and wealth, in which Abraham's reputation spread far and wide. The many people who visited the encampment were happily received by Abraham and his household, and they were treated to food and drink in a regal manner.

The smiling Bacol, daughter of Abraham and Sarah, born a few years after Isaac, served her father faithfully and happily. Abraham looked at his daughter, realizing that she had reached maturity, yet was still in her father's house.

He though, "but to whom can I marry her off?"

The question was a thorny one which gave him no rest.

He mused, "when she gets married she will have to go to her husband's house, and what will happen to her there? She will have to live among idolaters. Can she keep her faith in a place like that? Still, how can I prevent her from getting married? She's not a little girl anymore, and she hasn't been for a long time! I cannot afford to stay here in the land of the Philistines! I have lived in their midst for twenty-six years, and there is still not a single one among them who has begun to walk the straight path."

Abraham felt depressed whenever the subject came to his mind. He knew that the territory currently occupied by the Philistines would one day be a part of the land promised to him in the future. This fact had made him stay in the region for a long time. The thought that he might be able to change something in its people had prevented him from leaving; but now he had to worry about the future of his only daughter.

"Bacol, my dear," he said to his daughter, "could you please call your mother? Tell her I want her to come here."

The girl looked at her father lovingly and hurried to do his will.

"I do not know when my day will come to leave this world," Abraham said to his wife, who was gazing at her husband admiringly. "I am now one hundred and twenty-five years old, and no man knows the day of his death." Abraham looked at Sarah and saw that this was very disturbing to her as well.

"Here, in Gerar, she will never find a worthy husband," Abraham decided. "The people here do not want to change; they want to pursue their lusts! We must leave this land; we must go toward the territory of the Canaanites." A glimmer of hope and joy ignited in Sarah's eyes at the news. "In that country, there is hope that we may be able to find or attract an appropriate suitor for Bacol." Sarah nodded in agreement.

"Moreover, the Creator promised me that my children would inherit the territory of the Canaanites, so I do not want to be buried where we are. When I breathe my last, I want to be buried there, a plot of land far from here. My desire is to be interred in a holy and pure place, the sepulcher of Adam and Eve."

Sarah looked at her husband with a smile, knowing that he was about to reveal to her something from the depths of his heart. "And does my lord know where their burial place is?" She eagerly asked, wishing she, too, could have a place near the ancestors of humankind for her own eternal rest.

"Do you remember the day the three guests came and told us about Isaac's birth?" Sarah smiled, knowing the question was rhetorical. "That day, there was a runaway calf, and I pursued it into a cave. As soon as I stepped inside, I could smell the very scent of the Garden of Eden. I saw Adam and Eve there; it was like they were in a peaceful slumber, awaiting the day when they would awake from the sleep of the righteous. That was when I was struck by a proud yearning to one day be buried there."

She felt like she was floating in a dream, sailing toward remote districts in the depths of the past. Childhood dreams filled with the heroes of creation and the purity of their splendor. "If so, this place must be close to the Mamre Plains," she whispered dreamily.

"Indeed, on the border of the Mamre Plains and Hebron, in a cave hidden from the eyes of man, in a desolate and remote area — that's where it is," he whispered with heartfelt longing.

"Can I be buried there too?" She asked wistfully.

Abraham looked at his wife with a loving smile, "certainly, you and I will never part." Abraham began to speak decisively, "although the place is in Hebron, it seems to me that it is best that we move to Beersheba in the meantime, which is quite close to Hebron," he clarified. "Obviously, if we move to Hebron now, it will surprise the residents there, and perhaps they will not agree to sell me the burial place. Therefore, we will first move to Beersheba, and then I will see to buying the plot."

"I will tell the slaves to pack everything up…" Said Sarah, rising from her seat to do her husband's will.

"Kedar, I tell you, if you do not stop with your nonsense, I will chop your head off!" Nebaioth screamed at his younger brother.

Adbeel and Mibsam, their teenage half-brothers, were laughing. The three tykes, Mishma, Dumah, and Massa, looked into the distance, afraid to mock their oldest brother lest they too bear his wrath.

Kedar removed his hands from the camel's neck, and the poor animal snorted and choked, trying to catch its breath after the cruel attempted suffocation. "What happened? I'm just having some fun."

"Having fun?! Do you know how much this camel cost me?!" Nebaioth glared at his brother with a mad look, "now look what fun this is!" Nebaioth slashed the throats of five sheep in one stroke, with the dagger in his hand. "Do you want fun? Here's your fun!"

Kedar's eyes almost popped out of their sockets when he saw the massacre of his flock. "I will show you what fun is!" He screamed and drew his sword, beheading the camel, which had been sprawled on the ground in an attempt to recover. Then he ran towards the herd of camels standing in the corral, to the applause of Mishma, Duma, and Massa.

The hubbub of their shouts made Fatima leap up and rush out of the tent where her two babies, Hadad and Tema, were sleeping. "What the hell are you doing?" Her shout of alarm stopped the demonic prancing. The two young men stopped in their places, looking at the massacre each had committed among his brother's livestock

"Ishmael!!!" Fatima's furious call caused the two young men to shudder.

Nebaioth and Kedar were frozen in their places, anticipating the wrath about to fall upon them. A few moments later, Ishmael emerged from the tent, rubbing the cobwebs from his sleepy eyes.

Observing his bloodstained sons and the livestock, he shouted, "you blithering idiots!" He waved his hand at them scornfully. "Clean up this mess immediately, and then come to my tent."

From the door of Abraham's tent, a shocked Isaac watched the scene. He resolved to speak to his older brother, to beg Ishmael to invest more in his sons' education.

"Ishmael, my brother, unfortunately, I witnessed, today, the horrific spectacle of the behavior of your two eldest sons. I understand that it is not easy to watch and be attentive to children all day. I know you are very busy with your affairs and don't have much time to spend in the company of your wonderful sons, but I had a thought: if you could just make time every day to sit down with your boys to study, they would surely start to change." Isaac looked at his brother, saw his displeasure at where the conversation was heading. "You know that even just sitting in the company of a parent can allow children a lot of change in their behavior. I don't mean to be critical, but I thought that—"

Ishmael snorted derisively and cut off the lecture from his younger brother. "Boy, what do you understand about it? You are a bachelor, childless, and you mean to teach me how to raise my children?! Do you understand what it takes to educate them, to raise them?! No, you sit around like a parasite. You are a bookworm, always reading, not raising a finger to help someone in the pasture or with other chores, and you come to criticize my morals?! You patronize me, talking to me about investing time?!"

The veins in Ishmael's forehead swelled angrily as he raged at his kid brother's audacity. "You have no shame! You just take care of yourself, you sit all day and waste time instead of doing the things that we need, and you dare to lecture me on educating children!"

The anger in Ishmael's eyes grew as he screamed at his little brother. "You are just a spoiled and cowardly brat! Sitting all day, grasping your mother's apron strings, trying to please the whole world! Then you give lessons to those who come to Father's tent, as if you have ever done something of meaning in your life? I guess there are those who can, do; and those who can't, teach!"

In a barbed tone, Ishmael imitated Isaac, "the Creator must be worshiped with dedication! Surrender all of yourself to the Lord's work! Be willing to sacrifice yourself for him!"

Sarcastic laughter rose from Ishmael's throat. "You want to talk about dedication?! You are too lazy to even marry a woman and have children. Wasn't that the first commandment given to Adam? But you don't bother to fulfill it. Now look at me! I married as a teenager, accepted the yoke of matrimony when I was still a boy. And what about you? You are thirty-seven, and you're still not even considering it."

Isaac looked at his older brother, who was trying to tower over him; on the tip of his tongue was an answer he did not want to verbalize: Ishmael took his wives solely to satisfy his animalistic desires.

Ishmael continued shouting, "dedication! What do you know about it, boy? Or maybe I should call you a girl?!" Ishmael looked at his brother in disgust, seeing Isaac's delicate face looking at him in astonishment. "You even look like a powerless female! Sitting in a tent all day doing nothing, wearing clean and tidy clothes like one of the girls. Looking at your face, anyone would think that you are no man at all, but a girl playing dress-up! You know I was thirteen years old when Father said he wanted to circumcise me; I could have resisted, could have fought back against him, but I did not! You, you were only eight days old when Father circumcised you; you had no choice, you could not resist him at all! You condescend me? I dedicated myself consciously; I willingly sacrificed my body for the glory of the Lord when I entered His covenant!"

Isaac looked down, turning over Ishmael's reproach in his mind. It was true, he was lacking in proving his adoration of the Creator. The brain plumbed the heart, the heart sensed the brain. Abruptly, he met his older brother's gaze and declared, "do you boast because of one body part? If the Blessed Lord asked me to be slaughtered, I would happily lay down my very life!"

The howls of the jackals filled the night, as the last days of summer had arrived, carrying with them a pleasant coolness at the end of the oppressive hot days. A quiet wind carried on its wings the sounds of the whispering Beersheba desert, vibrating the leaves of the few trees.

"*Abraham!*" The familiar and beloved voice spoke within the heart of Abraham, who struggled to understand whether he was awake or asleep. The voice was rarely heard, so it drove, from his heart, any reality other than its presence.

"*Here I am,*" Abraham replied, still debating whether he was dreaming or awake.

"*Please take your son...!*"

Abraham heard the request, trying to understand why God couched this as a request and not as a command. He felt that inherent in the act, was some danger to his son. "Which of my sons? I have two sons," Abraham whispered, hoping to hear the opposite of what he knew he was about to hear.

"*Your only one...*" The voice said, drawing it out to increase the reward for following the word of God.

"They are both only sons, each one to his mother," Abraham maneuvered delicately, feeling in his heart that all his previous trials would pale in comparison to this.

"*Whom you love...*" God continued, giving Abraham the time to get used to and internalize whom they were talking about, stalling for time so that Abraham would not be struck mad by the very idea.

"I love them both," Abraham whispered, in fear of God's word.

"*Isaac...*" the voice finally spelled it out, rejecting the attempt to evade whom they were discussing.

Abraham filled his lungs with air, trying to calm his heart which was beating hard inside him by breathing deeply, attempting to assert control over his mind and accept things with equanimity and tranquility.

"*And go for yourself to the land of Moriah...*"

Abraham felt it as his heart skipped a beat. He thought, "I must take my son to the place of the altar built by Adam, the altar on which Abel and Noah brought their offerings. Perhaps the Lord wants me and my son to bring our offerings there as well."

"*And bring him up there as an offering, upon one of the mountains which I will tell you.*"

Deep shock gripped Abraham, terror and fear of doing such an awful thing. He had spent his entire life preaching, insisting that such an act was inappropriate and unwanted in the Creator's eyes. Now, he was expected to do that very thing to his son, whom his wife had borne to him when he was a century old? His heart seized up as he considered that he would have to tell his wife, who had given birth at age ninety, that her son was now to be bound to the altar.

Abraham lay on his bed trying to calm his racing heart, which seemed ready to beat straight out of his chest. Taking deep breaths and feeling the oxygen saturating his blood, instilled in him a feeling of drawing strength and confidence from his Creator. The mind asserted control over the heart banging against his ribs; he believed in the Creator, who would only tell him to do something if there were a worthwhile purpose. This thought brought him composure; he slipped back into deep slumber.

The rooster's crow awakened Abraham from his sleep, while the encampment was still in its deep slumber. Quickly, Abraham got to his feet, knowing his mission lay ahead of him. There was a sense of excitement about what lay before him; he recognized that the most difficult task before him would be to mollify Sarah as he prepared for the journey to Mount Moriah with his son.

Abraham hastened his steps towards his wife's tent, confident that she was already awake. He could hear the familiar sound of rattling pots in the tent which always remained illuminated by candlelight. Abraham cleared his throat, catching the attention of his bustling wife.

Sarah looked up in amazement at her husband, standing in the doorway of the tent. She arranged her head covering in her husband's honor. "It's still very early," Sarah noted, breaking her husband's tense silence. "Do you want to drink or eat something?"

"No, that's fine." Abraham tried to keep his voice calm, but his wife was alerted by the undertones; she knew the nuances of her husband's speech. "I just think that I am making a big mistake with Isaac.." His tone was thoughtful and indecisive, and Sarah nodded anxiously, awaiting her husband's elaborations.

"Our Isaac is already thirty-seven years old, and I still feel as if I have not begun to educate him in the service of the Lord. We had Isaac after so many years of marriage, and we have not yet brought a thanksgiving offering for the immense grace He has bestowed upon us," Abraham continued, ignoring the silence that prevailed in the tent. "I keep speaking about the need to thank God and the importance of gratitude for all that He grants us; I talk the talk, but I do not walk the walk. Almost four decades have passed, and I have still not brought a thanksgiving offering?" A sharp and penetrating pain was felt in Abraham's heart, knowing that his wife could not imagine what was going on inside him. He regretted having to mislead her and hide what he had been asked to do.

Sarah smiled at her husband with understanding. "My lord, do what you have to do. You know that I will not prevent you from training our dear son in the service of our Creator. Hurry up, and do what is needed."

Abraham stood rooted to his place, as his body refused to leave the tent. "I must go to the land of Moriah to offer the sacrifice there," he told his wife, "to the place of the ancient altar."

"Of course! Let me prepare some food for you. Such a trip will take you several days. My lord, I ask you to take at least two of our men with you, to help shall you need anything. I'll prepare everything you need, I'm sure it will not take me more than half-an-hour." Sarah turned her back on her husband happily, rushing to prepare everything necessary for her son's educational journey, training in the worship of God.

Abraham stared at his wife's back, a rebellious tear making its way to his cheek. He thought, "I wish you didn't have to go through this…"

He left the tent, gathering Isaac, Ishmael, and Eliezer. He made his way to the animal pens. Quickly, he approached the donkey and saddled it.

Isaac took the lead, while Ishmael and Eliezer accompanied the donkey, and Abraham brought up the rear.

"Well met, Lord Abraham."

Abraham looked beside him in amazement; an old man with a beaming face had suddenly arrived on his right. "Well met, sir," he replied. He thought, "I must have been so preoccupied that I didn't notice his approach. No one else seemed to notice him."

With a wide smile, the old man probed, "where is my lord going? If I may ask!"

Offhandedly, Abraham replied, "we are going to pray."

The laughter of the old man stopped him dead in his tracks. "Does one need a torch and a knife to pray?"

Abraham thought, "this old man is some sort of snoop. How can we get rid of this nuisance?"

Aloud, he said, "our journey will take several days. We need this equipment in case we find some animal or beast which we want to slaughter and cook."

The old man looked directly into Abraham's eyes, seeming to pierce his very heart. "You're a world-class idiot." The voice made his blood run cold. "You waited one hundred years for God to give you a child, and now on the advice of Satan you are going to slaughter him?! The Lord said: *'for in Isaac shall seed be called to you.'* Now, like a senile old fool, you are about to kill the gift he gave you?!"

Abraham looked at the old man; he was struck by the completely astonishing appearance of an elder who knew what was hidden from everyone else. "I follow the Creator's command!" He said confidently.

The cynical and cold laugh could be heard again, "you are a crazy and cruel old man! If you want to slaughter someone, if the madness enters you to murder someone, kill Ishmael!"

Abraham resumed walking, shouting to his three companions to continue on the path he had shown them.

The oldster's voice became pleading and soft, "do you not feel sorry for the unfortunate Sarah?! Do you think that if you kill your son now, she will bear you more sons?!"

"I follow the Creator's command!" Abraham said slowly, trying to strengthen his heart in the face of the attack that was tearing it to pieces.

"This is not the command of the Creator; it is the evil inclination which wants you to stumble. The Creator is disgusted by human sacrifices — isn't that what you tell everyone who will listen to your teachings? Obviously He cannot want you to slaughter your son Isaac, who is meant to perpetuate your legacy in the world."

Abraham felt the words trying to bore through the walls he had erected around his heart, against the claims wrestling within him. His thoughts had found expression through the old stranger's mouth.

"And even if he told you to slaughter Isaac, he did not tell you when! Abide a while, find Isaac a decent match, wait until his wife is pregnant, and then slaughter him." The old man was silent for a few seconds, giving Abraham time to think about his advice. "I tell you, listen to me. Everything you have done for more than one hundred and thirty years will be erased; people will think that all your words are hollow. All the many disciples who walk in your path will leave you after you have done this foolish act. Think of all you stand to lose out of your haste. How do you always put it? 'Satan makes haste!' What you're about to do is Satan's advice…"

Abraham felt his legs grow heavy, as if agreeing with the old man; he tried to refuse and keep going on the path outlined for him. His brain seemed to pulse rapidly and dizzyingly with thoughts that struggled against each other trying to break out of the skull. The old body trembled, trying to stop itself from going down the path of doom. The father's heart tried to take over the mind, which commanded the body to push one step further. The three escorts seemed far away now, as he had slowed his place. Abraham was coming to a halt...

The old stranger took a deep breath, "I'm glad you understood that this is Satan's advice," he said with a calm smile.

Abraham looked up, raised his sloping shoulders, "I truly understand, I understand that you are Satan himself, trying to keep me from fulfilling the command of the Creator!" Abraham's eyes flared and flamed. *"The Lord rebuke you Satan!"* He gazed into the perfect eyes looking back at him; his own eyes were two spears penetrating into tempered steel, diminishing it, obscuring its very being.

Isaac walked lightly, bounding from rock to rock like a graceful desert gazelle. Behind him were the figures of Eliezer and Ishmael, who were leading the donkey; followed by his father, walking slowly, who seemed to be talking to himself. He thought, "he must be communing with God as he walks."

The joy of what was to be done soon filled his heart.

"Well met, young master," came a cheerful, young voice a bit behind him.

Isaac turned his gaze in amazement at the voice. A handsome young man smiled broadly at him. "I hope I didn't scare you," he apologized with a smile.

"No, it's okay," Isaac smiled at the young stranger.

"Going for a walk?"

Isaac felt that the youngster was a special person. He thought, "perhaps he can be brought under the wings of the divine!" A feeling began to pulse within him. "No, we are going to learn how to prepare a sacrifice and make a thanksgiving offering to God," he said, as if revealing a secret, hoping that this would excite the man walking beside him.

"It sounds interesting." He looked at Isaac jokingly, "what are you offering for your sacrifice?"

"Lamb, kid, ram, something like that," he clarified happily.

"Very interesting, where is it?" The smile on his face widened.

"Ah... We did not bring any animals with us... We'll find something at our destination, I assume..."

The rolling peal of laughter froze Isaac in his place. "World-class idiot! You brought wood, even though there are trees all around; you brought fire even though it is easy to find kindling; you brought a knife. The only thing you left out is the most important, the one which is hardest to find in the middle of nowhere." The voice sounded cold, piercing like a blade. "Fool! You are the sacrifice! Your old father is going to slaughter you, so he did not bring any animal for slaughter! You are his beast!"

Isaac's heart skipped a beat; he had not considered any of this. Instead, he understood that he had to do whatever his father told him, without challenge or objection. The realization that the youngster was right struck him, shaking him to his very core. There was silence between the two youths as they stood opposite each other; the eyes of the stranger skewering Isaac's, penetrating into his innermost depths.

"Then... I won!" Said Isaac after long seconds, a seeming eternity.

"What did you win? Are you insane?! Your father went crazy and wants to slaughter you, and you say you won?!" The young stranger looked confused; he had not expected such a response.

The smile on Isaac's face widened, "if God commanded my father to bring me up as an offering, then there is no greater honor than that!"

"Your father has lost it!" The stranger shouted at Isaac. "He is insane! He has no control over his actions! He has fantasies and delusions in his head, so he is going to murder you!"

"My father is not sane?! I wish the whole world was as insane as he." Isaac gazed piercingly into the eyes watching him. "I know who you are! Get away from me immediately, Satan! You just want to keep us from fulfilling the commandment of God!"

The man's face looked bruised and sagging, "you are just like your father..."

Isaac laughed out loud as the figure in front of him began to dissolve, "I wish!"

The day faded, giving way to a starry night. The moonlight from above showed that a little less than half the month has passed. The light of the small fire cast flickering shadows in the darkness of the living desert. The father and son sat side by side, gazing at the sky spread out above them like a canopy. The rhythmic breathing of old Eliezer and Ishmael could be heard in the background, accompanied by the cries of the jackals and foxes.

"You see?" Abraham whispered and pointed to the vault of heaven. "This is Libra, the constellation that rules this month. The Creator arranged the twelve constellations in parallel to the twelve months of the year, and the shape of each teaches us what unique qualities that month has. The twelve constellations represent twelve states of running the natural world. It is possible and necessary to learn a great deal from the celestial bodies and their effect on ordinary human beings..."

"What do you mean 'ordinary,' Father?"

Abraham chuckled quietly, "'Ordinary,' meaning other human beings who allow naturalness to navigate their lives. People who live by nature are led by nature. I, too, was mistaken for many years; even though I worshipped the Lord, I was not enlightened enough to realize that the heavenly orbits are only milestones marking the path of nature. I lived with the understanding that it was impossible to deviate from the marked route, to veer off and blaze a new trail that no human or creature had ever walked: an unmarked way, a path never existed before, and which would cease to exist once I had passed."

"I'm not sure I understand," Isaac replied in confusion, trying to fathom his father's philosophy.

Abraham put his hand on his beloved son's shoulder, "an unmarked side path is not really a path at all. How do you think the trodden way differs from the untrodden?"

Isaac pondered the question, "a trodden path is actually a route which many people have walked, which has slowly become a road."

"Beautiful," Abraham grinned as if to himself. "Who says that's better than the untrodden road?"

"Many people have walked that path, and they have found it to be preferable. So we may assume that it is the best option."

"Ah, the wisdom of the crowd!" Abraham's voice betrayed his dismay at Isaac's argument. "Never, my son, never rely on that! You cannot accept something as true and right simply because that is how most people do it. All too often, unfortunately, the opposite is true. Every shepherd has a ram which leads the flock; the other sheep follow without thinking or exploring other ways. A wise shepherd will never let the ram lead his flock unattended, he will always check the way the lead ram goes, lest the entire flock follow it off a cliff.

However, most people are like the flock following the lead ram; they prefer to follow those who lead them without thought and without clarification of the truth. Once they have found someone who is willing to lead them, they will follow him with their eyes closed, unquestioningly. However, the Blessed Creator, because He loves His creations, outlines a path for them so they can avoid going over the cliff. This does not necessarily mean that they will choose the best path. If their leaders choose to mislead, to wickedly walk a crooked path, the Creator will remove those leaders — those misleaders, I should say! — from office; or He may give the followers sparks of inspiration to help them realize that they are going the wrong way. The natural choice of people is generally not the most correct path. Most of the time, a person chooses the easy, convenient track because it does not require him to think or investigate too much."

"So what exactly ought I to do?" Isaac watched his father, trying to figure out where he was heading.

Abraham laughed to himself, "you must constantly ask yourself whether you are on the right path! You should be willing to adapt with new information and innovation; you must not be afraid of what other people will say, even if the new understanding contradicts everything you have said all your life."

Abraham pointed to the sky again, "even if the new understanding contradicts everything, including what the celestial bodies and stars tell you, you must find the strength to change, according to the fresh realizations you arrive at — as I said, even if the new understanding contradicts everything you thought and told others to do, throughout your life!"

"I will go in first!" Abraham declared the next morning, looking at the raging river which cut him off from continuing on the path.

Eliezer looked at his master apprehensively, "my lord, this river is not supposed to be here! There has never been a river here, if there was a small stream, it was understandable, but this river... Please, my lord, do not try to ford it. You may drown!"

In measured steps, as if approaching a hostile castle, Abraham began to enter the water. The coolness seemed pleasant, but he rejected it as an enemy tactic, trying to lull him into a false sense of security.

He thought to himself fervently, continuing to advance into the raging water as he ignored the danger posed to his body. "There is no water! There is no river! There is no reality! The whole world is concealment, trying to make me falter and reject the desire to do the will of the Creator. The Lord has commanded me to do an act, and you, river, are trying to prevent me from doing it. You are nothing but the rind that covers and hides the fruit, a stumbling block trying to trip me up!"

The foaming water splashed on his face, wetting his beard.

Abraham protested silently, "you cannot stop me from doing my duty!

The cool water reached his mouth. *"The Lord rebuke you Satan!"* The scolding scream came out of his mouth, as if released by the roiling waters; his shout consumed them, erasing their existence, returning them to the nothing from which they had sprung.

Abraham stood in the heart of the vanished river, a torrent which had disappeared, leaving not one patch of mud or moisture.

Isaac, Eliezer, and Ishmael looked at Abraham, who stood in the heart of the vanished river, his clothes as dry as before he entered the water.

"We continue!" Abraham kept going on his way, as if everything were but a mirage.

CHAPTER THIRTY-TWO

The Binding

Three days had passed since Abraham left his house, his legs moving as if walking by themselves, towards the place where he was supposed to sacrifice his son. His body acted of its own accord, propelled by itself, repulsing the impediments that attempted to wash it away like waves trying to cover the shore.

Abraham was stopped on the spot, a man restrained by a force greater than himself. On the top of the mountain that towered in front of him, a pillar of cloud appeared before his eyes, as in his heart a burning fire roared, rising to the highest heaven. His eyes were fixed on the miraculous spectacle, his mouth open in astonishment. For a few moments he stood staring; then Abraham forced himself to look at his companions. He saw that Isaac was mesmerized, hypnotized by the sight atop the mountain.

"Do you see…?" He whispered to his son. Isaac nodded without taking his eyes off the wonder. Abraham glanced at Eliezer and Ishmael, surveying him and his son in bewilderment. "Do you see anything at the top of the mountain?" He asked, knowing the answer.

"You mean the trees there?" Ishmael asked, unclear why his father was so astonished.

"It doesn't matter," Abraham sighed deeply. *"Abide you here with the ass,"* he ordered Ishmael and Eliezer.

He thought to himself, "asinine people! The beast cannot perceive anything on the mountaintop, and neither can you!"

"Come, Isaac!" He said to his son, breaking his trance. Isaac went over to his father, who loaded him up with the firewood they had brought.

"I and the lad will go yonder; and we will worship, and come back to you," he murmured over his shoulder at the two men, who were watching their master and his son leave them and walk toward the mountain.

The father and son began to climb up the mountain, leaving their companions in the distance.

Abraham realized that his body kept moving unimpeded, and the thoughts of what lay ahead did not paralyze him; this filled him with confidence that he was doing the right thing.

Isaac, on the other hand, was quite perturbed by thoughts of the young man whom he'd happened across on the trail. With Eliezer and Ishmael present, he had not wanted to broach the topic of what they were meant to sacrifice, but now the time had come.

"Father," he began, causing Abraham to stop and look at his son, expecting a question that had been on the tip of the youth's tongue for several days. *"Behold the fire and the wood..."* He paused, for seconds that seemed to him like an eternity. He wanted to ask, but he feared that his question was unwanted. Finally, he concluded, *"... But where is the lamb for an offering?"*

Abraham breathed deeply, and a sigh emitted from his mouth. Time seemed to stand still as a mix of emotions trying to overcome each other stirred within the hearts of the father and son who stood facing each other. What prevailed, was a sense that all reality had been silenced, awaiting the father's answer. "*God will provide Himself the lamb* if there is to be one." The words tumbled out, becoming tangible, acquiring form and shape as they crashed down on Isaac. Abraham spoke like a man accepting a sentence which had to be carried out. "And if there is no lamb, then you are *for a burnt-offering, my son.*" An errant tear tried to break past the battlements of the father's eyes, torn as he was between his two great loves: for his son and for his father in heaven.

Seconds that felt like eternity passed within Isaac, his eyes closed, his heart striving to contain his father's statement. A deep breath helped him reconcile the necessity to do the last task assigned to him in his life. A slight smile rose on Isaac's lips and slowly it spread all over his face, "we have an important task to do, Father."

Abraham looked at his son, who suddenly seemed full of joy and gladness, "yes, we must continue on the path."

Abraham and Isaac continued to climb up the mountain, with smiles of happiness on their faces, indicating that they were satisfied with doing the duty placed on their shoulders.

Atop the mountain, the ancient altar appeared before the two of them. A large pile of stones placed there in times of yore to serve as a place for sacrifices. Sixty-two years had passed since Abraham had been there. The decades had taken their toll on the half-destroyed altar. Abraham began to rebuild the altar with a heart beating joyfully, while Isaac sat on the side at his father's command, lest he be wounded, God forbid; as being maimed would disqualify him as a sacrifice. The hands worked without inhibition, preparing the place where the father would sacrifice his son. The firewood, which they had carried with them from home, was arranged precisely and carefully.

Abraham and Isaac look at the altar with satisfaction, rejoicing in its configuration, perfect for sacrifice. Isaac began to climb carefully on the altar, realizing that this was the deed that had to be done. "Father, please bind my hands and feet," he asked calmly, "I cannot help you with this, unfortunately. Please bind me tightly, as fear may overcome me when I see the knife approach. I may inadvertently jerk, maiming myself and invalidating the slaughter."

Abraham went to work binding his son on the altar. The ropes were stretched taut, tying Isaac's hands and legs behind him. Shouts and screams were audible inside the father's head, trying to dissuade him from doing the deed which no sensible person would do. The sound of weeping and pleading from obscure and unseen sources, begging the Master of the Universe to have compassion on the bound boy. There was a feeling that the whole celestial entourage was yelling and pleading for the cruel act not to be done.

The father looked at his bound son, trying to transcend his mercy and do his duty, without letting his feelings interfere with the word of the Creator.

"Father," Isaac whispered to his father, who was gripped by these passing thoughts. Abraham momentarily became disconnected from the spot, looking at his son, hoping he would not ask him to stop.

"Please, after you offer your sacrifice, take some ashes for my mother, so she can have a souvenir of me," the son's lips murmured as he lay on the altar.

Abraham went to take the knife in his hand. He tried to reach out, but his arm refused. The brain commanded the hand to take the knife with which the sacrifice was to be slaughtered, but it sensed the body's resistance to its action. Knowing that all his deeds so far had been done without resistance on the part of his body, Abraham began to suspect that a heretical thought had entered his mind.

A fierce struggle broke out between the body and the soul that commanded it. Sweat beaded on his forehead, his hands trembled slightly in an effort to subdue the body. The rebellious hand gripped the knife, approaching the bound boy. The legs were heavy and refused to carry the weight of the body which bore down upon them. Abraham feared that his powers might depart from him before he could carry out the commandment of his Creator. The mind screamed at the body, trying to subdue the animalistic impulse, to transcend the emotions at play. The heart tried to stop the legs, slowly approaching the only son of Sarah, the love of his life. The mind ordered the father to do his duty. The heart ordered the father to spare his son.

Abraham looked at his beloved son, who lay with his eyes tightly closed on the firewood, his neck stretched out in anticipation. A slight tremor passed through the son's body, with the father's loving hand resting on his neck. They mobilized all the powers of their souls to soothe the tremors that gripped the hands and the whole body.

Abraham began to compel his right hand, grasping the knife, forcing his hand to approach the neck ready for slaughter. Screams filled his head, "Nooo!"

In his mind, he yelled back, "I must!" The eyes were flooded with tears, flowing in the grooves of the face, running down the beard. The knife was set on the place of slaughter, all the hand had to do was the will of its owner. Abraham felt a spirit of peace enveloping him suddenly; his heart filled with joy for the impending sacrifice, for his son being chosen for this purpose.

He thought to himself, "now…"

He felt his body relax. Beneath his hand, holding his son's neck, he sensed that the boy had calmed down as well. Abraham moved his hand, felt the warmth of a liquid covering his hand. He realized that his hand has begun to cut into his son's flesh, knew that a few seconds separated him from the end of the unbearably difficult experience.

"*Abraham! Abraham!*" The penetrating voice burst into the depths of Abraham, freezing him in his place, restraining his hands from continuing his action. The oozing drops moistened his fingers, which were still on his son's neck. The voice, caressing and soothing, spread warmly throughout his limbs, ripping him from the hallucinatory experience in which he had been immersed.

"*Here I am!*" He whispered, understanding that all of this had been a trial to test him.

The heavenly voice commanded him, "*lay not your hand upon the lad!*"

"But…" Abraham felt overwhelmed by confusion. Nullification of the order given to him to slaughter his son, a complete abrogation of the royal decree? In order to carry it out, he'd had to mobilize all the powers of his soul — in order to overcome the compassionate impulse pulsating within him; in order to succeed in his mission, now brusquely interrupted. The exhausting internal struggle had stretched his soul taut, like two people at tug-of-war, ending when one side abruptly relinquishes the rope. Abraham felt himself thrown back, sprawling, by his own power, when told to let go.

"In the past You said to me, '*For in Isaac shall seed be called to you;*' then You said to me: '*Please take your son;*' and now You say to me: '*Lay not your hand upon the lad*?!'" A feeling of insane frenzy gripped him. "I cannot understand this!" He tried to say, knowing that he had succeeded in conquering his virtues in order to fulfill his task; he would certainly be happier to accept the current directive, to keep his son alive! He felt a struggle between his two halves — complaining, so to speak, about the revocation of the order to kill his son.

"Did I tell you to slaughter him? No, I said *'And bring him up there as an offering, upon one of the mountains which I will tell you.'* You brought him up; now take him down," the voice calmed him, resolving the contradictions.

Abraham, whose eyes had hitherto been closed in the completeness of the act of slaughter, opened them slowly, expecting to see the blood of his son flowing through his hands, which were still holding the knife and Isaac's neck. His eyes widened in astonishment, realizing that the liquid that wet his hands were his tears seeping slowly through his sealed eyelids. Isaac, lying still on the altar, seemed otherworldly. His face was as serene as a servant willing to do his duty unquestionably. Abraham gazed at Isaac, who had always looked gentle and even a little girlish; but now his features were different. The girlish look has been replaced by the look of a man of strength, who could handle unbearably difficult trials.

Abraham thought, "something great happened to my son today."

"Maybe I'll slaughter a little?" Abraham whispered

"*And do nothing to him;* do not injure or maim him at all!" the voice ordered. Knowing that father and son were fully prepared to do the deed, it continued, "*for now I know that you are a God-fearing man, seeing you have not withheld your son, your only son, from Me.* I know that if it were up to you, you would execute the task fully, but I do not want that."

Isaac blinked, feeling the burning in his eyes, wet from his father's tears. His gaze was glazed, as if he did not know where he was. Was he alive? Was he dead? He felt his heart beating in him differently, remembering a vision he had witnessed, being ready for slaughter. The pulsating sights he saw in the worlds beyond, as his heart blossomed within him, merging with his God, nullifying his very being. His eyes gazed at his beloved father's face, to see him looking back at him. "It's over..." His father whispered. "The trial is over..."

Abraham loosened the ropes that bound his son. Isaac descended from the altar, feeling a new spirit pulsing within him. Suddenly, he felt like a person who would be able to withstand any ordeal and any challenge that the future might hold for him.

A rustling sound diverted the attention of the father and son, who had been looking at each other. They turned to the side, their eyes falling upon a ram, caught in a thicket by its horns. The father and son approached the ram to bind it and bring it up as an offering.

"May it be Your will that this be considered as if I offered my son before You..." Abraham whispered a prayer.

"May it be Your will that this be considered as if I were offered as a sacrifice before You..." Isaac appealed.

"May it be Your will that if my descendants sin in the future, You will remember for them this binding — that I bound my son on the altar before You — and You will forgive Your children for their sin," Abraham pleaded.

Abraham heard the voice, "*by Myself have I sworn, says the Lord, because you have done this thing, and have not withheld your son, your only son, that in blessing I will bless you, and in multiplying I will multiply your seed as the stars of the heaven, and as the sand which is upon the seashore; and your seed shall possess the gate of his enemies; and in your seed shall all the nations of the earth be blessed; because you have hearkened to My voice.*"

Abraham and Isaac watched the blazing fire envelop the sacrificed ram. Slowly, the flames faded, as the smoke rose to the top.

"Let's go back to our men," Abraham said to Isaac as the fire subsided, "and we will return to our home in Beersheba."

CHAPTER THIRTY-THREE

The Announcement

"Sarah! Sarah!"

The urgent voice at the door of the tent made Sarah jump. She quickly ran out of the tent to see who was calling her. An old stranger, resplendently dressed, looking into her eyes with a cheeky smile.

"Yes, my lord, can I help you with anything?"

The smile turned into an annoying grin, "you want to help me?! You are the one who needs help!"

Sarah looked at the oldster, trying to figure out what his object was. "If so, you know nothing!" He contained with a laugh.

"And what do you know?!" Sarah tried to stop the anger that was about to erupt at the stranger, who seemed to want to tease her.

"Where is Isaac?" The old man asked, about to burst out laughing.

Sarah felt a tremor in her heart, "he went with his father to pray," she said in an attempt to put the man off.

The old man put his hand over his mouth, as if trying to conquer his laughter. "To pray?!" He chortled briefly. "Not to make a sacrifice?"

Sarah hesitated for a few seconds before answering, "yes, to make a sacrifice," Sarah said, wondering to herself how the stranger knew of it. "And so what if my husband and son went to make a sacrifice?"

"So what? So what, you ask?!" The man's eyes suddenly looked full of malice, intending to tear the flesh of the woman standing in front of him to pieces. "Really, if it was a sacrifice, then so what…" The man stretched out his sentence, seeing the tense face of Sarah, about to explode. "Do you know what the sacrifice is — I ought to say, who it is? The coot slaughtered his son!" shouted the oldster, trying to instill doubt in the heart of the aged mother in front of him. "This madman tied up your son and slaughtered him, as if he were some sort of beast! He tore his flesh to pieces and burned it on the altar he made!"

A shriek of pain rose from her; she felt as if the knife was rending her flesh, dismembering her body. Bacol rushed out of the tent to see what was going on with her mother. She saw the old man laughing madly at Sarah's horror. The stranger, who seemed to enjoy hearing the cries of pain and sorrow from the bereft mother, went on, "you know what little Isaac said? 'Father, Father, please spare me!' Oh, how he begged!"

Sarah fell to her knees, sobbing painfully in the arms of her daughter, who wept with her.

"'Please have mercy on me!'" The old man imitated Isaac's voice, "'I will be a good boy, Father', your son begged. But the old man just tore him to pieces and burned him with pleasure on the fire," he went on to describe the horror. "He took the knife and slaughtered him cruelly, then tore him limb from limb…"

"Enough!!! Get out of here, evil Satan!!!" Bacol got to her feet, rushed at the old man who so relished the torment, ready to strike him; but the old man vanished and disappeared.

Bacol leaned over to her mother, hugging her, trying to calm her down and comfort her. "Mother, he's lying! Father would never do such a thing!"

"Isaac, my love, if only I could have died in your stead! I am so sorry; I raised you, I nurtured you, and now I must mourn you!" Sarah wept, throwing dust on her head in grief over the death of her son.

"Mother, he's lying!" Said Bacol, her voice now unsure.

"No, he's not!" Sarah sobbed. "I felt something terrible was about to happen when your father came to me and told me that he would teach Isaac the sacrificial service. I sensed in his words that he was not revealing to me the whole truth. But I decided to be silent instead of asking questions, and now my son is dead!"

Weeping and sobbing, the two women shivered for long hours. People from all over the encampment sat around Sarah and her daughter crying over Isaac.

Time passed, the fountain of tears ran dry, pain pounding fiercely on the heart so accustomed to bitterness and sorrow. Sarah, holding her daughter like a lifeline, tried to gather the crushed fragments of her limbs and recover.

"If this is what I am destined to experience in my life, then I accept the judgment upon myself... and I will try to accept it with love. The commandments of God have been executed by my husband and son, and who can transgress the word of our God? You are righteous, for all Your deeds are good and righteous. Because..." Sarah's voice broke. "I, too, have rejoiced at Your command." Sarah filled her lungs with air. "Though my eyes are bitterly weeping, my heart is glad..."

She could hear the slaves crying, from a distance. Finally, she got to her feet. "I must go see my husband; I must see what has happened to my son," she whispered in a shaky voice. Sarah walked slowly to her tent, collecting her belongings.

The journey began, Sarah set her sights on Hebron, the place that Abraham had spoken of, where he had wanted to be buried at the end of his life. She thought that her husband would take his son's ashes to his grave, what he saw as his resting place after death. All the slaves and handmaids accompanied their mistress in the tragic funeral procession for the young master sacrificed in his youth, the son she had finally been blessed with at age ninety. Merchants and nomads who crossed their path were asked about Abraham and Isaac, but they were unable to provide any information.

The last of the caravan entered Hebron at dusk. The horizon was painted in shades of fiery red and ashen gray, but it seemed to the travelers mundane and meaningless. The tear-stained eyes barely saw the setting sun in the distance.

The peddlers folded their wares and rushed to their homes, seeing that the convoy entering the city did not want to purchase their goods but to ask them annoying and meaningless questions.

"Sarah... Sarah..." The notorious voice stopped Sarah in her tracks. Sarah looked up, seeing the old man who had joyfully told her about the sacrifice of her son.

"What do you want now?!" She asked angrily.

"It's not nice to talk to friends like that," the oldster sneered at the angry voice. "Do you not know me well? I came to tell you about the evil of your husband's deeds!" Venomous laughter erupted from him.

Sarah felt the hatred rising inside her, toward the man who was so happy for her sorrow. "No, I have no gratitude towards you!" she hissed between her lips ferociously.

"So, maybe I should not tell you the good news..." The man sounded offended by Sarah's reaction.

"What good news?" Sarah demanded. Much as she detested this vile individual, he might have information about her husband's location.

The man began to laugh madly at the astonished Sarah. "You and your pride! Small and insignificant people who hold themselves up as role models and paragons! Tell the truth, when I told you that your son was sacrificed by your husband, did you not feel proud that your son was a perfect offering to the Creator? Your prideful heart was happy that your son was found worthy of being sacrificed to the Lord!"

Sarah felt the venomous laughter penetrate her innards, touching the very vessels of her soul. The sorrow for her son merged with self-flagellation, lest, in the depths of her soul, be hidden some improper traits of pride, as the oldster claimed. The slaves, who had seen the man abusing their mistress, began to walk towards him with clenched fists, with looks of uncontrolled rage.

"Then know that he really is not worthy of sacrifice! That is why he was not brought as an offering at all! Your son is alive!" Said the old man defiantly to Sarah, as if he were a harbinger of bad news. Sarah felt her heart happily skip a beat at the news that her son was alive.

"Your weakling of a son did not agree to your mad husband's plan and he resisted by force. So, in the end, he was not offered to God!" said the oldster, firing an arrow towards her heart.

The heart full of joy suddenly felt the pain of sadness, over not having raised a son willing to give his life for the sanctification of God. Conflicting emotions hit her chest hard. The joy and sorrow that struggled with each other pierced the old heart. Sarah lifted her hand heavily towards her sternum, feeling the sharp pain piercing her. Slowly she imploded, falling to the ground.

Bacol, her daughter, fell at her feet with cries of sorrow and grief, her soul breaking its earthly bonds to accompany her mother to heaven. Mother and daughter breathed their last, pure souls ascending, leaving behind a full entourage of slaves and handmaids, weeping bitterly in front of the corpses lying on the arid sand. They sought the old reprobate to bring him to justice, but he had vanished like a mirage.

CHAPTER THIRTY-FOUR

Hebron

On the journey back to Beersheba, they travelled much more quickly. Abraham and Isaac were walking on air, rushing to make it back to the encampment. Ishmael and Eliezer straggled behind; they thought the whole exhausting excursion pointless.

Abraham and Isaac hurried their steps, confident that just beyond the next hillock, they would see the encampment which they had left, a few days earlier. However, they were brought to an abrupt halt as they finally crested the hill and saw the camp empty and abandoned. The only figures visible were a few of Ishmael's children, who seemed to be looking for items left behind. The four men made their way urgently down the slope to the encampment to see what had happened to Sarah and her household.

"What are you doing here?" Fatima asked Isaac, shocked by his appearance, ignoring her own husband.

"What am I doing here? What do you mean? Why would I not be here?" Isaac was surprised by his sister-in-law's question.

Fatima, in apparent disbelief, replied, "but you're dead. That's what I mean! So what are you doing here?"

Abraham, his face grim, approached his daughter-in-law, "who told you that he was dead?"

"The old man who came here, he told us that you… That you murdered Isaac!" She whispered, in trepidation, as she saw Abraham's forbidding expression.

"Where has Sarah gone?" He demanded, beginning to understand what had occurred while they were far away, knowing he had to move swiftly.

Fatima's whole body trembled, as she felt that her father-in-law's flaming eyes were scorching into her. "As far as I know, she set out in the direction of Hebron. You know she does not like me very much. She didn't bother to tell me where she was going, nor did she invite us to escort her. So I stayed here, to guard the place."

"Come!" Abraham turned away from his daughter-in-law and toward Hebron, hoping that he could make it there before his wife.

The four men began to run in the direction of Hebron, knowing that it was a long journey, but ignoring the great difficulty. It was many long hours of running, but the flaring pains in their thighs were forgotten amid the rush of their troubled thoughts. Finally, the city wall of Hebron rose before the four of them, a high, fortified barrier which surrounded the town on all four sides.

The four of them entered the city gate and began looking for Sarah and her men. From a distance, they could hear cries of sorrow and grief. Abraham and Isaac hurried towards the sound with heavy hearts. Then they fell to their knees, realizing that they had come too late. The pain and anguish overwhelmed their bodies, which they had pushed beyond the breaking point in order to reach their destination. Abraham felt that his heart was torn in two, part of it lost forever. The tears poured from his eyes like a wellspring, flowing over the lines in his face etched by a life of hardship, heartbroken at the realization that his actions had caused the death of the love of his life. Their spiritual bond was sundered, only to be reforged when Abraham, too, would leave the material world.

Meanwhile, a mass of grief arose from the very being of his son, rising above the mind which refused to believe that his mother had been taken from him. The pain was concrete and palpable, tearing through his heart and bursting through his eyes in a flood of tears. His hands, as if on their own, grasped the top of his robe and tore it deeply, exposing his chest, heaving with grief. In a voice choked with bitter tears, he proclaimed, "blessed be the true judge."

A short time had passed since they had arrived in Hebron. The sun inclined towards the west, as if in a hurry to bring the terrible day to an end. Many people came to the place to see Abraham, who was renowned throughout the land, seeking to help the esteemed man.

The Hittite king who ruled over the city arrived, reverently, to offer his assistance to the wealthy man who had come to his town under tragic circumstances. He pondered how he could keep the man in his city.

"My Lord Abraham," the Hittite king advanced toward him with a downcast face, "is there anything I can help you with?"

Abraham looked at the man, wiping tears from his eyes. "I must bury my wife and daughter. I need a burial plot to bury them," said Abraham, determined to bury his wife in the Machpelah Cave, the burial place of Adam and Eve.

"Surely, my lord, I will immediately tell one of the ministers to find a place for two graves in our cemetery. *Hear us, my lord: you are a mighty prince among us; in the choice of our sepulchers bury your dead; none of us shall withhold from you his sepulcher, but that you may bury your dead."*

Abraham bowed in gratitude to the Hittite king, knowing that in this way he would be able to get what he wanted. "Thank you, my friend," he said humbly, "but my friend knows that our way is a little different from yours. If it is your desire to bestow upon me a true act of compassion, I want to bury my wife in a separate burial plot. If you want to do me an eternal kindness, please help me find a plot of my own, from among your people's territory."

Thoughts rushed through the king's head, realizing that if only he could accede to Abraham's request, he and his people would be able to enjoy the man's legendary wealth. Although the thought that he was not willing to bury his wife alongside the townspeople was a little insulting, the king would gladly bear it in order to bring the foreigner's wealth into the city. "Certainly, my lord, is there a particular place you had in mind?"

"My friend, if you wish to do me a favor, please put me in touch with Ephron son of Zohar, as I wish to bury my dead in a field which he owns. I would like to purchase the whole field, as well as the cave at its edge, which will serve well as a family burial plot. I am prepared to pay the full market value of the field and the cave, if it pleases him."

The Hittite king nodded in assent, turning to one of his servants, commanding him to summon Ephron urgently.

As Abraham waited for Ephron, the minutes seemed to stretch out before him. In his heart, Abraham came to the decision that he would buy the cave at all costs. "I will pay him a thousand silver shekels, even though it is not worth ten!" Abraham thought, firm in his intention to fulfill Sarah's desire to be buried in the Machpelah Cave.

A short, bald man, leading a large entourage, arrived with the messenger. His small eyes darted in all directions with a sly expression, his hands rubbing each other with pleasure. He looked down to the ground as he approached Abraham, only occasionally revealing his cunning eyes. He could barely contain his joy, knowing that because an important man like Abraham needed him, he would rise to greatness.

"Your Majesty summoned me?" He asked, with flattering humility.

"Indeed, my friend Ephron," said the king with a tone of respect. "Lord Abraham the Hebrew wants to buy a plot of land for his wife, who sadly passed away today."

Ephron nodded, as if not understanding the connection to him.

"Abraham wants to buy from you the Machpelah Cave and the field that surrounds," the king told his subject.

"Ah, yes... the Machpelah Cave, and the field..." Ephron looked thoughtful. "Yes, the field and the cave are very important to me... I inherited them from my father... It is difficult for me to part with it..." Ephron glanced at Abraham's face, trying to stand his ground.

He thought, "this lunatic is willing to buy the cave, in cash! Does he not know that it is a place of darkness and demons?!"

He hid the smile trying to take over his face. "But surely, if my lord desires this cave and this field, I will not withhold it from him, though I have very deep feelings for the field and the cave, which are the inheritance of my ancestors to me," Ephron said aloud. "But, here in the sight of all my people, I will give it to you for free!"

Abraham laughed inwardly, bowing to the seemingly generous man, even as he recognized his deceitfulness, greed, and hunger for honor. Abraham thought in his heart, "his name is quite apt, as his initials spell out 'profit.'" In a voice loud enough to reach the entire crowd, he declared: "*But if you will, please hear me: I will give the price of the field; take it of me, and I will bury my dead there.* I am not asking for a gift; I want to pay you for it. Tell me how many silver shekels you would like, and I will happily pay."

Ephron looked up and slowly approached Abraham, happy at the juicy prey that had fallen into his hands.

Abraham bowed his full height toward Ephron, who signaled that he wanted to whisper something to him. "Between two friends like us, is four hundred silver shekels too much for such a piece of land? Then you may bury your dead."

A smile spread across Abraham's face. He thought, "friends like us? I am a friend of God, while he has no friend but cold, hard cash!"

Abraham patted Ephron affectionately on the shoulder. He thought to himself, grinning, "if you were silent and unwilling to set a price, I would give you a thousand shekels for it; *but he that makes haste to be rich shall not be unpunished.*"

"Eliezer!" Abraham called out to his faithful servant. "Run and bring me four hundred shekels of silver to pay my friend Ephron for the field and cave. Please hurry, so that I can bury my wife before sunset."

The crowd was shocked to hear this, a hubbub running through it. "Four hundred silver shekels! That's fifty times what the field is worth."

Ephron seemed pensive, regretting not asking for more; his little eyes looked narrower than ever. "And maybe we'll make it six hundred?" He asked, embarrassed.

The king glared at Ephron, angry at his excessive impudence.

"Ah... I was just kidding... We'll leave it at four hundred, but my lord..." Ephron whispered to Abraham, "please ask him to make sure the coins are new and shiny, not worn and scratched."

"Eliezer!" Abraham exclaimed with a laugh at his servant, "be careful to bring *four hundred shekels of silver, current money with the merchant.*"

Eliezer returned with a cart full of silver coins, as commanded by his master. The money was given to Ephron, who avidly scrutinized each coin. The Machpelah Cave was thus purchased by Abraham, in full and in cash, as witnessed by all the citizens of Hebron.

The funeral procession set out, Abraham and Isaac following the coffins of Sarah and her daughter, followed by all the noblemen of the land: Shem and Eber; King Abimelech of Gerar; Eshcol, Aner, and Mamre; and all the kings and ministers of the cities near Hebron.

"Do not weep too much, my son," Abraham whispered to Isaac, "lest the people think that we are sorry for the trial we went through, in the aftermath of which your mother died. Our Father in heaven and she both know our sorrow for the bitter loss and our joy at the trial... Once our days of mourning are over, I want you to go to study at Shem and Eber's academy, where you may stay until I summon you to return."

Abraham stood before the great crowd, tearing up, as he delivered a eulogy for the love of his life:

A woman of valor who can find? for her price is far above rubies.

The heart of her husband does safely trust in her, and he has no lack of gain.

She does him good and not evil, all the days of her life.

She seeks wool and flax, and works willingly with her hands.

She is like the merchant-ships; she brings her food from afar.

She rises also while it is yet night, and gives food to her household, and a portion to her maidens.

She considers a field, and buys it; with the fruit of her hands she plants a vineyard.

She girds her loins with strength, and makes strong her arms.

She perceives that her merchandise is good; her lamp goes not out by night.

She lays her hands to the distaff, and her hands hold the spindle.

She stretches out her hand to the poor; yes, she reaches forth her hands to the needy.

She is not afraid of the snow for her household; for all her household are clothed with scarlet.

She makes for herself coverlets; her clothing is fine linen and purple.

Her husband is known in the gates, when he sits among the elders of the land.

She makes linen garments and sells them; and delivers girdles unto the merchant.

Strength and dignity are her clothing; and she laughs at the time to come.

She opens her mouth with wisdom; and the law of kindness is on her tongue.

She looks well to the ways of her household, and eats not the bread of idleness.

Her children rise up, and call her blessed; her husband also, and he praises her:

"Many daughters have done valiantly, but you excel them all."

Grace is deceitful, and beauty is vain; but a woman that fears the Lord, she shall be praised.

Give her of the fruit of her hands; and let her works praise her in the gates.

Made in the USA
Las Vegas, NV
10 November 2024

11496940R00203